D1001661

THE TEACHINGS OF POPE JOHN XXIII

THE TEACHINGS OF POPE JOHN XXIII

Edited by
MICHAEL CHINIGO

Translated from the Italian by
Arthur A. Coppotelli

A GINIGER BOOK
published in association with
GROSSET & DUNLAP

THIS BOOK IS PUBLISHED BY GROSSET AND DUNLAP, INC., 51 MADISON AVENUE, NEW YORK 10010, IN ASSOCIATION WITH THE K. S. GINIGER COMPANY, 1140 BROADWAY, NEW YORK 10001.

ORIGINALLY PUBLISHED IN ITALIAN BY CASA EDITRICE LICINIO CAPPELLI, BOLOGNA, ITALY, UNDER THE TITLE GLI INSEGNAMENTI DI PAPA GIOVANNI.

LIBRARY OF CONGRESS CATALOGUE CARD NUMBER: 66-25714.

PUBLISHED SIMULTANEOUSLY IN CANADA

Nihil obstat: JOHN M. T. BARTON, S.T.D., L.S.S.
Censor

Imprimatur: PATRICK CASEY
Vic. Gen.

WESTMINSTER, *14th November, 1966*

First American Edition 1967

PRINTED IN THE UNITED STATES OF AMERICA

CONTENTS

NOTE

In the Bible passages, use has been made of the Westminster version.

THE TEACHINGS OF POPE JOHN XXIII

[I]
PREFACE

The Surprising Pope

"*Pastor et Nauta*" (Shepherd and Pilot), Malachia's prophetic description of Angelo Giuseppe Roncalli, figured conspicuously in the first newspaper and radio–TV reports that went around the world soon after his election. But it was enough for the new Pontiff—while he was explaining his choice of the name John—to make just passing mention of the fact that "almost all his predecessors with this name had a brief pontificate," to cause the so-called experts in Vatican affairs to dismiss Malachia's controversial remark. They thought up instead "The Compromise Pope" and "The Transitional Pope" and re-emphasized the eternal question: "Is he going to be political or pastoral?"

The attempt to summarize the Pope's entire policy in a single slogan was not new. The age-old history of the Church and the Papacy offer abundant precedents.

Unusual and disturbing, however, was the outbreak of political speculation in the written and spoken statements that were pouring out, and in the contradictory interpretations of supposed disclosures about the election itself. These "disclosures," facilitated in a sense by the absolute secrecy in which the events of the Sistine Chapel are held, really expressed the desires and interests of those who had written or spoken them. Desires and interests directed openly toward "mortgaging" the activity of the new Pontiff, if not actually toward monopolizing him for their side.

John XXIII was struck by the universal interest his election had stirred—which he was quick to attribute not so much to his own person as to the institution of the Papacy—but he was resentful of the biased reports to the extent that he made it clear immediately on his coronation:

"During these days of great mystery and trepidation, keeping an ear open to the voice of the world, We have been comforted and encouraged—on the one hand—by the universal joy and delight with which Our elevation to the Supreme Pontificate has been greeted, while, on the other, We are perplexed and made anxious by the variety of burdensome tasks which weigh on Our shoulders . . . tasks which are attributed to Us from here and there, each person taking on himself to assign Us one within limited horizons according to his own personal attitudes, according to his experience, and according to his own way of conceiving individual and collective life. There are those, in fact, who expect the Pontiff to be a statesman, a diplomat, a scientist, an organizer of our life in common, indeed someone whose mind is open to all the standards of progress of modern life, without any exceptions.

"These people are off the right path, because their way of conceiving of the Supreme Pontiff does not fully conform to a true ideal.

"The new Pope, during the course of events of his life, is like Jacob's son, who, upon meeting his unfortunate brothers, reveals to them the tenderness in his heart and breaking into tears says: 'I am your brother Joseph.' The new Pontiff, let us repeat again, embodies most of all that splendid image of the good Shepherd which is described to us by St. John the Evangelist in the very words that came from the lips of the Holy Redeemer. He is the gate to the fold: '*Ego sum ostium ovium.*'

"Into this fold of Jesus Christ no one can enter if not guided by the Supreme Pontiff; and men can surely attain salvation only when they have united with him, because the Roman Pontiff is the Vicar of Christ and represents His person on earth. . . .

"Especially dear to our heart is the task of being Shepherd to *the whole flock*. The other human qualities—scientific knowledge, diplomatic skill, organizational talent—can succeed in enhancing and rounding out pontifical direction, but they can in no way replace it.

"But the main point is the Good Shepherd's zeal, ready for any sacred, direct, constant act of courage, even the ultimate sacrifice: 'The Good Shepherd gives his life for his sheep'. . . .

"Then the horizon widens: 'and I have other sheep which are not of this fold, and I must lead them too; and they shall hear my voice and there will be one fold under one shepherd.' This is the missionary problem in all its vastness and beauty. This is the concern of the Roman Pontificate, the prime one if not the only one: it combines with many others of equal importance.

"But more than simply doing, we are concerned with the spirit of the doing. Every Pontificate takes its stamp from the features of the man who embodies and represents it. And certainly all the faces of all the popes are reflected and must be reflected in the face of Christ. . . .

"Now the divine teaching and its great lesson are expressed in His words: 'Learn from me who am meek and humble of heart.' " Therefore great meekness and humility.

"Pious souls, fervent souls of the whole world, We beseech you to pray always to God for the Pope, to obtain for him the practice of perfection of meekness and humility."

An illuminating speech on his coronation, as we can see. It presented to the world the Pope's dearest aspiration, to be above all "a Good Shepherd, meek and humble."

On that day of his coronation, the dual figure of John XXIII emerged clearly: the one "official and biblical, the son of Jacob," the other, paternal.

In fact, after his address, he spoke to the people of Venice and of Bergamo as if to his family, going back in time to his memories of childhood, once when he was watching from his father's shoulders a celebration by the Catholic Action of his native town. He concluded, his voice choked with tears, that now he was to be carried by the Heavenly Father.

It is difficult to say whether—as sometimes authoritatively it has been claimed—during the very first weeks it was "his prepared oratory . . . noble, contained, discreet" or whether it was "his spoken word, spontaneous, immediate, directed to his listeners, emphasized by the wide gesturing of his hands, the movements of his eyes, the frankness of his terms, by his firm yet pleasing voice that was penetrating and persuasive," that produced throughout the world a real wave of sympathy and support for the new Vicar of Christ. It is difficult to say because whoever was fortunate enough to be near him in different situations cannot but believe that the two figures of the Pope complemented each other, in the larger frame of the "Good Shepherd."

The Pope himself was aware of this growing wave of sympathy and with perfect candor referred to it some weeks after his elevation to the Chair of Peter: " . . . besides, in our knowledge of ourself, although imperfect, and in the humility of our spirit, We feel we must acknowledge it is not simply for the friendly and human traits of our modest person that We have so quickly gained the sympathy of the people and the governments of the world . . . but through a renewed outpouring of the grace of the Holy Spirit which was promised the Church by our Lord."

For the thousands of pilgrims in St. Peter's or outside in the embrace of the twin colonnade, who came to visit the Pope " . . . not for curiosity . . . but as a father, with love and trust" John XXIII soon became the "*Papa Buono*" (the Good Pope), as he is known even now.

In the fatherly conversations already mentioned, the Pope loved to quote the Gospel for the day and then wittily and gently impart the appropriate lesson or moral.

But on November 25, 1958, in amplifying the major lines of the policy he spoke about in his coronation address, the Pope indicated clearly that "if all the concerns of a pastoral ministry are dear to us and We are aware of its urgency, We feel above all the duty to arouse everywhere and by continuous effort an enthusiasm for Holy Scripture, which was written to enlighten the course of life, from infancy to old age.

"And so an instructive apostolate . . . this is the appeal, this is the task of the book open on the altar: to teach the true doctrine, the right discipline of life, the forms of man's ascent toward God.

"The primary glory of every pontificate is in fact to carry out the command of the Gospel: 'Go and teach,' to the farthest places. . . .

"The altar: it is from this holy height that we must look on earthly things, lead them, and make use of them."

Already in his first radio message to the world, the Pope had said " . . . and with equal, fatherly affection We embrace the Eastern Church, and We open our heart and our arms to all those who are separated from this Apostolic See where Peter himself lives among his successors."

This appeal, which every Pope had made to the schismatics, even though more insistent, was not immediately interpreted as a sign of great new plans in the offing.

Nor was anything seen in the remark "Go and teach . . . to the farthest places . . . " which he made at the end of November.

His first Christmas Message renewed the appeal to the separated churches and added:

"Still alive in our mind is the memory of some ten years ago when several representatives of the Orthodox Churches, with the practical cooperation of several governments, thought to provide for the bringing together of civilized nations, and began with an agreement among several Christian confessions with different rites and separate histories.

"Unfortunately, more pressing concrete interests and nationalistic concerns overrode those intentions which in themselves were good and worthy of respect.

"And the painful problem of the broken unity of Christ's heredity always remains disturbing and prejudicial to that same effort towards resolution, along the road of heavy difficulties and uncertainties.

"The sadness of this grievous acknowledgment does not stop, nor will it ever stop, We trust in God, our soul's effort to carry out the loving invitation to our dear separated brothers, who bear as well the name of Christ before them. . . ."

It was at this point in history in the opening days of John XXIII's pontificate that we had the clear feeling something extraordinary was about to happen. But for the world in general it was a complete surprise when, on the following January 25, the feast of the conversion of St. Paul, the Pope announced the convocation of a diocesan synod in Rome and of an Ecumenical Council of the Universal Church.

The Pope himself described the Council as "one of the more significant notes" of his reign. And without doubt his announcement was the most far-reaching news of the first year of his pontificate. And so he was proclaimed on several sides the "Pope of Unity" and the "Pope of Pacification."

Chronologically, however, the first change he made was in the structure of the Sacred College—the "*plenum*" to be exact—which, by tradition, was limited to seventy cardinals. John XXIII increased the number to seventy-four in the first consistory, and in the following consistories to more than eighty, to make the Church more universal, and to answer the needs of the broadening apostolate.

For his major speeches, the new Pope quickly took to the modern media which science had put at the disposal of faith.

This immediately earned him the name of the "Innovating Pope" which he himself decided to clarify during the audience for the rectors of seminaries in June, 1959:

"Some claim that the traditions of the past should be considered obsolete and that new ideas and new systems should be adopted. No one would reject whatever development is sound in the means for arriving at the great goal . . . but it is not difficult to guess the sad consequences that usually derive from such a premise. One must be careful, even when the prospects seem rosiest and most satisfying."

Therefore, tradition when it continues to be fruitful, as in the past. Changes, yes, but only on due reflection. And so no dramatic changes. There in brief was the Pope's thought.

In the first days of his pontificate, John XXIII surprised everyone, including the personnel of Vatican City, when he began visiting methodically all the offices and learning personally about the various facilities of the Apostolic Palace itself. At first these visits almost seemed like the flight of a bird from a golden cage. They were never announced in advance, and they were always joyful events for those on whom the Pontiff paid a call. Gradually people understood that the Pope was becoming informed about the conditions under which his family—the clergy and lay employees of the Vatican—worked, about their morale and their economic situation.

And so came about quite quietly what was to be called the "internal economic peace" of the minuscule state.

One of the most moving sights that had ever been seen in the Vatican by the people who write on such matters, and perhaps the first of its kind in the history of the Church, was the ceremony which took place in St. Peter's on a Sunday morning, October 11, 1959. The Pope personally gave a silver pectoral cross, which he himself had blessed, to each of the 510 missionaries from various countries who were now going out to all parts of the world. While the Pope was greeting with fatherly solicitude each of the priests and nuns and blessing them, it seemed as if the biblical scene were repeating itself, when Jesus said to His Apostles: "As God has sent me . . . so I send you . . . into the world."

Missionaries had been particularly important to Angelo Roncalli, the priest, the monsignor, the bishop. He would say that his work as apostolic delegate in Bulgaria, Greece and Turkey had had primarily a missionary character. Now, as Supreme Pontiff, he wanted to emphasize that the future of the Catholic Church, of humanity itself, is based on the eagerness with which missionaries bear the word of God to the unbelieving.

His gesture was perfectly linked to the intention he had announced earlier: that is, "The primary glory of every pontificate is to carry out the command of the Gospel: 'Go and teach . . . to the farthest places.' "

The Pope was unsparing of himself in running the many daily affairs of the Church, while, at the same time, dedicating his energy to her revitalization and to that of the faith, to the Union of Christians and to harmony in the communities and in the world.

Papal policy was detailed in his first encyclical, *Ad Petri Cathedram*, issued on June 29, 1959. In it, the Pope deals with "The knowledge of the truth, especially revealed truth," emphasizes that "the truth of the Gospels leads to eternal life," recalls the press to its duties "in relation to the truth," condemns "religious indifferentism," urges men "to be brothers and to base peace on truth," and encourages "unity and harmony among peoples, among social classes." He then turns to the "pastors, the clergy, to the religious and the missionaries, both men and women, to Catholic Action," pointing out to each the paths to follow and the goals to attain in a renewed fervor for the faith.

He addresses "the afflicted and the oppressed," "the ranks of the less fortunate," "the refugees and emigrants," comforting them all and giving them his valuable paternal advice. And finally he describes his grief for the "persecuted Church" and urges the faithful in every corner of the world to pray for her.

After this great plan for his apostolate, others followed, while the best and most qualified minds prepared for the Ecumenical Council.

The great encyclical, *Mater et Magistra*, issued on May 15, 1961, "summarizes," as the Pope himself said, "the thought of two thousand years of Christianity's history" on the social question.

The essence of the encyclical is admirably expressed in the words "*Pax vobis*" (Peace be with you) because it deals with the social problems of the modern world with absolute frankness, as well as with the solutions necessary to peaceful coexistence between employers and labor.

The widespread agreement and the immediate effects it produced are clear signs of the opportuneness and validity of this singular document.

And then, after years of patient preparation, the Second Vatican Council was inaugurated by the Pope on October 11, 1962. In his memorable addresses to the bishops, to the diplomatic representatives extraordinary of eighty-six governments and international bodies, to the fifty and more observers to the Council, sent by various Christian groups not joined to Rome yet desirous of confirming Christ's exhortation that "They be one," John XXIII defined the essence, the goals, the intentions of the Council. He recalled the foundations of Catholic teaching and explained the contribution the Council would make to peace among peoples and to social harmony. He repeated the pastoral concern that Christ's heritage everywhere should set out on the road to unity and take the Glad Tidings to all those who are waiting for God's hour.

The descriptions of the "political Pope," the Pope of the Council," "the Pope of unity," and "the Pope of peace" were in all the press reports that went out to the whole world.

And so we come to the last great document of John XXIII's pontificate: the encyclical, *Pacem in Terris*, issued on April 11, 1963.

The problem of peace among men and among nations found in Pope John a tireless advocate, from his very first message to the last words he uttered before dying. His appeals, his exhortations, his advice he repeated frequently, in every Christmas and Easter message, and at every moment of danger.

The encyclical, *Pacem in Terris*, traces the guidelines for a lasting peace "founded and developed only on a full respect for the order established by God." In it, John defines "Order among human beings," "Relations among human beings and among public forces within single communities," "Relations among political communities," and "Relations of human beings and political communities with the world community." He concludes with a "Pastoral Summons" directed to the faithful and intended to contribute to the creation of a world in which it would be possible to establish lasting peace "in full respect for the order established by God."

The great plan for peace outlined in the encyclical, which was to be Pope John's last act, was received with eager attention throughout the world. But as happened on his election to the Chair of Peter, and to an even greater extent, political speculation arose to exploit for one side or another this or that section of the unified, coherent plan which had been intended for universal application, as a single, indivisible body.

The arrival in Rome of Nikita Khrushchev's son-in-law and his wife and their audience with the Pope combined with the biased interpretations of the encyclical to create widespread confusion and to stir up controversy throughout the world.

I shall here quote Monsignor Loris Capovilla, Pope John's private secretary, who "revealed"—several months after the Pope's death—what went on during the audience that was the cause of inferences and controversies so saddening to the Pope.

"The Pope received the Adjubeis in his private study. On the walls of that study there were many portraits of saints and popes. The Pope described to his guests the lives of each one of them. After which he sat at his desk and asked the Adjubeis to be seated.

"The Pope: 'Now, according to protocol, I should give you a medal or some stamps. It's the custom for non-Catholics. But I don't like protocol. I prefer giving you a more valuable gift: if you will permit me, I should like to give you a rosary, dear children, so that our Mother, the Virgin Mary, will always be near you.'

"Mrs. Adjubei murmured a thanks in French, and took the rosary in her hand. The Pope asked her: 'Tell me the names of your children. Don't think I do not know them,' he went on smilingly, 'in fact, before receiving anyone, I always inform myself about his family. But the names of children always acquire a special sound from the lips of their mother.'

"Moved by such delicacy, Khrushchev's daughter murmured the names of Nikita, Alexis and Ivan.

"The Pope: 'What beautiful names! And how fortunate your children are! Nikita, the endearing form for Nicholas. St. Nicholas is a great saint, loved and venerated in the East especially. And Alexis! How many times—when I was in Bulgaria—did I stop to pray in the churches, in the convents and in the monasteries dedicated to that great martyr of the Church. But it's Ivan I love most of all, your son who has my name. May they all be blessed, but to Ivan I send a special blessing. Embrace him for me when you see him again; you'll see, the others won't mind.'

"The Pope's paternal gentleness had moved Mrs. Adjubei to the point of tears. Adjubei then said: 'Holy Father, tell us the way our now separated worlds can meet, understand one another and therefore love one another.' And the Pope answered, "You are a journalist and so you know the Holy Bible. The Bible says that Our Lord created the world in six days. The days are certainly ages, an infinite space of time. On the first day, God said, Let there be light! Today we are at the first hour. It is God Who gives us light. Do not doubt, my son, that He will give us the rest.'

"It was a great example of pastoral liturgy and holy diplomacy . . . you see, the controversies and the inferences . . . had no reasons for being."

I have set down Monsignor Capovilla's disclosures here because they clarify an episode that saddened the Pope . . . but also many men the world over. It is a pity that the necessary reserve in this case evidently was such as to cause arguments which even a brief but timely explanation might have avoided.

I have set them down, more particularly, to stress the dangers there are in "working" partial statements wrenched out of the context of Pope John's entire thought.

In this volume, I have done exactly the opposite. That is, I have put all the Pope's teachings on a single subject together, or else I have chosen the most complete expression of them.

It is to be noted that beside the encyclicals, the major speeches, the radio messages, the formal addresses, I have found some valuable moments in his "fatherly talks," which, perhaps more than anything else he did, made the Pope universally popular and beloved.

I have been encouraged too by prelates of the Holy See,

who furnished me with abundant work and study materials. To them go my thanks.

It is evident that the breadth of Pope John's undertakings—expressed in the convocation of the Ecumenical Council and in the encyclicals—will resound through the world in future years. The "tone" of that resounding will depend on the way in which men apply or fail to apply, in all or in part, the principles and the directives contained in the two major encyclicals.

For his humility and for the gentleness of manner which distinguished him and drew him close to men as a simple country priest—a role he himself preferred—and for the variety and the uniqueness of his undertakings, as well as for the strength of his dedication and his willingness to act . . . right to the end of his days, John XXIII deserves each one of those descriptive titles given him during the course of his brief but productive pontificate.

But instead we prefer the one that summarizes all the Pope did and wanted to do. And also because it corresponds perfectly to what he himself had to say about his life; that is, "it's been a series of surprises."

Michael Chinigo

[II]

THE ECUMENICAL COUNCIL

We think it an inspiration from the Most High, the thought We have had even since Our Pontificate began, to call together an Ecumenical Council. From this great assembling of bishops around the Roman Pontiff, the Church, beloved bride of Christ, can acquire fresh and greater splendor in these agitated times. And there shines again the hope that those who, although taking pride in the name Christian, are yet separated from this Apostolic See, will listen to the voice of the Holy Shepherd and come to the only Church of Christ. [1]

The Ecumenical Councils of the past were mostly concerned with questions of doctrinal exactitude, the various and important ones concerning the *lex credendi* (the law of what to believe), because heresies and errors were trying to penetrate the early Church in the East and the West.

At Nicea the divinity of the Divine Word—made Man for the salvation of the human race—was put into question: the Arian heresy. At Ephesus there was great concern about the unity of the person of the Word in his two natures, and about the divine motherhood of Mary, the Theotokos. At Chalcedon, further quarrels and discussions about the distinctness of these two natures. In the sixteenth century, the constitution of the Church was compromised at its very base, and at Trent everything had to be and was re-established on the old bases: faith, worship, sacraments, discipline; everything was brought back to a firm foundation and a very clear light. The first Vatican Council, in the brief space of time allowed to it, took another and vigorous look at the divine constitution of the Church, with special attention to the *infallibility of the Roman Pontiff in matters of faith and morals.*

The occasions for the meeting of the other fifteen Ecumenical Councils, beside the five mentioned, were prompted by various circumstances and by the concern to safeguard, it is true, the purity of the Church's teaching. But they were also concerned to strengthen and to guide the consciences of men who had been disturbed in the face of religious and political events that were taking place in various countries under differing circumstances. Their concern was always directly tied to the Church's main purpose to teach the blessings of equilibrium and peace in the service of order.

In the modern world, whose face has been so profoundly changed, a world which is straining to hold itself together in its dangerous yet fascinating search for material wellbeing, when the principles of the spiritual order that characterized the growth of Christian culture are forgotten or enfeebled, more than one point of doctrine or ecclesiastic regulation must be recalled and re-examined in the pure light of Revelation and tradition. The issue is whether or not to restore value and splendor to the substance of the humane and Christian way of thinking and living, of which through the centuries the Church has been the depositary and the teacher.

Furthermore, out of our sense of duty and the seriousness of the situation, we must deplore the waylaying of the human spirit, which has been tempted by and urged toward the enjoyment of worldly goods alone, goods which modern scientific research has put at the disposal of all of the children of our time. God save us, however, from overstating its proportions to the point of believing that God's heavens are closed over our heads forever, that truly *tenebrae factae sunt super universam terram* (darkness has closed over the whole world), and that there is nothing left for us to do except shed tears on the laborious road of life.

We must instead take heart.

No; Christ, the Son of God and our Redeemer, has not left behind the world he saved. And the Church he founded, one, holy, catholic and apostolic, always remains his mystical body, of which he is head, to which each of us turns, to which each of us belongs. This is the great truth that every baptized person must bear in mind: that belonging to the Church of Christ is not simply an individual act, but pre-eminently a social one for everybody. And this is the meaning of *catholic man*, *catholic world*, of the *Catholic Church*, which is to say that each of us is—in Christ Jesus, in his Church—truly of the same divine family, we are sons and brothers: *For those whom he (the Father) foreknew he also predestined to be conformed to the image of his Son, in order that he might be the first-born among many brethren* (Romans 8, 29).

Every faithful believer belongs to the whole catholicity, just as every priest does, and—with a proper distinction in responsibilities—each bishop. This relationship takes place with respect to the divine whole which Jesus, the Son of God and Founder of the Church, impressed onto the institution he made for universality and eternity.

The Council has its own circumscribing purpose, as a *civitas in monte* (a city on a mount), that is, to occupy itself exclusively with what concerns the Catholic Church, our mother, and her present internal organization.

We expect great things from this Council, which will want to bring new vigor to the faith, to doctrine, church discipline, the religious and spiritual life, and to contribute to the reaffirmation of those principles of Christian ordinance upon which the developments in civil, economic, political and social affairs depend as well. The commands of the Gospel must reach even here, envelop and penetrate everything, even when there comes to us *the dew of heaven and the fatness of the earth* (Genesis 27, 28). Yes, reach even there, which means that all elements of the social order must participate conscientiously, seriously, sincerely—the priesthood and the laity, and constituted authorities, the intellectuals, labor—the entire social order must concern itself with the perfect conjunction between heaven and earth, between the uncertain and perilous present and eternal and joyous future, in proportion to our response as men and as Christians to the Lord's gifts of grace and mercy.

Looking over several essays from the copious literature concerning the last Vatican Ecumenical Council convoked by Our Predecessor of venerated memory, Pius IX, in 1869–70, We happened upon a printed address by one of the more excited and applauded spirits of that definitely anti-Roman era. The address was dedicated with tasteless irony to the bishops who were coming to the Vatican from all over the world, and compared them with the ancient bishops of the East who convened in Nicea in 325 for the first Council.

"You are gathered today at the latest and last council in Rome. The first one, the Nicean, was solemn in venerating the baptism of triumph and of ordered unity, the religion the times wanted. This last council, yours, that is, will attest—no matter what you intend—to the immense fact of a dying religion, and thus inevitably, to the rise not far off of another" (from *Scritti editi ed inediti di G.M.*, Vol. LXXXVI [*Politica*, Vol. XXVIII] Imola, Cooperativa Tip. Ed. P. Baleati, 1940, p. 241).

These are authentic words of challenge and prophecy.

At a century's distance we realize their insanity, and what these prophets of Baal deserve—and there is always one around—*who saw the false and stupid for you* (cf. Lam., 2, 14). Let them talk; it will be an exercise of vigilance and patience for us, *ut promissionem reportemus* (so that we may bring back the promise). We remain faithful to Christ's word, the last with which Matthew draws to a close his Gospel, the assurance of victory for Christ's Church, our Church, right to the end of time.

A council of the Catholic Church must study a whole complexity of relations involving not only individuals and families but all nations as well, relations that are pivotal in human society.

From the Ten Commandments of Moses to the four Gospels, everything takes its meaning from Christ and from his Church, at the center of which Christ is present in the act of repeating the great words: *I am the light of the world. I am the way, the truth, and the life* (John 8, 12; 14, 6). The last words of the Gospel according to St. Matthew put the divine seal on them and what they mean: *Lo, I am with you always, to the close of the age* (Matthew 28, 20).

What wonderful work this will be!

Just thinking about it moves the spirit to exult and to thank God for the clarity and spiritual beauty the Holy Church will acquire before the whole world, for its enlightenment and encouragement.[2]

With the grace of God, We shall call the Council, and We intend to prepare it with the purpose of reconsolidating and invigorating what is necessary in the entirety of the Catholic family, in conformity with Our Lord's plan. Then when we have realized this large task by eliminating everything—on the human side—that could hinder our way forward, we shall present the Church in all her splendor, without blemish or wrinkle, and we shall tell all those who are separated from us, the Orthodox, the Protestants, and the others: See, brothers, this is Christ's Church. We have worked to be faithful to it, to ask the Lord for the boon that she always remains thus as he wanted her.

Come, come: this is the way to the meeting, to the return. Come to take or take again your place, which for many of you was the place of your father of old. From religious peace, from a re-united Christian family, what joy, what prosperity—for the civic and social order as well—can we allow ourselves to expect for the entire world![3]

Everything must be well prepared, with the greatest love and cognizance of the people, with an awareness also of the sons of a very old tradition, who now need to be understood and attracted by proof of brotherhood, tenderness and peace. Without doubt, the Lord will intervene with his grace and grant us great consolations, even if it will be others in the future who will enjoy the fruitful results. History has attested by the events of this or that country how the Church has remained faithful to her mission unswervingly, through vicissitudes and conflict, and has kept a steady course.

We hope and pray that the Council will renew, first of all, the sight of the Apostles gathered in Jerusalem after Christ's ascension into heaven: a unanimity of thought and prayer with Peter and around Peter, Shepherd of the lambs and the sheep. An offering of energies that will be resharpened and renewed to search for what will best answer the needs of the apostolate today.[4]

The Council, by God's grace, should be a point of departure for a general renewal, a fresh, vigorous spreading of the Holy Gospel throughout the world. Holy Mother Church will bear its message, make it known and explain its lessons.[5]

The salient point of this Council is not the discussion of this or that theme of the Church's fundamental doctrine; that is, a diffuse repetition of the teaching of the Fathers and of old and modern theologians, which is supposed to be present and familiar to the spirit.

The Council was not made necessary by this. But from the renewed, calm, tranquil adherence to the Church's teaching in its wholeness and precision, as we still see shining forth from the conciliar acts—from those of Trent to those of the First Vatican Council—the Christian, catholic and apostolic spirit of the entire world awaits a leap forward toward doctrinal understanding and the guiding of consciences. Thus there will be greater fidelity to authentic doctrine, and that doctrine itself will be studied and exposed through the methods and the language of modern thought.

The substance of the ancient doctrine of the *depositum fidei* is one thing; quite another is the way in which it is restated, and it is this restatement we must—with patience if necessary—take great account of by measuring everything by the extent and the means of a teaching mission that is predominantly pastoral.

At the opening of the Second Vatican Council it is more evident than ever that God's truth lies in eternity. We see, in fact, as one age succeeds another, how the opinions of men are always being replaced by new ones; no sooner do errors appear than they disappear, as fog in sunlight.

How to overcome errors

The Church has always opposed these errors; often she has even condemned them with the greatest severity. Now the Bride of Christ prefers to use the medicine of mercy rather than of severity. She believes in meeting the needs of today by demonstrating the validity of her doctrines rather than by renewing condemnations. Not that there is a lack of fallacious doctrines and dangerous opinions and conceptions to be on guard against, which need to be eliminated. But they are in such obvious contrast with a strict standard of honesty and have been so disastrous in their results that by now men are ready to condemn them, it seems, on their own. We speak especially of those ways of life which despise God and his law, of excessive trust in the progress of technology, and of the well-being founded wholly on life's comforts. They are more and more convinced that the dignity of the human person, his perfecting and the commitment it requires are matters of the utmost importance. What counts even more, experience has taught them that violence inflicted on others, force and political domination, are of no use in finding a happy solution to the problems which beset them.

Things being as they are, the Catholic Church raises, by means of this Ecumenical Council, the torch of religious truth and shows that she is the loving mother of all, benign, patient, merciful and good, even toward the children separated from her. To mankind, weighed down by so many burdens, she says, as Peter said to the poor man who begged alms of him: *I have no silver or gold, but I give you what I have; in the name of Jesus Christ of Nazareth, walk* (Acts 3, 6). That is, the Church does not offer passing riches to the men of today or promise them just earthly happiness. She shares with them the good of divine grace which raises men to the dignity of God's children and thereby provides a worthy means and help for a more humane existence. She opens the fount of her life-giving doctrine which allows men enlightened by Christ to understand what they really are, their high dignity, their purpose. Through her children she spreads Christian charity everywhere, and nothing is better than charity in removing the seeds of discord and in establishing harmony, a just peace and brotherhood.

The unity of the Christian and human family must be promoted

The Church's concern in promoting and defending the truth derives from the fact that men cannot, according to the plan of God, "who desires all men to be saved and to come to the knowledge of the truth" (I Timothy 2, 4), arrive at a complete and solid unity of spirit to which is joined true peace and eternal salvation, without the help of all of revelation.

Unfortunately the entire Christian family has not fully reached this visible unity in the truth.

The Catholic Church believes it her duty, therefore, to do all she can to bring about the wonder of that unity, for which Jesus Christ prayed to his heavenly Father just before his sacrifice. She enjoys great peace knowing how closely related she is to that prayer, and she takes great joy when the prayer has had beneficial effects, even on those outside her care. In considering carefully this unity Christ sought of his Father for his Church, there seem to shine from it three great rays: the unity among Catholics themselves, which must serve as an example; the unity of prayer and desire among the Christians separated from the Apostolic See to join us; and lastly the unity of esteem and respect toward the Catholic Church on the part of those who follow religions not Christian. And here we must note with sadness that the majority of mankind—albeit all men who are born were redeemed by Christ's blood—do not share in those sources of divine grace which they have in the Catholic Church. St. Cyprian said: "The Church, surrounded by divine light, extends its rays throughout the world; she is a single lamp that spreads light everywhere without losing her oneness. She sends branches out, and rivers as well, to the whole world by her fruitfulness, but all the same their head is one, their source is one, she is the only abundantly fertile mother. We were born of her, we are nourished by her milk, we live by her spirit."[6]

What does it matter if these eyes see it take place and conclude? It is enough for the confident serenity of Our soul that We simply fulfilled a happy inspiration and that We be ready to do and dare everything for its success.[7]

[1] *Motu Proprio*, June 5, 1960. [2] Speech, November 14, 1960.
[3] Speech, August 4, 1959. [4] Radio broadcast, April 23, 1959.
[5] Conversation, July 27, 1960. [6] Address, October 12, 1962.
[7] Address, November 11, 1960.

[III]

CHURCH RENEWAL

The Adolescent

The adolescent! Jesus too, the Divine Teacher, looks with special benevolence on this important and marvelous age, and the theme of the "Adolescent" reappears often in the Gospels, each time with a different tone, as a fresh coloring which makes those pages more alive and unforgettable.

Sometimes it is an appeal of absolute generosity, as when Jesus invites the young man to leave everything and follow him, and he looks into his eyes and shows him his love: "And Jesus looked on him and loved him" (Mark 10, 21).

Another time it is a powerful command to arise which restores life to two young innocents crushed by death. And it is so moving to think that of the three commands to arise recorded in the Gospels, two are addressed in almost equal terms to two children. In fact to Jairus' daughter Jesus says, "*Talitha cum,*" which means, "Maiden, I say to you, arise! (Mark 5, 41) and to the son of Naim's widow, "Young man, I say to you, arise!" (Luke 7, 14).

Again it is an invitation to work together, almost a precursor of Catholic Action in its function of working together with their bishops. In fact, it was a boy who gave our Lord the few loaves of bread and the fish that were necessary for his divine intentions (cf. John 6, 9).

Life is not made just to close oneself within oneself, in

selfishness and irresponsibility, but to move out, to teach, to do good.

Life does not mean inertia, laziness, paralysis, but rather generosity and enthusiasm. This Jesus expects from you and this his humble vicar, the Pope, asks of you.

Just as to the young man in the Gospel, Jesus appeals to you to be generous, for some of you will be called to higher ideals and may put into practice the letter of the passage from the Gospel: "Go, sell all you have . . . and come, follow me" (Mark 10, 21).

There is nothing indeed more beautiful than a religious and missionary vocation. But from all of you he asks without distinction this generosity: to leave the attitudes and empty demands of the world to serve him more closely, to know him more deeply, to love him and to make others love him more intensely. All this certainly requires sacrifice, but no one more than you young people can be as enthusiastic in following our Lord with a fervid heart, a clean mind, and tenacious will, without putting limits on your own generosity.

Just as he calls the adolescents of the Gospels, Jesus calls you to *life*, to the joy of living in grace, to know that you are the living temples of the Most Holy Trinity whch resides in the souls of the just. A life of prayer, of confession and spiritual direction; a life of Mass and of frequent communion that is always more devout. A life of faithfulness to the divine commandments, because this is the only condition for keeping to the fount of life itself, to Christ the Redeemer, just as the shoots are attached to the vine, bearing their golden clusters in abundance.

Just as he calls the young man of the Gospel, Jesus calls you to work together to offer your strength, your labor, your intelligence to spread his Kingdom. Let no one think he is not yet able. With five loaves of bread and two fish, Jesus fed a multitude, and he will know how to use your contribution to the apostolate, small as it may be, to work miracles.

All of you feel the holy desire to help Jesus by working together with the Catholic clergy, putting into practice what is asked of you, participating in group life, with all of its activities, and trying to set a good example wherever you live and work.[1]

[1] General audience, September 29, 1960.

To Youth

As Abraham predicted, the peoples of the earth have become as numerous as "the stars of heaven and as the sand which is on the seashore" (Genesis 22, 17). And We are gladdened by the sight of the modern generation who are the promise of the future.

Above all, you are *young*, and so aware of beauty, holiness, justice. Discouragement and destructive pessimism have not yet blurred your vision, as they so often do in later years. Preserve this clarity, this courage in facing the most trying tasks, this interest in the good things in life. In the orderliness and tranquillity of your youth lies the secret of the peaceful growth of the society which awaits you.

Despite the criticism one hears these days about modern youth, We retain our trust in them. We often repeat it, and again today: We trust in your capacities of mind and heart, and in your ability to meet the challenge of future responsibilities.

Once again: you offer a guarantee of peace because you are *willing*.

Your constant efforts to improve your knowledge of the faith and to excel in your studies are meaningful proofs of your good intentions. You will be asked, with God's grace, to contribute to the building of a national and international community where selfishness and mistrust will give way to charity and concord. And Holy Church expects much from your good will.

Your generous nature—We are happy to predict—will not disappoint us. You will cultivate the talents God gave you.

You are guarantors of freedom because you want *to learn.* You are willing to deepen your knowledge of life's essentials as they are presented by Divine Revelation and taught by the catechism.

In that small but great book are contained all the answers to the questions that have bothered men through the ages. It is the fount of living waters, which satisfies every thirst. So many souls have sought for it in vain, despite their intelligence, because they looked in the wrong place (cf. Jeremiah 2, 13).

By studying the catechism during your productive and decisive years, you are heading straight toward the essence of things; you will understand where to find the truth. We trust you will refer to it in your need, as the Psalm says: "Thy word is a lamp unto my feet and a light to my path" (Psalms 118, 105).[1]

There are three qualities a young person should have: joy, wisdom and strength, which he expresses with dignity and courage.

First of all, joy, the expression of a healthy life motivated by grace. A young person should be happy, enthusiastic. For that matter, everyone should be; old men are much more charming when they reveal some inner jocundity. But when a young man is not happy, it is especially desolating.

There are people who are not extraordinarily endowed, but whatever one had, he must make it worth something, because everything we have is given us by God. It is for this reason that life is worth living serenely. Our daily experiences teach us this. Whenever we meet someone who is sad, as good

Christians we immediately reach out to understand the reasons why. This basic act of charity we do especially for the young. If it is illness that is the cause of unhappiness, we try to help cure it; if it is a spiritual matter, we try to identify and eliminate the cause. It is part of our Christian mission.

Then, of course, we must speak of *wisdom*. We say a man is wise when he can see ahead, study the task to be done and bring it to completion. We do not have to give in to subconscious, irrational stimuli—and We say this particularly to the young—nor must we give in to the impulses inherent in our own character, the character we love so much, too much. Everything should be looked at carefully. How often we hear it said that a boy is good, and very promising, but a little strange, peculiar, willful. No, this should not be; the essential point is to keep your balance, internally and in your relations with your fellows.

Now, where can we find this valuable possession? We can really find it in the Lord's teaching: the Gospels, the Old Testament. There is the way to wisdom. When we have to make a decision, we can turn to the Lord's teaching and we will make a right one, because his Name, his law, and fear of him are the sources of wisdom.

In examining one's own conscience and looking at the conditions of one's life, its inevitable uncertainties and inadequacies, one is bound to ask, what must I do, what can I do? God has given me certain talents and opportunities, and I know what it is to do good, but at times I lack the courage to take a firm stand. This is the reason we need fortitude, strength. To sustain us in all our difficulties. God will help us if we are determined to do right. . . . [2]

Young people are very critical of themselves, perhaps because they are so impatient: their behavior, their language, their tendency to criticize. That is why one must go slow, holding on to some certainty, being faithful to all one has been taught. We must know how to wait for the Lord's grace to descend on us. Moderation is the key. This is true even of self-discipline and self-denial; it does not mean being lazy or slacking. . . . It means being sure we are using every way possible to reach God, according to his teaching.[3]

[1] Speech, April 10, 1959. [2] Speech, September 17, 1961.
[3] Speech, July 18, 1962.

Guardian Angels

One of the tenets of our faith teaches us that each person is not alone. As soon as a soul is created by God for a new human being, especially when the grace of the sacraments surrounds it with ineffable light, an angel is called forth from the pious, peaceful and jubilant hosts in heaven who will remain at our side during our entire earthly pilgrimage. It is fitting to recall this reality in the presence of Our Lady of the Angels in the church dedicated to her, and it is for good reason that the first note of our daily round is the greeting to the Blessed Mother, *Angelus Domini nuntiavit Mariae.*

When the Holy Father was called to Rome in October, 1958, and had to receive the vows of obedience that began his pontificate, he received a letter from a dear and devoted bishop in which he was reminded—as if it had been revealed to a chosen soul of great virtue—that upon the election of a new pope no less than twelve angels are sent by God to assist him in fulfilling his great mission. We are not dealing here, obviously, with an article of absolute faith, but doubtless this pronouncement reflects a doctrine which is consonant with all the rest. Now being content with simply the one angel each of us has means that We are providently anchored to that which is a guarantee and a trust, and therefore an incalculable treasure.

While in conversation one day with a very great pontiff, Pius XI, the Holy Father listened to him explain a very beautiful secret confirming that the protection of the guardian angel always gives joy, and resolves every difficulty and lightens every burden. When I have to speak to someone with whom I know it is difficult to argue, Pius XI confided, and for whom I have to choose especially persuasive language, I always turn to my guardian angel and ask him to speak to the other person's guardian angel, so that once the two spirits agree, our conversation is made easier and turns out for the best.

Queen of the Angels, Queen of the Angels! What enchantment, what a foretaste of heaven even in exercising our devotion to Mary, the Heavenly Mother, who is always surrounded with legions and legions of angels.

Let every believer take care to remember the important greeting, for his sake and for the sake of others, especially infants, not only in the morning but also in the evening. Greet your guardian angel so that he will watch over you and know how grateful you are for his care. In that way, you have the means to dissipate the cloud of whatever unhappiness took place during the day and to restore inner peace.[1]

[1] In St. Peter's, September 9, 1962.

Adversity

Here we have heaven and earth. We possess heaven in our minds, and something of it also in our hearts, especially when we feel a great love for God. Furthermore, Christian doctrine, in which we have been educated, imparts an incomparable lucidity to our minds, since we know where we come from, we know our final end and the right path to follow to it. Then we are always informed of what is most important to us: to honor oneself in Jesus Christ who saved us, in Christ crucified, and to carry out what we are taught by Jesus' mother, who—on Calvary—became our mother as well. What sublime thoughts!

Heaven and earth. We walk on the earth and encounter difficulties, bitterness, hardships, but we can face anything if we have faith in our hearts and confidence in our spirits, when we are certain that the Lord rules everything, that our final and real goal is Paradise, towards which everything and every means is coordinated.

Many times there are misfortunes in the family and we weep. But here is faith to show us that if God has allowed grief, he will sustain us: he shall come at the hour he has fixed to count us and raise us.

This reminder of security and inner peace is fundamental in the life of a Christian.[1]

[1] Audience, September 10, 1960.

Pain and Resignation

We know it by experience. Without pain, without resignation, true spiritual tranquillity—in the home and in society—cannot be hoped for, nor the merits for the hour when we shall pass over to the life that knows no twilight.

What began as an expression of triumph at the gates of Jerusalem ends on the fatal mount of Calvary. Shortly will sound the Hosannah at the entrance to the holy city, only to be followed by the curse and malediction which epitomize ingratitude and ignorance. From glory to ignominy. From *Hosannah!* to *Crucify him!*

Dearest children, that in a word is the summation of life on earth. Those who take it with love enjoy inner riches that thrive in peace and serenity. The others who go on fretting become subject to all the upsetting changes: personal bitterness, and a visible withering of their characters and traits.

On the accepting of the Christian calling, and following Jesus, who comes humbly astride an ass, depends the order of family life, of the community, of civil society itself.[1]

[1] Speech, March 19, 1961.

Lust and Desire

Triple lust: money first of all has a terrible power of attraction; thirst for power is insatiable; and the pleasures of life lead to indulgence and weakness.

The temptations are strong, the dangers serious. So they were yesterday, are today and shall be tomorrow.[1]

Whoever has had responsibility for directing souls, of the family and of religious, civic and social bodies, feels imperatively the duty to resist the collapse the three kinds of lust threaten man with. He is duty-bound to recall those ancient words that sound so unpleasant to some, the invitation to discipline and penance.

Discipline and penance, in fact, lead to an increase of social well-being and the assurance of peace.

This and nothing else is the reality: without discipline there is no man; without penance there is no Christian.

We must all fight against desire. Many dream about and

desire material riches, money. And St. Francis teaches everyone from all walks of life to fight against the lust of the eye, which is a great deceit, a great vanity. The wealth of Christian life does not consist in money and the pursuit of it. Money is necessary to live, true, but we do not have to be magnetized by it. Before his father and the bishop, Francis renounced even his clothes, so great was his love of poverty.

When Providence gives someone more than he needs, his surplus becomes an invitation to redistribute it, to help the poor, to contribute to the great works of brotherhood. This precept applies to everyone, especially those who have consecrated their lives to God.

Whoever has ample means must give more generously, and give for those who do not have so much. The commandment applies not only to two brothers, two families, two cities, but to the whole world. Because it can happen that a rich man feels strong and boasts of his strength, closing his eyes and his ears to poverty, to those who are forced to live out miserable lives, while brotherhood would help them have at least what is necessary to live. If we want to find a little joy on earth too, we must follow St. Francis' example, which was the same as Christ's, who performed miracles to help the starving.[2]

[1] Speech, March 19, 1961. [2] Conversation, October 4, 1961.

The Devil

Facing man, the Christian, and especially the priest, stands the enemy of the good: *seeking someone to devour* (I Peter 5, 8). He tries to subvert the order God ordained. Every weapon is useful to him, from scorn of the eternal laws (as if they were superstitions of the ignorant) to the pettiest spiritual sloth, from the hectic pursuit of personal interests to facile and rebellious demagogy, from the temptations of solitude to those of intellectual pride and cultural intolerance.

But our weapons are more powerful than those of the prince of this world. They demand constant vigilance: *Be sober and watchful . . . resist him firm in your faith* (I Peter 5, 8–9).[1]

The so-called lord of the world dared in his audacity to approach the Son of God, who in his infinite humility permitted him to, knowing well how inane the gesture was, but desiring to show us how to behave when evil tempts us, as it always does even though the prince of evil knows his works shall earn eternal malediction.

Jesus' answers to the three temptations of the devil are clear, explicit, peremptory right to the last ringing command: "Thou shalt love the Lord thy God and serve only him."

We are speaking of the problem which always arises between truth and error, good and evil, humility and pride, selfishness and charity, love and betrayal.

Jesus' enemy persists in his attacks, even though he knows in his desperation that he will never have a final victory. He will not have it because there is someone stronger than he is. And the human beings who are his victims hear the loud voice of Christian teaching, the Gospel of grace, the Gospel of penance. They hear Christ's warning not to be deceived, to have faith in him who will always and in eternity be the victor.

Everybody has faults and peculiarities, and unfortunately can lapse into blame. But it is always possible to raise oneself again—it must be done immediately—through Christ, through his crucifixion, his teaching, the certainty of his forgiveness.

And so the great virtues which the lessons of the Holy Savior impart thrive in the Christian soul. The soul is strengthened in that profound and active union which is most clearly demonstrated in the person of Christ's Vicar.

The Pope hears the prayers of his children join his own, every hour of the day and well into the night. These prayers draw upon the moving parts of Holy Scripture: O Jesus, near you my mouth is still, but even my silence speaks to you: *silentium meum loquitur tibi*.

From the uninterrupted prayer spring even greater fruits for God's Church. The gifts of humility and meekness increase, and above all the gift of a constant and persuasive patience, the undoubted sign of fresh victories.[2]

[1] Speech, April 2, 1961. [2] Speech, March 11, 1962.

Against Bad Habits

The Catholic doctrine concerning the immaculate conception of the Virgin Mary praises her splendor and is well known to every good Christian, a joy to noble souls. It is in the liturgy, in the writings of the Church Fathers and in the hearts of so many who would hold up her purity as an example to raise the level of private and public morals.

This is truly a great task for us, to work together, all of us, with the help of Mary Immaculate and in the light of her teachings, toward a purifying of public and private life.

We know we are striking a sad note, but Our conscience compels Us to do so.

The forgetting of purity, the perversion of morality that is everywhere displayed and praised through so many forms of seduction and prevarication, is a source of grief to the priest —and imagine of how much greater bitterness to the Pope.

As We go back over the long course of Our life and recall its encounters and its various impressions from so long ago, We are still moved in remembering the numberless brides and mothers, the humble housewives and consecrated virgins whose charitable and prudent service was the strength and true nobility of the family and the helpmeet of the priest's mission. Their silent work was performed in the light of divine law, as an expression of human and Christian virtues, which flower from the dignity and purity of morals.

The traditions of Our good Christian people are still in the main sound and firm, anchored to a sure faith and to an awareness of the truth and wisdom the Church so jealously guards as her greatest spiritual treasure. It is necessary, however, for all those who really care about the fate of the family and society that they express greater firmness in the face of the unprecedented attempts to defeat morality. In this common effort to which are called all men of good will, especially the fathers and mothers of families, a help against defeat, a bright and powerful inspiration to keep faith and to remain strong in this worthy battle, is Mary Immaculate. We must ask her to protect us, to provide an example for us, to be our comfort in this guiding and apostolic work.

Mary Immaculate, morning star who dissipates the shadows of the dark night, to you do we turn with great trust. *Vitam praesta puram: iter para tutum.* Free our paths from the seductions of worldly interests, sustain the energies not only of youth but of all ages, exposed as they all are to the temptations of evil.[1]

[1] Address, December 8, 1960.

Immorality

Containing the desires of the flesh

To know how to mortify the desires of the flesh which daily tempt us in this earthly existence. This is the discipline that every mortal must learn to impose on himself. And those who have authority and responsibilities must feel more vividly the sacred duty to oppose immorality.

The love of purity is the honor and the most precious possession of Christian families, the surest sign of earthly and heavenly blessings.

Declining the glory of the world

God's gifts are priceless claims to honor for those who realize they have received them from the Creator and who accept them humbly, without boasting. But indulging one's vanity and trying to justify one's conceit in the eyes of the world are signs of an impoverished spirit that can only arouse compassion and derision. In the Catholic Church, the examples set by Christ and his blessed Mother are the real signs of greatness. There are two particular expressions of them: Learn from me your Teacher, *for I am gentle and lowly in heart* (Matthew 11, 29), and the other concerning our Mother—the Mother of the human race regenerated in Christ: *Behold the handmaid of the Lord*; for me, the word and the goodness and the example of the Lord *be done unto me, let it be to me according to your word* (Luke 1, 38).

Not desiring the goods of others

The great precept and the great temptation both face us all: not to steal, not to defraud workers of their due, not to oppress the poor, not to pursue intemperately the passing riches of the world. Considered carefully, this is the trouble with the whole world. We do not mean that in political and economic relations—or disagreements as the case might be—there are not honest people who respect the rights of others, but in fact one of the greatest temptations in life to which a large number of men succumb directly or indirectly is this; that is, to covet and to steal. Anything can become robbery or its accomplice under various terms; everything is desire, greed and often horrible violence, once we have felt the dark skills and the subtle deceit of the initial craving. From there we go to abomination which becomes the extermination of cities, countries, peoples.[1]

[1] Appeal, April 8, 1962.

Marriage

There is unquestionably something in the air these days which is very subtly aggravating the dangers that the institution of the family faces. Its effects are being more widely felt, yet are more insidious and undermining than they were in the past.

The Church has already expressed its alarm in the face of this erosion of conscience, both individual and collective, in a matter of such vital concern to the well-being of society. The encyclicals, the pronouncements, and the speeches of Our Predecessors attest to the maternal concern of the Church. And today too she will not fail in her duty, given to her by Christ himself. The Church will continue to teach the lesson she must, no matter how severe.

For this reason, We intend calling the attention of all men of good will—magistrates, sociologists, educators, and the faithful generally—to the serious problem which menaces the sanctity of marriage, so that they will be moved to do something about it. We would like to suggest some simple points for common consideration. These three points concern pastoral practice and an authentic sense of mission: (1) everyone must be instructed; (2) those who instruct, counsel or judge must have a firm doctrinal grounding; (3) the fatherhood of God must always be borne in mind.

(1) In the first place, the necessity of instruction concerning the dignity and the obligations of marital life.

Speaking to a group of newly-weds on April 22, 1942, Pius XII reminded them that "matrimony is not simply a function of nature, but also a great sacrament, a great sign of grace, something very holy, as is Christ's marriage with the Church, which he made his with his blood in order to regenerate the children of men who believe in his name. . . . The seal and the light of the sacrament which, so to speak, transform the natural function; the sacrament ennobles marriage, endowing it not only with indissolubility, but also with the meaning of sacrament itself."

This Christian viewpoint on marriage must be continuously passed on to the faithful in every walk of life. It is particularly necessary that the young, who are about to be married, be instructed to make them aware of the deep responsibilities they are entering into and their religious significance.

We are very conscious of the various undertakings these days to provide instruction to engaged couples: scientific publications, marriage counselors, courses, lectures. We are grateful for these experimental efforts when they are undertaken with due caution, delicacy and the consent of ecclesiastical authorities, because they promise to yield valuable results.

We must be energetic and sincere in wanting to deal with this problem; the times are more pressing and impatient. The age of youth, especially when the young are engaged to be married, sometimes blurs the clarity of ideals in the mists of sentiment and passion that are not understood or controlled. We are not far from the truth in this: we have evidence of it over the radio, in the press and the movies, and in the other vacuous and immoral offerings of the day. The artificial world contrived out of a thousand seductive ploys—which are really violations of the conscience—mitigate against traditional customs and, worse, mislead youth.

The seriousness of this problem lies not so much in the many varied instances that can be easily identified, as in the general relaxing of moral barriers. For this reason, We urge all pastors to use every means at their command to inform parents and children of their duty.

We extend this invitation to anyone who has some say in public affairs, so that they will strive to clarify and not obscure the important ideas at stake: the integrity and respectability of the most valuable social good, the inviolability of marriage.

(2) In order to carry out this obligation, those who are professionally or by vocation concerned with marital problems must have strong doctrinal grounding.

This is especially true of the judiciary who must bear in mind the demands of the law they are administering and the necessity not to give in to weakness or sentimentality, but at the same time to be perfectly balanced in their judgments in the light of the conditions of our time.

Doctrinal strength in educators and doctors. We can never deplore enough the damage done to marriage and to the concept of family by naturalistic and inevitably materialistic viewpoints. By trying to diminish the role of the Church and reducing marriage to a purely human institution, these viewpoints have slowly but surely eroded its structure and stability.

We cannot emphasize enough that morality and the sound education of the feelings, along with the appreciation of human values as consonant with the supernatural, will resolve right from the start those difficult situations marriages sometimes face. Even when the courts have arrived at some solution to them, the wounds they cause never heal. In part, we must recall the conditions imposed by original sin: the need, in short, of grace. Grace alone can restore the injured man, and when we ignore it willfully, we deprive married life of its strongest support.

This is a consideration that doctors and educators must bear in mind, too. They must not think of their professions from just a single point of view, but rather with thought to man's entire condition, in which he can only regain health through the harmonious action of both his physical and his immortal parts.

The irresponsibility that is so frequently shown in marital problems, and the slackening in moral standards We have already mentioned, are caused not only by a worrisome deficiency in religious training, but also by the lack of clear ideas on the part of those who are professionally involved in advising young people about marriage. Their lack of conviction, their superficial advice, and even their mistaken philosophical and religious ideas, along with—and We say this with great sadness—frequent hostility to the Church deal the first blows to the moral standards of these young couples. At times, these young people are influenced the wrong way by anti-Christian doctors and teachers.

Strength of conviction, of will, of doctrinal orthodoxy, coupled with continuous application and study, and humility, will teach that real knowledge can never contradict the dictates of Revelation and the precepts of the Church.[1]

Amid the doctrinal uncertainties which are here and there disrupting public opinion, a solemn and serious reminder of the principles behind the Church's views on matrimony is absolutely necessary. In protecting the indissolubility of the bond and sanctity of the great sacrament of marriage, the Church is not only defending an ecclesiastic and civil right, but above all, a natural and divine one. These two great goods, which passion and prejudice sometimes obscure, are required by natural law, impressed on man's conscience, and by the law of our Lord Jesus Christ, even prior to any concrete, human law. This is not a matter of rules and prescriptions dictated by circumstance and changeable in the course of time, but rather of divine will, in the intangible order established by God himself to safeguard the family, the nucleus of civilized society. Matrimony is a matter of primordial divine law, which Christ brought to completion in the fulness of time, *but from the beginning it was not so* (Matthew 19, 8).

The Church is not defending class interests, nor outmoded traditions. She aims only at fulfilling the plea in the Lord's Prayer: "Thy will be done on earth as it is in heaven." The Church is interested in defending God's will on earth, and in that will is found peace, serenity and even material prosperity for all her children.

A large effort to teach and to illustrate the truth, through the Church's traditional methods, and through the modern communication media, is therefore very necessary. We must study new methods to deliver this teaching, particularly to the young people who are about to be married.[2]

There is only one reason for saying all this. And that reason is the Church's purpose throughout the ages, the salvation of souls. She is motivated only by concern for all her children. This is the informing spirit of the Church's tribunals; this spirit guides the ecclesiastic judge, the defender of the bond, as well as the promoter of justice and the lawyers. It is the ministry of the truth, because it seeks the salvation of the souls of those who must have recourse to these tribunals.

The Church does aim at the eternal salvation of the individual, even when she must limit the right of accusal and issues a sentence of guilt; indeed, the guilty spouse never loses access to the means to escape eternal damnation.[3]

[1] Allocution to the Sacred Rota, October 25, 1960.
[2] Allocution to the Sacred Rota, December 13, 1961.
[3] Encyclical, *Ad Petri Cathedram*, June 29, 1959.

Sin, Sinner, Forgiveness

St. Luke recounts a singular episode in his Gospel. It is a delicate, important subject, not to be taken lightly or commented upon inexactly.

Mary Magdalene, a sinner, throws herself at the feet of Our Lord, who had been invited to the house of a chief Pharisee, Simon. She repents her sins; she has faith in the Savior, the Son of God. He addresses a word of true rebirth to her: "Your faith has saved you; go in peace."

Naturally the rest of the guests began to murmur at this unusual scene, and wonder at the Lord's words. Jesus did not ignore their complaints; reading the thoughts of his host, he explained to him his goodness, his compassion and his forgiveness. The Lord forgives the sinner who has repented and leads him to salvation.

For twenty centuries, this episode has echoed in the history of the Church. Numberless souls have been able, like Mary Magdalene, to throw themselves on the infinite mercy of God.

It is the same mercy that, operating through the Sacrament of Penance, absolves all sins, no matter how large or small. The Divine Teacher, a few days before the episode St. Luke recounts, speaking to his disciples, had explained how they should pray: "Our Father, who art in heaven . . . forgive us our trespasses as we forgive those who trespass against us. . . ."

In the greatest prayer of them all, the Our Father, priests and faithful alike invoke the Lord's forgiveness, "forgive us our trespasses," but add as the absolute condition for that pardon, "as we forgive those who trespass against us." The Lord absolves our sins but demands we do the same for those who have offended us.

If this doctrine were applied universally, it would facilitate and fructify the labors of the statesmen and diplomats who meet throughout the world for the purpose of ending war and securing the peace. If the principle that God will forgive us if we forgive others were a living reality in the world, there would be universal respect and tolerance between men. Forgiveness informed by faith in God would open the heart to his grace, and therefore to the possibilities of justice and fraternity.

The Church has always taught these goals, beginning with forgiveness itself. She has pointed the way, in so many cases, to the attainment of God's mercy. What in fact are the Holy Years, the Jubilees, that Pope Boniface inaugurated in 1300, if not solemn and grand occasions for imploring divine clemency and fostering the Christian spirit of brotherly love?

Whoever turns to God with contrite and humbled heart, whoever forgives those who have offended him, will surely be embraced by the Lord. Thus on earth would have begun the canticle of joy which is the eternal reality of paradise.[1]

. . . We must never . . . confuse the error with the erring, even when the error, or the inadequate knowledge of the truth, is religious and moral in nature. The person who errs is always and above all a human being and retains, in any case, his personal dignity. He should always be considered and treated as befits such dignity. In every human being, furthermore, the need for truth never ends. And God's action within him never fails. For this reason, the person who does not possess the clarity of faith at one point in his life, or who subscribes to mistaken opinions, can be enlightened to the truth at any moment. The encounters and the dealings in various sectors of the temporal order between those who believe and those who do not, or who do not believe adequately, can be occasions for discovering the truth and honoring it.[2]

[1] Speech, July 22, 1961.
[2] Encyclical, *Pacem in Terris*, April 11, 1963.

Penance

To do penance for our sins as Jesus explicitly bade us is the means man the sinner has to obtain forgiveness and to attain eternal salvation. The attitude of the Catholic Church is, therefore, as evident as it is justified; the Church, dispenser of the fruits of Redemption, has always considered penance as the indispensable condition for the perfecting of her children's lives and for a better future.

Now if we consult the Old and New Testaments, we will find that every meaningful encounter has always been preceded by the call to prayer and penance. Moses, in fact, does not deliver the tablet of the Ten Commandments to the Hebrews until they have done penance for their idolatry and ingratitude. The prophets unceasingly exhort the people of Israel to pray to God with contrite hearts so as to fulfill the design of Providence that is present throughout the history of the chosen people. A moving voice among them is that of Joel, which resounds in the holy liturgy of Lent: *Yet even now, says the Lord, return to me with all your heart, with fasting, with weeping, and with mourning; and rend your hearts and not your garments . . . Between the vestibule and the altar let the priests, the ministers of the Lord, weep and say, "Spare thy people, O Lord, and make not thy heritage a reproach, a byword among nations . . .*' (Joel 2, 12–17).

Rather than diminishing, these calls to penance take on new meaning with the advent of the Son of God on earth. St. John the Baptist begins his sermon with the cry, "Do penance, for the heavenly kingdom is at hand." Christ himself does not begin his ministry with the immediate revelation of the sublime truths of faith, but with the call to purify the mind and the heart of whatever might hinder man from understanding the glad tidings: "From that moment, Jesus began to preach and to say: Do penance, for the heavenly kingdom is at hand." More than the prophets ever did, the Savior demands of his followers that they transform their spirits completely, in recognition of God's claims: "Behold, the Kingdom of God is with you." Penance is a power against evil; Jesus himself taught us, "The heavenly kingdom is won by force, and is prey to those who use violence."

The same call reappears in the sermons of the Apostles. St. Peter spoke to the crowd after Pentecost to convince them to accept regeneration in Christ and the blessings of the Holy Ghost: "Do penance, and be baptized, each one of you, in the name of Jesus Christ, for the remission of your sins, and you will receive the blessing of the Holy Spirit." The Apostle warns the Romans that the Kingdom of God does not consist of arrogance and indulgence of the senses, but in the triumph of justice and in interior peace: "For the Kingdom of God is not food and drink, but justice, peace and joy in the Holy Spirit."

You must not think that the call to penance is directed only to those who are about to enter the Kingdom of God. All Christians, in reality, have the duty and the need to chastise themselves, in order to drive back their own spiritual enemies, to preserve their baptismal innocence, or to acquire again the grace they lost by transgressing against God's commandments.

Interior penance is needed, above all; that is, penitence and absolution of one's own sins, which is achieved especially by good Confession and Communion, and by attending the Holy Sacrifice of the Mass. For this kind of penance all the faithful should go to the Novena to the Holy Spirit. All the external acts of penance would be in vain if there were not at the same time a true humility of the spirit and true regret for one's sins. In this sense, Christ warns us severely: "If you do not penance, you shall all perish." May God keep this danger from all those who have been entrusted to Us.

The faithful must be urged to external penance as well, in order to submit their bodies to the dictates of right reason and the faith, and to expiate their own guilt and the guilt of others. St. Paul, who had gone to Third Heaven and touched the verge of saintliness, does not hesitate to say of himself, "I mortify my body and keep it in slavery," and elsewhere warns us, "Those who belong to Christ have crucified their flesh with their desires."

The first external penance we must perform is to accept all the pain and grief God sends us in life with resignation and faith, and to carry out our obligations regardless of the work and the inconvenience they cause us, in our daily occupation, in our place in society and in the exercise of Christian virtues.

Beside the penances we must necessarily perform for the inevitable griefs of this mortal life, Christians must also be prepared to offer God their voluntary mortifications, following the example of Our Redeemer. As St. Peter said, "He died for our sins once and for all, he the just for the unjust, to bring us back to God; he was put to death in the flesh, but arisen to life in the spirit."

"Since Christ suffered in the flesh," let us too arm ourselves "with the same thought." Let the saints of the Church be examples, for the mortifications they inflicted on themselves, although they were often innocent, fill us with wonder and admiration.[1]

[1] Encyclical, *Poenitentia agere*, July 1, 1962.

Goodness

Nothing has more excellence than goodness. Human intellect can appraise other important qualities, but none compares with goodness. It is connatural with the Son of God made Man and with what he explained and showed to us: the practice, that is, of brotherhood, of patience; constancy in enduring and suffering, in the inner discipline of our own natures and in our social relationships, just as he pointed them out to us.

Jesus did not tell us: Learn from me that I am the son of the Heavenly Father. He did not teach us how to create the sky and the earth or how to ignite the sun, but rather he taught us to be meek and humble of heart. And here is the foundation of goodness. By filling ourselves with it, we shall be taking the surest way to overcome the pitfalls and the meanness of this earthly existence.[1]

[1] Conversation, March 10, 1960.

Good and Evil

Good and evil prevail and will remain in the future, because the human will shall always have the freedom to express itself and also the possibility of losing itself. But to Christ and to his Church shall be the final and outward victory in each elected soul and in the elected souls of every people.[1]

[1] Radio broadcast, September 11, 1962.

To the Seminarians

The seminarian's rosary . . . reminds Us of all the young men who are preparing for the priesthood both in the countries that have long been Christian, and in missionary lands. The sight of these young souls who aspire to the highest ideal on earth leads Us to say something which may be useful to you, a message dictated by the desire to meet today's needs and to fulfill the Church's intention to gather her forces, so that she may be of greater service and attraction to the world.

Our advice is inspired by the three favors We always ask of God through the intercession of Mary Immaculate, Our Lady of Good Counsel, of the holy Apostles, Peter and Paul, of St. Charles Borromeo and of all the patron saints of the dioceses and seminaries: that is, We ask for purity of heart, strength of character and love of charity. They will renew us, even when our age and our labors have lessened our physical vigor.

Above all, *purity of heart*, that which becomes, with careful vigilance, the order and clarity of our whole life, of every word, of every act. This is one of the chief virtues of Christian families, where it flourishes, for the family is its natural home. And it is the soul's relentless attraction. Passing like white snow over mud, which unfortunately covers so much of this poor world, *all of which is in the power of the evil one* (1 John 5, 19), purity of heart touches even the most distant, even those who may at times have derided it, but who have need of it.

Purity of heart assures serenity to whoever has a serious vocation, the soil from which grow all of our inclinations. It is certainly not the prime virtue, in the sense that whenever God may no longer be present, it would provide some kind of natural perfection; rather, it is the breath of God's love and the indispensable condition a priest must observe if he is to fulfill his ministry and his disinterested service to his fellow men. Purity of heart enables him to have those incomparable conversations at the foot of the Tabernacle; it enables him to feel the meaning of the apostolate and of charity; it inspires a continuous serenity, which is never defeated by adversity nor interrupted by joy. Purity of heart puts an unmistakable stamp of calm, reserve, discretion on everything the seminarian or the priest does, or says.

Live by this virtue in the freshness of your years; remember it in your prayers, in your self-discipline, in your studies. Because it is the virtue which gladdens your religious preparation, your training for the modern world, since your theological, pastoral and ascetic studies do not lack a modern literature, in several languages, that is readily available. These are the things priests of the Lord ought to read, and not the tiresome and harmful literature which wears away the conscience, which disguises itself as knowledge while it is actually an exercise in *subtiliter fornicare*. This kind of reading seriously weakens the priest's capacity to inspire his parishioners to higher things, the capacity which is the source of his own inner joy and of the purity of his look and smile.

From this awareness of purity proceeds the strength of character of which We spoke as the second endowment of your vocation. The Church wants strong and staunch men, who are prepared in heart and mind. Fortunately, the time when candidates for the priesthood were weak and incomplete, almost spineless beings, the time, that is, when the vigorous and impelling reality of the Church was not recognized, has passed. Belonging to the Church demands a well-tempered character and will, firm self-discipline, and with God's help, self-domination. If this is true for the man who wants to live as a Catholic in the real sense, then it is even more true for the man who feels the call to the priesthood, to which only a limited number of the resolute and strong are chosen. These are the men who can follow the Lord's call without hesitation, or compromise, giving up even their permissible joys in order to lead as pure a life as possible on earth.

The Church wants you this way. Future priests must learn to resist the attractions of the secular world. They must train their senses so that they are always master of themselves wherever they may be. They must have the natural virtues as well, because we would seek the Christian and the priest worthy of his vocation in vain, if they were not equally endowed with natural virtues. Thus it is your duty to be sincere and impartial, just as God is; God, before whom there is no partiality (cf. Romans 2, 11); your duty to keep your word, to be forthright and not devious, and not to conceal cruder motives by calling them charity or worship.

Finally, you must love *charity*, which perfects everything you do.

Love is "the fulfilling of the Law" (Romans 13, 10); you must feel charity in order to perform your daily tasks meaningfully, from the smallest to the most important. Love enables you to obey your bishop willingly, and to work enthusiastically in your parish, without worldly concerns, or desire for ephemeral praise. The seminarian who feels this charity is not alarmed by the difficulties he must inevitably encounter; he gives himself over confidently to God, who called him, and whom he would not want to displease. The seminarian distinguishes himself in his discipline and orderliness; he makes the sacrifices which are inherent in his way of life without realizing it, and willingly offers the Lord the renunciations he makes of the worldly things that would frequently overwhelm him. Through charity, he makes prayer and the sacraments the center of his life.

The sublime beauty of the priesthood. We would not have dared describe its essential characteristics, which make it an almost superhuman calling, if We had not known that God is near us. He calls us to his service, and provides us, at the same time, the strength to meet the call. The Heart of Jesus inspires us; from him proceeds charity, justice and love.

The priests who have drawn on the Sacred Heart have found there the source of their sanctification. Suffice it to recall the Curé of Ars, whom We have cited as an example for all priests in Our recent encyclical, *Sacerdotii Nostri Primordia*. Every diocese has the names of great and humble priests in its registers, names which may not have official recognition from the Church, but which nonetheless embody the spirit of sanctity and dedication, even *beyond the confines of earthly life.*[1]

[1] Speech, November 22, 1959.

The Priesthood

Today as always, high ideals sustain Our priests. They want to carry out their vocation without ever compromising with the secular spirit of the times. They want to consolidate the bonds of brotherhood with other priests so that they can overcome the narrowness of solitude and develop their spiritual and pastoral interests more fervently and effectively. They dedicate themselves to identifying and resolving the constantly changing problems the modern apostolate must confront.

We are very pleased with them. By the same token, We are not unaware of the dangers that the enemy is always sowing, even in the best of works. It has not escaped Our attention either how a mistaken sense of accomplishment and a willful search for novelty can seriously threaten the loss of a priest's real qualities.

We should like to present you with some thoughts to remember this day, so that the consideration of the greatness and obligations of our common priesthood will encourage you to remain strong in your commitment and to perfect the work the Lord has entrusted to you.

The priest is—above all—a man of God. This is the way Christians think of you, and this is what God willed you to be. Try to confirm your lives with the pure implications that that definition alone causes in your hearts. By saying "man of God," one excludes everything which is not God. The true priest is he who, like Abraham, chosen to be "the father of many tribes," has abandoned everything for ever in order to follow the divine call. As we read in the Bible: "Go from your country and your kindred and your father's house to the land that I will show you" (Genesis 12, 1). For the true priest, this promised land promises a cross. He seeks nothing but Christ and this cross. Eternal and invisible, God reveals himself in Jesus, and the priest must try to discover the *Mediator Dei et hominum* (Mediator of God and men), who will point out the Father. "Have I been with you so long, and yet you do not know me? . . . He who has seen me has seen the Father" (John 14, 9).

May your lives, therefore, be filled with Christ, with ardent love for him who leads us to the Father. This is the real basis of life for the priest who is concerned with his own peace and with the welfare of souls. We say to you, "The love of Christ and the love of silence." Let Christ be your only friend and counselor, during your vigils before the

Tabernacle, while you work at your desk, or helping the poor or curing the sick or preaching. Seek only him, consider human things in his light, to conquer them for him. Take his gentle yoke upon you by practicing the virtue that is proper to a consecrated life; that is, dedication to the Lord and to his people, untiring efforts for the Church, the performing of the fourteen works of mercy, prompt and sincere obedience to your bishop, and manly respect for holy things.

Jesus cannot be found in a dissipated life, even if the most sacrosanct reasons of the ministry were appealed to. And for this reason, We have said to you, "the love of silence." Silence is the sure guardian of all the virtues, especially of chastity and charity; it is a guarantee of effective pastoral work.

Be men of God in all things, silently committed to the search for perfection and charity "in Christ Jesus Our Lord."

Another thought We want to leave with you, Venerable Brothers and dear children, We have already declared to the faithful of Rome and the world the day We took possession of Our Cathedral, St. John Lateran. In explaining the meaning of the solemn liturgical rite, We pointed out the two most precious objects on the altar, the Holy Scriptures and the Chalice. And We said, "The bishop and all the priests working with him express the primary character of the Church's pastoral mission—the teaching of sacred doctrine. Here in the Missal are the two Testaments, here in the call to the people is the principal and highest point of the Catholic priesthood. . . . It is here fitting to affirm the sacred nature of the pastoral ministry, a strong, splendid and compelling catechesis."

Today too, as We repeat these words, We want to stress that the sacred books are the principal source of true doctrine and inspiration in your pastoral mission. Anthologies of sermons, or even the most complete theological reviews and periodicals, are not enough, if there is not the foundation. Even less sufficient to your spiritual and intellectual life is the popular press, which can be subtly distracting, but which interferes with the meditation and the dialogue the consecrated soul has with God. As Our Predecessor, St. Gregory the Great—whose feast-day is today—warns, "*Valde namque inter humana verba cer defluit: cumque indubitantur constet quod externis occupationum tumultibus impulsum a semetipso corruat, studere incessabiliter debet, ut per eruditionis studium resurgat*" (*Reg. Past.*, p. II, Chap. XI).

We recommend, therefore, that you assiduously study Sacred Scripture, theology, the sacred sciences, all in the light of the Church's living interpretation, which will keep you always young in spirit, and which will prevent you from instructing others imprecisely, vaguely, presumptuously . . . or monotonously. People seek Christ's words, and it is the duty of the priest to communicate them in their wholeness and freshness.

Next to the Bible, the Chalice.

The most mysterious and sacred part of the Eucharistic Liturgy centers in the chalice of Jesus, containing his sacred blood. Jesus is our Redeemer, and we participate mystically in his Body, the Holy Church. Christian living means sacrifice. Through sacrifice which is motivated by love, we approach most closely the ultimate purpose of Jesus' life on earth. We urge you to make the Sacred Mysteries the center of your day. We do not gain perfection or true love for God and Christ without profound devotion to the Eucharist, which is the life of all the faithful, particularly of the priest.

Our last recommendation: another great love which must transfigure your lives—the love for men's souls. We know this is your ideal, but do not think Our recommendation superfluous. It is prompted by a consideration that pains us all: why is it that after so many efforts and sacrifices, after so much work, the results are so unsatisfactory? Why is it that despite everything the apostolate can do, the dead sons of the Church do not arise, as we read in the lenten liturgy about the son of Elisias' servant, the boy who lay still?

"The boy does not arise!" At times spiritual miracles do not take place because the intention is not pure; perhaps because it is not always and solely that the good of souls is sought after, for which we are prepared to sacrifice ourselves; or perhaps because we have too much confidence in means that resemble human means, and are therefore inadequate, and we have not based our work on prayer and total sacrifice.[1]

The uncontaminated glory of the Catholic priesthood throughout the world, and in all the activities of the apostolate in which they are engaged now and will be in the future, is their spotless lives; that is, the purity of their minds and hearts, their spirit of meekness and humility; the perennial flame of action and sacrifice.

Do not let yourselves be attracted or persuaded just by currents of thought or by anything that takes away from the integrity of this teaching, which must take precedence over any other. Any concessions on this point, or any compromise, however slight, always lead to deception and disappointment.

My sons, how sad is withered conviction. From conviction, we expected beauty, and general edification. But instead, it is dried up and blown away by any wind.

Our youth is unhappy whenever this happens; how painful and slow the progress through life, through the years, of the man who did not fulfill the great promise of his total consecration to God.

A spotless life is always poetic and fresh, happy and enthusiastic, and always the source of attraction for the souls of others.

Another precious aspect of the priestly life is meekness and humility. When the Son of God came on earth to instruct mankind, he taught no lesson clearer than this: the humility of the spirit, of the mind, in word and in attitude.

Often this humility is silence; this meekness can appear to be weakness. In reality, it is strength of character and the great dignity of life, an indication of certain value, even as a sign of the beginning of free and peaceful relations among men.

Success is always assured to the humble of heart. Whoever is not so, whoever gives in to presumptuous pride, is destined to live through bitter days, empty-handed, and discouraged.

Study too, inspired by divine wisdom, puts the assurances of true and deep knowledge within our grasp, and must be prized when it is motivated by the decided intention of learning, spreading, defending the truth.

The young man who feels the call to the universal apostolate, to the transmission of grace from his heart to his brothers' hearts, so that everyone can know Revelation and Christ's glory, must study and prepare.

As the Apostle said, "You are blessed, young men, because you are strong."

Such strength is most gloriously enacted in the spirit of sacrifice, which is the mortification and the denial of the self, offered to God's will and to the true edification of souls.[2]

The great happiness We felt as a young priest just beginning his ministry is linked in Our mind with the deep emotion We felt once, in St. Peter's, on January 8, 1905, on the occasion of the beatification of the humble village priest, Jean Marie Baptiste Vianney. Having been ordained just a few months earlier, We were struck by the description of this admirable priest that Our Predecessor, St. Pius X, the former pastor of Salzano, had so happily given as an example to other priests. Even after so many years, We cannot recall that event without thanking Our Savior for the spiritual inspiration We received at that moment, right at the beginning of Our work.

In speaking of St. Jean Marie Vianney, we describe a priest who was extremely disciplined, who, for the love of God and the conversion of sinners, would deprive himself of food and sleep, chastise himself and deny himself to an heroic degree. True, the faithful are not generally asked to do this, but Divine Providence has arranged that there be such men in the Church, who, guided by the Holy Ghost, do not hesitate to take this path of self-sacrifice, because it is such men especially who work wonders of conversion.

Our Predecessor, Pius XII, desired to clarify this doctrine and allay any misunderstanding; he said specifically that it is false to affirm that "the clerical state—in itself and insofar as it proceeds from divine law—by its nature or by a postulate of the same nature, demands that its members observe the advice of the Gospel." The Pope concluded rightly: "The clergy, therefore, is not obligated by divine law by the poverty, chastity and obedience prescribed by the Gospel." But it would be a large misunderstanding of the Pope, who was so concerned for the holiness of priests and the consistent teaching of the Church, to believe that the secular priest is called to perfection any less than the religious. On the contrary, the carrying out of his priestly functions demands of the priest "a greater degree of interior sanctity than that required by the religious state." And if by virtue of the clerical state the priest is not compelled to practice what the Gospel advises in order to arrive at this sanctity, he must realize, along with all of Christ's followers, that practicing what the Gospel teaches is the royal way to Christian sanctification. It is a great assurance to Us to note how many priests today have realized this, because even though they remain in the ranks of secular priests, they ask to be guided and upheld in the ways of perfection by pious associations approved by the Church.[3]

[1] Speech, March 12, 1959. [2] Speech, November 20, 1958.

[3] Encyclical, *Sacerdotii Nostri Primordia*, August 1, 1959.

The Religious Orders

We greet the members of religious orders, who in embracing one of the various states of Christian perfection, vow to live according to the Rule of their order, and in obedience to their superiors. We encourage them. May they always be enthusiastically dedicated to fulfilling the ends of their orders, principal among which are prayer and penance, education, aid to the young, assistance to the poor, and the other purposes prescribed by their founders.

We know, too, that many of these sons of Ours find themselves—under present circumstances—called upon to minister to the faithful, with great benefit to religion and to the Christian way of life. We urge them wholeheartedly—albeit We are confident that they do not need to be urged—to add to the merits of their orders and institutes by voluntarily lending their help to meet the impelling needs of the faithful, in fraternal collaboration with other priests, as best they can.[1]

Holy Church is adorned by the chastity of the young girls who consecrate their lives to prayer and sacrifice, and to performing the fourteen works of mercy.

You know well that today as in the past, the voices of so many privileged souls who ask to belong to holy and approved societies, who await encouragement and the assignment of new tasks determined by the needs of the times, are always welcomed benevolently. After examination and the long test of experience, which are necessary preliminaries to such important and responsible work, the Church accepts as her own many magnificent institutions, whose diverse purposes serve a great variety of needs.

These admirable women, who offer their natural endowments in the service of the Church, endowments so liberally bestowed on women by God, are truly worthy of consideration, respect and honor before the whole world. We shall never stop repeating it.

We should like to quote a few words from the *Imitation of Christ*, which are certainly familiar to you, and apply them to your lives and to the apostolate to which you are dedicated.

At the end of Chapter 48 of Book III, which asks us to love the things of heaven and to place our hearts there forever, we read: *Beatus ille homo, qui propter te, Domine, omnibus creaturis licentiam abeundi tribuit* . . . "Blessed is the man, O Lord, who for your love abandons all creatures and fights his nature, and in the fervor of his spirit crucifies the lusts of his flesh so that he can pray to you with serene conscience and be worthy to stand with the angelic chorus, free inside and out of earthly things."

From this splendid passage, We point out four themes which are the invisible ornaments of your religious habit: detachment from creatures, strength of character, unceasing prayer, and heavenly life.

Detachment from creatures

The *Imitation of Christ* speaks first of all of complete detachment from creatures, "to bid goodbye to all creatures." This is, after all, the prime characteristic of the religious life, the leave-taking—glad and willing—of the things of this world in order to consecrate oneself with perfect purity of heart.

You each come from different places, from the city, from the country, from Our beloved and honored villages, in surprisingly large numbers. You are from different social conditions, you are for the most part young, although there are older novices, and many of you have already served the apostolate in other areas of militant Catholicism.

Amid these differences, there is one consistent note which unifies those who are consecrated despite their diversity; that is, their chastity. We want you and the whole world to hear, on this occasion, that virginity is appreciated and glorious.

Chastity opens your hearts to the truest, broadest, most universal love that can exist on earth, in the service of Christ. You have not sought earthly love, or your own home, or the accomplishing of personal tasks. These are all things which—despite being right and just—could not satisfy the yearnings of your heart. You have chosen instead the heavenly Bridegroom and the Church.

From this general consecration stems the particular vocation of each religious family, which is embodied in the service to God and to your fellow man in the form of the fourteen works of mercy.

Holy, knowing, generous chastity, at the call of the sick, the old, the poor, the orphaned, the widowed, adolescents and infants, Holy chastity which works through the heart to enlighten the ignorant, advise the doubting, warn sinners, console the afflicted, guide the erring, and to arouse enthusiasm in the great missionary tasks.

In paying homage to this beautiful vocation, which the charity of Christ allows to the Church, let Us note that chastity cannot remain attractive and strong whenever there is not sufficient moral, ascetic and even psychological training.

Strength of character

The *Imitation of Christ* is eloquent in this matter: *naturae vim facere*, to do violence to nature.

We are speaking, first of all, about interior strength, which is employed to know one's own nature and to turn it to the service of God and souls, and at the same time to know one's weaknesses so as to compensate for them in the long and patient exercise of virtue that is nourished by trust and abandon in God.

This strength upholds humility because it is aware of its own limits and weaknesses; it generates meekness, conduces to obedience, the sure lesson for strong souls. It does mean to bow down in order to serve better, to control oneself in order to draw people by gentleness to God, to win out over oneself so that the virtue of Christ will be in us (cf. 2 Corinthians 12, 3).

Fortitude insures the equilibrium of the intellect, the will and the sensibility, and shapes the ideal of the *brave woman*, which Holy Scripture speaks about with admiration (cf. Proverbs 31, 10 ff.).

While on this subject, let Us say something about the confidence that has come out of Our long experience. It can happen that an outburst of sadness, discontent or pessimism breaks through our self-control and creates a sense of unease in the person who witnesses it, or an impression that is not favorable or opportune. Certain bitter words, expressions of distrust, or even complaints are not appropriate coming from someone who has dedicated himself to an institution that is not just human, even as noble an institution as the family or society, but to God.

When the value and extent of chastity is understood, as well as the meaning of service to humanity and the self-denial which does not seek human recognition but God's eye alone, then these motives for sadness will not find a place in the heart of the person consecrated to God. And if temptation strikes, it will be quickly beaten back.

The great and strong soul never becomes prey to sadness, not even in the hour of its fiercest tribulation. A sign of perfect chastity and tried strength can also be found in the joy of the spirit, in discourse and in work, in the complete detachment from every claim of the self. This in order to serve man and God, almost like a "busy bee," in the words we use to honor St. Cecilia.

Unceasing prayer

These are qualities that cannot be developed in just a few weeks. We must persist in asking the Lord for them. And so to the advice We have already given you, We must add: Pray incessantly. Notice the delicacy of Thomas à Kempis's expression: *Serenata conscientia puram offerre orationem:* "to offer a pure prayer with serene conscience." Prayer is not offered simply out of success, or out of deep woe, or out of mechanical duty. It finds expression in sincerity and in love toward all, in the purest charity, inspired by the message of St. Paul in the First Epistle to the Corinthians: "Love is patient and kind; love is not jealous or boastful; it is not arrogant or rude. Love does not insist on its own way; it is not irritable or resentful; it does not rejoice at wrong, but rejoices in the right. Love bears all things, believes all things, hopes all things, endures all things" (1 Corinthians 13, 4–7).

Prayer rises from this serene conscience, its purity is to listen to God, talk with God, and be silent in him, and to ask for what pleases him. A prayer of adoration and thanks, more than one of petition. The Lord knows what we need. How beautiful are the words of the Curé of Ars concerning the prayers of the chaste: "God contemplates with love," he says, "a pure soul, and grants it all it asks for. How could he resist a soul that lives just for him and in him? The soul seeks him, and God shows himself; it calls him and God answers; it is at one with him . . . the soul is near God like a child to its mother" (A. Monnin, *Spirito del Curato d'Ars*, Rome 1956, pp. 57–58).

We should like, therefore, to ask you, with paternal insistence, to meditate on the subject of prayer, because you will not be able to teach others to pray—and this will often be your task, to help parents and priests—if you yourselves have not learned it well first.

And on this matter, you must be watchful and cautious, so as not to teach the recital of prayer alone, but the practice of the Our Father and the Credo.

Heavenly life

And finally, a heavenly life. *The Imitation of Christ* treats the essence of your vocation: "to be worthy to stand with the angelic chorus, freed inside and out from earthly things."

Here we are then, back to our point of departure: a chaste life is a heavenly life. In this way, you who are leading active lives are in perfect harmony with your sister nuns in the cloistral and contemplative orders: *oportet semper orare*, according to the teaching of Christ (cf. Luke 18, 1). Cloistered nuns have their place near the Tabernacle, but you must move from the Tabernacle toward fulfilling your mission.

This unceasing prayer will render your lives "worthy of the angelic chorus"; it will add the final touch to your perfection, embodied in interior order and in exterior grace and simplicity.

In outlining the qualifications for choosing deaconesses, St. Paul says explicitly to Timothy, "The women likewise must be serious, no slanderers, but temperate, faithful in all things" (1 Timothy 3, 11).

This is the habit you must wear on the inside: reserve, measured speech, a welcoming attitude, fidelity in your daily duties.[2]

[1] Encyclical, *Ad Petri Cathedram*, June 29, 1959.
[2] Allocution, January 29, 1960.

Catholic Action

The burgeoning activities within the Church today make so many demands that it appears the clergy and the religious orders are unable to keep up with them. And what is more, priests and the religious do not have access to everyone; some paths are closed to them, for after all, there are those who do not care or whom the priests miss, and unfortunately those who are distrustful or downright antagonistic.

For this reason, Our Predecessors called upon the laity long ago to participate in Catholic Action and to share in the work of the apostolate. And today, the many activities which churchmen cannot perform can be handled quite well by Catholic men and women, always in coordination with their pastors and in due obedience to them. We are always consoled when We think of what was accomplished in the past, even in missionary lands, by these valuable collaborators. Coming from every social group, these men and women of all ages have worked hard and well to teach the truth to the world and to make known the wonderful feeling of Christian virtue.

Large areas where there is much to be done are opening up to them, because there are still too many people who need their help and their example. We trust that all those who militate in the ranks of Catholic Action will keep up their invaluable work. The greater the demands of our time, the greater will be their efforts, their concern, their generosity. May they work together, because, as we all know, unity is strength. Let them give up their personal opinions when it comes to furthering the cause of the Catholic Church, which must have priority. This involves not only doctrine, but also the regulations issued by the Church, to which everyone must conform. Obedient to their bishops, let them march in close ranks to new conquests. Do not spare any effort, do not refuse any discomfort, as long as the Church's cause triumphs.

In order to assure that triumph, they must take care—and they themselves know this—that they have a good moral, Christian and intellectual education. Only in this way will they be able to pass on to others what they themselves already possess.[1]

The teachings of Pius XI and Pius XII are closer to us and relevant to the needs of our times; they provided the guides to insure that Catholic Action would always be on the right course. With their teaching in mind, We want to point out the most appropriate qualities of Catholic Action which are demanded by today's conditions, and which are useful to the church hierarchy. Catholic Action must reflect ordered and disciplined unity, it must be an example for the whole world.

1. Catholic Action is the clergy's partner. That is to say, the work laymen can do to assist their pastors and bishops in the apostolate, according to the classic definition of your society. This help is not merely a momentary enthusiasm, nor is it intended merely to care for old and dear traditions, even though such work may be praiseworthy in other areas. Catholic Action is an expression of unity with the Catholic priesthood in working toward fulfillment of the plea "Thy kingdom come" over the whole earth.

This assistance can only come about if the members are completely prepared and are aware of their other duties, which they must accept as if they were a holy vocation. They must face new and sacred tasks with love and missionary zeal.

The younger members of Catholic Action, the children, are its great hope. Their duties, at first, will be light. But as they grow older, they must be willing to make greater and greater contributions to the work their bishops entrust to them.

2. Catholic Action must reflect ordered, disciplined unity. The concept of unity, as you know, is something We frequently talk about. Unity represents the hope and the promise of efficacious pastoral action and apostolic mission.

Unity is needed in order to insure lasting success to the various undertakings of Catholic Action. Whatever is too localized, individualistic, opinionated is contrary to the spirit of unity and tends to create confusion and to lessen enthusiasm. Too much discussion and arguing waste precious time which should be used to assist the clergy. It is necessary, therefore, to have agreement and a single line of thought, unified intention and unified policies, if there is to be success.

3. Lastly, Catholic Action must be exemplary, "the luminous sign" of modern times, consisting not of complicated things, or showy uniqueness, but of a clear policy, goodness and direct language.[2]

The ecclesiastical assistant in Catholic Action must remember how important a role he must play. He must sanctify his soul, and the souls of those he works with, whether they be students who are preparing for a profession or career, or humble workmen, whose contribution to life is equally noble and important. Everyone must be treated and encouraged according to his own talents and vocation, but always with the help of divine grace, which alone can enable us to fulfill our various tasks.

Consequently the ecclesiastical assistant must be a very devout priest who is deeply aware of the inner life of those who are called to divine service; his whole being must be penetrated with the life of our Lord, Jesus Christ. Otherwise, he might be a very charming person, bright, persuasive, even momentarily compelling, but there could not be that crucial foundation, which inevitably must be recognized; that is, the love of God.

We do not have to go to the distant past to find lessons in the good. From the apostolic era to our own day—in which, thank God, there are many fine works being performed—there has been a marvelous development of spirituality, of ennoblement. The bases for this growth are always the same. We have the Lord's Prayer, the holy Eucharist and the Breviary always with us. We have Holy Scripture, especially the evangelical books and the books of Wisdom, which must be the daily sustenance of our hearts and minds. Not to mention the other wonderful works in which ascetic literature abounds, such as *The Imitation of Christ*. Thus, we must be familiar with the great expressions of Christian piety, not as superfluous accessories, or worse, as a burdensome heritage, but rather as the most deeply felt and committed part of our faith.

The ecclesiastical assistant must strive for a unified spirit and intention. In emphasizing this essential point, the Holy Father is trying to concentrate, by virtue of his Apostolic Office, attention on religious unity, and to eliminate any waste of energy or any deviation from the right road.

Mercy is the eternal fount of grace and joy to the young priest, who gains thereby peace and calm, and the motivation to win souls everywhere he goes.

Now that these truths have been recalled, and we are convinced of them, it is easier to look to the future with great confidence. We can at last understand that what counts now is action.

But this action can also mean to let someone else act, to encourage others to do, to stimulate dulled motivation, to guide those who want to dedicate themselves to the apostolate. And so, at night, when we examine our consciences, the results will be positive; we shall not need to reprove ourselves for having indulged worldly interests, but rather we shall be able to appreciate the effects our advice and our example have on others. We shall be imitating the ecclesiastical assistants of Catholic Action, who have left brilliant memories of resolute courage and meaningful contributions.[3]

[1] Encyclical, *Ad Petri Cathedram*, June 29, 1959.
[2] Speech to Catholic Action, January 10, 1960.
[3] Allocutions to ecclesiastical assistants, July 7 and 17, 1959.

The Militant Catholic

The things We should like to say to you are inspired by the Epiphany of Our Lord, a dazzling manifestation of his glory to the whole world. The three kings came to bring their gifts to the child Redeemer from the East, following the star on their long journey. From the shores of Palestine, the Lord's word has spread to all the peoples of the world. The Church rejoices in that long procession of the faithful who move through the centuries toward God become man. "Arise, shine; for your light has come, and the glory of the Lord has risen upon you . . . And nations shall come to your light, and the kings to the brightness of your rising. Lift up your eyes round about, and see; they all gather together, they come to you; your sons shall come from far and your daughters shall be carried in the arms" (Isaiah 60, 1, 3–4).

In the perspective of her mission, one can readily see the relationship between the Church and the world in which she exists. Men are all moving toward God; many of them unknowingly. And the star lights their way.

The words of St. Leo I

Dearest Children, your task must be to study society, to learn of its aspirations, its triumphs, its direction, and then to convert it to Christ. We can only urge you to continue your efforts, which cannot fail to yield happy results. May We remind you of several things that will help you succeed, thoughts that arise in these particular days of meditation. They are taken from the pages of Leo the Great, from his Eighth Sermon, delivered on the occasion of Epiphany (*Sermo* XXXVIII, In Epiphaniae sollemnitate VIII; Migne, PL 54, 260–63). He says very pertinent things about the spirit which must move Christians in their religious mission: a pure heart, pure intention, bountiful charity. Let us look a moment at each of these qualities.

Pre-eminence of supernatural values

1. *A free heart.* Listen to the intensity of his appeal: "Let us not occupy ourselves with vain and passing things; let us rather choose what has no end." Earlier he had said, "A free heart, detached from things of the senses, must follow the light of intelligence as a guiding star." This then is the first requisite of religious mission: a heart freed from earthly attachments, material interests, and vanity itself. True, we must acknowledge the claims of the reality around us, but our hearts must remain free to dedicate all to the promises of Christ. The heart must be able to look beyond life and beyond this world. Haste in succeeding may conceal a desire to be recognized, and certainly is never consonant with the action of Providence, which teaches us to proceed with calmness, confidence and measure.

As you can see, it is always the priority of supernatural values that is at stake. We never tire of urging this truth to the clergy and the laity.

The hope of supernatural life, and the great means of sanctification each one of us can count on, gives you the ideas, the conviction, the large possibility of commitment you need. It follows then that you will be able to exercise a sense of delicacy and mature judgment; that you will be ready to obey; that you will be charitable. Here is the secret behind a real and lasting religious mission; from this point, every worthy enterprise is born and blessed by God.

Disinterestedness, integrity, sincerity

2. *Pure intention,* the only true condition of inner freedom. St. Leo says in his sixth sermon: "He who really wants to know if God abides in him—the God who is terrible in his sanctuary (Psalms 67, 36)—must scrutinize his soul and ask with how much humility he resists pride, with how much benevolence he fights envy, and how truly indifferent he is to the flattery of his adulators; indeed, does he rejoice in the good of others?"

This, my dear children, is the spirit with which you must approach your brothers, even those furthest from understanding. You cannot teach the word if your heart is burdened with envy and pride, if you are self-complacent, selfish, and self-seeking. The witness every Christian must bear is informed with disinterestedness, integrity and sincerity. If these are lacking, the results you seek, no matter what your efforts may be, will be prejudiced.

God's message of love

3. A free heart and pure intentions lead to a spirit of charity, the basic motive for every sacrifice. St. Leo continues, "Lest a too rigorous examination of the conscience exhaust itself, look into your soul for the mother of all virtues, charity, and if you find there the desire to love God and your fellow man with all your heart . . . rest assured that God will lead you and abide in you. . . . Seek therefore charity, so that the souls of all the faithful will be united in a single feeling of chaste love."

After the omnipotent help of God and his grace, the most effective means for overcoming the dangers of mutual distrust, of theoretical and practical materialism, and of religious indifference is the felt and renewed awareness of the supernatural joined to the real exercise of charity. The love of God and of one's fellow man, *toto corde* as St. Leo says: love of God to sanctify his name, to extend his kingdom, to do his will on earth as it is in heaven; the love of men in order to meet the needs of the moment, to be truthful so as not to delude, to be charitable so as to make the sacrifices we must make in order to build. This is the message that will touch all hearts, and this is the message that will recall to the faith all those who are trying to find justice and peace without it, outside the Church.[1]

[1] Speech, January 5, 1962.

The Rosary

As a devotional practice among the faithful of the Latin rite, who form a notable part of the Catholic family, the Rosary—for the clergy—takes its importance after the Mass and the Breviary, and for laymen, after participation in the holy sacraments. The Rosary is a devout form of union with God. and is always spiritually uplifting.

Words and contents

It is true that some people who were not taught to pay other than lip service will recite the Rosary as a monotonous series of prayers, the Our Father, the Hail Mary, and the Gloria, arranged in the traditional set of fifteen decades. Without doubt, even this recitation is of some value. But—and We must stress this—it is only a beginning, an external ritual of confident prayer rather than an uplifting of the spirit to communion with God, whom we seek in the sublimity and tenderness of his mysteries, in his merciful love for all humanity.

The true substance of the Rosary, if it is meditated upon, lies in three relevant acts which give unity and coherence to the saying of it; that is, *mystical contemplation*, *intimate reflection* and *pious intention*.

Mystical contemplation
First of all, a pure, luminous, rapid contemplation of each mystery; that is, of those truths of faith which describe the redemptive mission of Christ. By contemplation one can get closer in feeling and thought to the teaching and life of Jesus, the Son of God and Son of Mary, who lived on earth to redeem, to instruct, to sanctify—in the silence of one's hidden life, made up of prayer and hard work—in the pain of his blessed Passion—in the triumph of the Resurrection, just as in the glory of the heavens, where he sits at the right hand of God the Father, ready always to help and to quicken—through the Holy Ghost—the Church founded by him and advancing in his path through the centuries.

Intimate reflection
The second act is to reflect; reflection fills the soul of the man who prays with the light of Christ's mysteries. Everyone can find in those mysteries an example he can make his own, related to his own purification and to the conditions in which he lives. Enlightened by the Holy Ghost, who, from the depths of the soul in grace "intercedes for us with sighs too deep for words" (Romans 8, 26), everyone can face his existence with the renewal that springs from those mysteries, and he can find endless applications to his spiritual needs, as well as to his daily life.

Pious intention
The last is *intention;* that is, to name the persons, the institutions, the social causes, the personal needs that represent, for a devout and active Catholic, an exercise of charity toward

his fellows, the charity that is the living expression of communion in the Mystical Body of Christ.

In this way, the Rosary becomes a universal plea, from individuals and from the immense community of the faithful, who are united no matter where they are by this single prayer, whether it be for personal intentions, or personal gratitude, or as part of the unanimous voice of the Church for the intentions of all of humanity. As the Redeemer himself willed it, the Church lives amid the contentions, the adversities and the opposition of social disorder, which often becomes a frightening threat, but she looks undaunted ahead to the eternal finalities.

Spoken and private recitation

This is the Marian Rosary as we see it in its several aspects, which find a single expression when it is recited aloud.

Vocal prayers have their own importance, especially prayers on Sunday, which give the Rosary tone, substance and life, and in coming immediately after the announcement of the single mysteries, marks the passage from one decade to the next. Then the angelic greeting, resounding with the exultation of heaven and earth as the life of Jesus and Mary unfolds, and finally the triad, recited in adoration of the Most Holy Trinity.

The Rosary takes on beauty from its reciter: the innocent child, the sick person, the young girl who has consecrated her life in a cloister or in the apostolate of charity, the man and woman who are parents, both urged on by their great sense of responsibility, the modest families who are faithful to the old tradition of the home—these souls gathered in silence, freed from the distractions of worldly life which they have renounced, and although they are compelled to live in the world, they do so as anchorites, amid its uncertainties and temptations.

This is the Rosary as the devout say it, in their deep

preoccupation with their own fates and with their surroundings.

Praying solemnly together

In paying respect to this old, time-honored and moving form of Marian devotion, according to each believer's own personal situation, We should like to take note that the changes of modern life that have taken place in all areas of society, scientific advances, the revolution in working conditions which has enabled man to penetrate his world with greater awareness, have had their effects even on the functions and forms of Christian prayer. Now the person who prays does not feel alone any more, interested in his own spiritual and temporal concerns, but feels more than ever before that he belongs to a society, with whom he shares responsibilities, enjoys advantages, and faces the same uncertainties and dangers. This is, besides, the character of the liturgical prayer contained in the Missal and the Breviary. At the beginning of each prayer, marked by the words, "Let us pray . . . " there is presupposed the sense of community not only of the priest who is praying, but also of the person or persons for whose intention the prayer is offered. The multitude is praying as one single supplicating voice for brotherhood in everything man does.

The Rosary is the means at hand for praying, publicly and universally, for the sake of the ordinary and extraordinary needs of the Church, and of the world.[1]

Whoever has great feeling for the family and for the Gospel feels a deep necessity to be familiar with the Holy Rosary. It is enough to point out that the many pilgrims who come to Rome to venerate the martyrs and to greet the Holy Father bring their Rosaries with them, in token of the great events it celebrates.

Without wanting to disparage the past, We observe that

Marian devotions are more frequent in our times, especially the group devotions in church, as well as those in the home and in other places. This gives us some idea of how devoted the faithful are to Mary, in the remembrance of the events in her son's life—the baby, the boy, the adult—the course of a sacrifice, from Bethlehem to the Cross. The world is not sufficient to contain the energy of so much goodness, and so we look ever upward to Mary. The Church celebrates her triumphs in the Glorious Mysteries. From the third Mystery celebrating the descent of the Holy Ghost on Mary and the Apostles we begin the fourth, the Assumption of Mary in body and soul to Heaven, and finally to the fifth, where her glory is celebrated by the angels and the saints.

What sublime events, what sublime lessons! And yet the Rosary is a simple prayer, inviting us always to internal peace, to abandonment in God, to trust, which is the sure way to obtaining the grace we need.

Thus we can understand why the great purposes of the Church, which teaches, guides, inspires and encourages, can always be found in this form of prayer.[2]

[1] Apostolic Letter, September 29, 1961.
[2] Conversation, October 13, 1960.

The Lay Apostolate

In the service of the hierarchy

The lay apostolate, in putting itself at the service of the Church fathers, will want to act with the same conviction. The layman who devotes himself to working for the Church and with the Church knows the basic premise: all men without any exceptions belong to God's great family, into which Christ came to lead and to reign evermore.

With what spirit can one profess great charity? Charity teaches us mutual understanding, patience, respect for our fellow men, even when they have not yet attained the light. Charity strengthens us when we are confronted by inevitable trials. If in fact evil is a sad reality, today as it was yesterday, it will never succeed—as we well know—in winning out over the good.

The apostle looks to the good and so is determined to help it anywhere he can, even where it has barely sprouted.

The apostolate takes on many forms. Its fulfillment is available to whoever chooses to follow in the path of the famous missionaries, for example, St. Francis Xavier. And what is more, there is always the possibility of action, no matter what the time or place, for all those who determine to nurture the spirit of charity, which is immensely superior to all the human achievement resounding through the ages.[1]

In the mission territories

Faithful Christians, just as a living organism, cannot close themselves off and think that by looking to their own spiritual needs they have done enough to fulfill their duty. Everyone, on the contrary, must do his share in spreading the reign of God on earth.

Everyone must participate in a contest of holy emulation and give witness to his concern for the spiritual welfare of his neighbor, for the defense of his own faith and for making it known to whoever is ignorant of it or to whoever does not know it well and so misjudges it. Even in the youngest Christian communities, it is necessary that the clergy, the families and the local missionary organizations inculcate this sacred duty from childhood and adolescence on. There are then several happy occasions particularly suited to this training for the apostolate, on which it can find its most convincing expression. For example, preparing the young or the newly baptized for the sacrament of Confirmation, when "a new strength is infused in the faithful to defend Mother Church and the Faith which they have received from her." This moment of preparation is particularly fitting, especially where local custom provides initiation ceremonies for preparing for the official entrance of the young into their social group.

The catechists

We cannot fail at this point to emphasize the work of the catechists, and we urge them to think always on the spiritual happiness of their condition and never to stop making efforts to enrich and to deepen—under guidance of the Church fathers—their education and moral development. Catechumens must learn from them not only the rudiments of the faith, but also the practice of virtue and great and sincere love of Christ and of his Church. Every effort dedicated to increasing the number of these invaluable assistants to the hierarchy and every effort to train them adequately, indeed every sacrifice the catechists make to carry out their task in the best and most useful way, will be an immediately effective contribution to the founding and the development of new Christian communities.

In public life

The "holy struggle" for the faith is carried on not only in the depths of the conscience or in the intimacy of the home, but also in public life in all its forms. All the countries of the world face problems of various kinds, to which solutions often are sought from only human resources and in conformity to principles that are not always in agreement with the demands of Christian faith. Many missionary territories, furthermore, are undergoing "a phase of social, economic and political evolution which is laden with consequences for their future." Problems which have already been solved in other countries or which can be solved in part within the tradition of those countries appear in some nations to have an urgency that is not by any means free of dangers, in the sense that hasty solutions borrowed with deplorable facility from ideologies that have no respect for or perhaps directly oppose the religious interests of individuals and of peoples are forced by that urgency. Catholics cannot ignore such problems, for their own good or for the public good of the Church, nor can they allow these problems to be solved prejudicially, so that the solutions themselves will require much more than mere straightening out in the future and in fact will ultimately prove to be barriers to the evangelization of the world.

Laymen in missionary countries have their most direct and vital role in the area of public affairs, and it is of the utmost urgency that the Christian communities be able to offer to their native countries men who can do honor to the various professions and activities at the same time as they honor, with their solid Christian conduct, the Church that has brought them to grace.

Especially in the areas of education, social welfare, labor relations, politics, the presence of expert native Catholics might have a felicitous and worthwhile influence because they will know how to inspire their purposes and their work with Christian principles—as their duty demands, which they cannot neglect without being guilty of betrayal. History has shown how those Christian principles have been effective and decisive in bringing about the common good.[2]

In social education

Educating people to conduct themselves as Christians in their economic and social dealings will not be a successful undertaking if they do not take an active role in preparing themselves, and if education as such does not take place through action.

It is said rightly that we cannot acquire the ability to exercise our freedom justly unless we learn its proper use. Analogously, educating ourselves to behave as Christians in economic and social activities cannot be achieved unless we practice our Christianity in those areas.

Therefore an important task in social education awaits the groups and organizations concerned with the lay apostolate, especially the ones whose main purpose is to revitalize the Christian principles in those two areas of the temporal order. In fact, many members of those organizations can make valuable use of their daily experiences in teaching themselves and in contributing to the education of youth.[3]

[1] An audience, February 17, 1962.

[2] Encyclical, *Princeps Pastorum*, November 28, 1959.

[3] Encyclical, *Mater et Magistra*, May 15, 1961.

Easter

Easter is the most splendid holy day in the Sacred Liturgy. The two weeks of the Passion which precede it renew the meaning of the belief in the redemption of mankind, the Lord's lesson to every good Christian to save himself and to purify himself in expectation of heaven, and an affirmation of Christ's triumph in time, a temporary triumph in earthly terms, but certain and final in eternity.

From Palm Sunday to this day of Christ's Resurrection, how great the history we rehearse. St. Leo the Great declared that the *Paschale Sacramentum*, the Easter celebration, is the most important one in holy worship.

The liturgy's contents are the most intimate and sacred; they penetrate and vivify the depths of the souls touched by grace. The liturgy is complemented by ceremonies that strike the eye and reach to the heart.

1. The entry of Christ into Jerusalem: what a glorious and happy spectacle! Just a few days from his crucifixion which

will inflict so much ignominy on him in the eyes of the world, Christ prepares a triumphal entry for himself. Proclaimed a wonder-worker by the crowds and acclaimed as king, greeted as the Messiah by the good people, and adored by his followers as the Christ, the Son of the Living God, what honors would have sufficed? Who was worthier than he of royal receptions and profane exultation? But he would have none of it.

St. Ambrose tells us Jesus prepared his triumph through his own humble people. He said to his two disciples, "Go into the village opposite you, and immediately you will find an ass tied, and a colt with her; untie them and bring them to me" (Matthew 21, 2).

2. The second great image rekindled for us during Holy Week is that of mankind's grief, embodied in the suffering Christ. We have been told that the faithful participated more meaningfully and fully in the ceremonies of Holy Week because of recent liturgical reforms. This feeling is a psychological phenomenon that the doctrine of the Mystical Body enlightens and enables. We hear Christ's moans as he shares men's woes in the hour when throughout the world their freedoms are being destroyed or suppressed or continually threatened.

We turn again to the words of Our Holy Predecessor, St. Leo the Great: "The Cross of Christ is a sacrament and an example for us" (Sermon 72). A sacrament which contains and transmits the virtue of divine grace to our souls, and an example that urges us to patience, the patience of which Christ was the supreme exemplar.

Human knowledge glories in its errors and follows its teachers blindly. What communion do we have with Christ if we do not unite inseparably with him, who said of himself, "I am the way, the truth and the life" (John 14, 6)? The way of holy discourse, the truth of divine doctrine, the life of eternal happiness.

3. Here we recall the Gospel according to St. John, the most eloquent introduction to the event of centuries, Christ's Resurrection. Life and death locked in a fearful struggle. The Master of life triumphed over death, and his victory becomes the Church's victory through the ages. Let us free our spirits of all cares and open our hearts to the brightest hope for the future. We may be harried by the world, and we shall continue to be for certain. Before leaving, Christ said, "Have faith, I have won the world." It is true, a combatant remains on the terrible field of battle, and we refer to him often by name. He is a prince; the Holy Rabbi of Nazareth called him "the prince of this world." Christ carries on the struggle against him, humbly but effectively to affirm justice and peace. The infernal adversary hates peace and justice, and at times his tactics cause such confusion that those who fight against him falter.

Every good Christian trusts Christ, fulfills his duties according to the laws of his conscience, before God and before men. The Christian is unwavering and uncompromising; he walks undaunted and secure. He works for peace.

To strengthen himself against error and evil, he prays. He invokes the heavenly aid of grace which enlightens and sustains the strong.

We know that Christ truly arose from the dead. Christ's victory over death is the guarantee that the obstacles to human efforts for the defense of justice, liberty and peace shall be overcome.

Christ, you are not the mock king, as Herod the tetrarch of Galilee tried to present you to the people. We have complete faith in your word. We shall call upon you always for justice, liberty and peace.[1]

At Eastertime, the Church will resound with the joyous news, "The Lord has truly risen!" And this must be said of his brothers as well, "He is truly risen!" He who sinned is truly risen. And risen are those who doubted, feared, vacillated. Arisen are the troubled, the suffering, the oppressed, the miserable![2]

[1] Radio broadcast, March 28, 1959.
[2] Sermon, March 29, 1959.

The Lord's Prayer

Remember the petitions contained in the Our Father. They are replete with understanding and meaning.

The Holy Church keeps on this right road, and the life and history of the world are directed on it. This continuity of light, strength and grace sustains permanent value; that is, knowledge, progress and true Christian culture.

These are goods of a temporal nature as well, but they prepare us for the eternal ones which await us.

1. Before everything, the name and worship of God.

The name must be respected and the acts of worship brought back to their ancient beauty or given new arrangements, as modern life sanctified in holy doctrine might also suggest.

Next to worship, discipline—the strength and unity of the Church as Christ constituted her, the source of fresh energies in the evangelical mission, and the security for the promises Christ made to his followers and to the depositaries of his heritage.

2. God's kingdom. When we speak of God's kingdom, we should not confuse it with the political structures man builds, as frequently happened in history, just as here and there it

happens today, the expression of human and material arrogance.

Thy kingdom come (Matthew 6, 10), as Christ said, and as the Liturgy sings in one of its greatest moments: *the reign of truth and life, the reign of sanctity and grace, the reign of justice, love and peace.*

The holy mysteries that express the "either-or" of every individual's life, of the life of families, of nations, of the whole world.

Therefore we must be either on Christ's side, with some of the weight of the Cross on the shoulders of each of us, or we must be without him, lost in uncertainty, in hazard, in disorder and in the universal abyss.

3. God's will. *Thy will be done* (Matthew 6, 10). The Lord's will inspires and guides us. It marks our efforts to purify ourselves, as it was written—"For this is the will of God, your sanctification" (1 Thessalonians 4, 3).

4. And the great question, seeking our daily bread? That too is part of Christian action and prayer. The Lord gives us bread, as a reward for our labors, as strength to the intelligence of numberless souls who conscientiously seek even material prosperity, so that the body can better respond to the demands and to the splendors of the spirit.

Knowing that so many refuse to draw strength and edification from the teachings the Church can provide for the resolution of problems created by economic conditions and the search for temporal well-being, saddens Us greatly. Once our eyes are closed to evangelical law, it is only natural that all human efforts will be in vain, even those in pursuit of economic improvements. They can never fully satisfy the needs of living together in its broadest implications.

5. The Catholic Church and the Christian clergy are very

concerned, along with carrying out their ministry, with the individuals and the nations who seriously reject or despise the sanctity of life's basic laws; that is, whether God will ever forgive them.

6. The prayer Jesus taught us on the Mount, which should be our daily inspiration and guide, concludes with a powerful plea to God to save us from malignant forces: "Save us from evil" (Matthew 6, 13).

Human nature is subject to temptation, and in giving in to it, man threatens his freedom and dignity. Unfortunately, "we know . . . the whole world is in the power of the evil one" (1 John 5, 19). We are saved from such misfortune by God's mercy, but we must do our part by firmly opposing evil and its seductions.

In one of the most sacred moments of the Mass, just after the Our Father, the Church continues the supplication that has become universal: "Free us, O Lord, from all evils, past, present and future". . . .[1]

[1] Exhortation, October 28, 1959.

Our Daily Bread

After twenty centuries of progress in the sciences, the arts, economics and culture generally, and of change in political and social realities, Christ's words have not lessened in value: "Truly, truly, I say to you, unless you eat the flesh of the Son of man and drink his blood, you have no life in you. . . . This is the bread which came down from heaven . . . he who eats this bread will live forever" (John 6, 54, 59).

We want to emphasize the three prerogatives of that "Daily Bread" which the children of the Church must ask and wait for with faith and desire from the Heavenly Father's providence.

(a) It must be our own bread; that is, asked for in the name of all. "The Lord," St. John Chrysostom tells us, "taught us by the Our Father to pray to God in our brothers' name as well. He does not want us to pray to him for our own interests alone, but for our neighbor's too. Thus he intends to combat hatred and to put down arrogance" (*In Mattheis* VI, Hom. XIX).

(b) It must be a nourishing bread, sufficient, that is, for our needs. Since man is made up of a body and an immortal spirit, the bread we must ask for should not be just "material" but as St. Thomas observed, "spiritual" bread, which is God himself, the truth to be contemplated and the goodness to be loved, and it should be "sacramental" too, that is, the Body of the Savior, the sign and the viaticum of eternal life (cf. *Commentatio in Mattheis*, c. VI).

(c) The third but not least quality of this daily bread is that it be *one*, the symbol and cause of unity. "*Quemadmodum enim corpus illud Christo iungitur, ita et nos per panem hunc unimur*"—continues St. John Chrysostom—"Just as that body is united with Christ, so too we are united by means of this bread" (*In Epistola I ad Cor. Homil.* XXIV, 2).

The eucharistic bread is unquestionably the image and fount of unity in the Mystical Body, both for the minds it enlightens and leads to the profession of the same divine truths, and for the wills it inspires to love God and neighbor.

If only the Eucharist were better understood by Christians, and more worthily and frequently received! How much greater would be our share of concord, peace and spiritual rightness, for the Church and for the whole world! All the problems that preoccupy us would be more readily resolved, thanks to the spirit of sincere and complete brotherhood which would prevent dangerous undertakings and preserve us from compromising with the forces and seductions of this world.[1]

[1] Radio broadcast, September 13, 1959.

Ailing Humanity

In observing recent events, we would say that our age is marked by anguish and fear. Perhaps many people are not even aware of it, but you can see it in their relationships, and the effects are felt on all levels, in family, social, national and international disturbances.

This realization becomes even more painful when we think that the Creator willed that men understand one another and unite to work together, to settle their differences and to distribute their goods equitably, according to standards of justice and charity.

The prophets tell us this clearly, as do the Psalms. Isaiah asks, "Is not this the fast that I choose; to loose the bonds of wickedness, to undo the thongs of the yoke, to let the oppressed go free, and to break every yoke? Is it not to share your bread with the hungry, and bring the homeless poor into your house; when you see the naked, to cover him, and not to hide yourself from your own flesh? . . . And the Lord will guide you continuously, and satisfy your desire with good things" (Isaiah 58, 6–7, 11).

If we consider the relations among nations today and the results of their international meetings, we can understand how far we still are from God's word as it was recorded for the ages in the Old Testament, and as it triumphed in the advent of Christ. There we read of the beatitude of peace, while in the international councils we hear beautiful words (when good form is being observed, but even that is frequently neglected), which only mask a spirit of contention.

It is only the pride of the strong that subjugates, the insatiability of the greedy, who close their hearts against their brothers (cf. 1 John 3, 17); it is the insensitivity of the well-off, who ignore the sufferings of the world. It is the selfishness of those who think only of themselves.

What is always missing is Christ's goodness. In that goodness we would find the antidote to all this contrariness and implacability; with it we are led to a more reasonable view of things.

Having to deplore evil is very sad, but deploring is not enough to eliminate it. We must will it, act on it. We must proclaim goodness before the world; we must do what we can to teach it to all; it must become part of our lives.

The individual must be good, because he is the embodiment of conscience, where duplicity, calculation and hardness should not penetrate. He must be good because his purpose is to perfect himself; good because he is faithful to his purpose.

The family is a good one if there is mutual love among its members. With a sense of goodness, they more readily accept the father's authority and the mother's discretion. Goodness modifies the unruliness of the children, and enables the family as a whole to face necessary sacrifices.

Goodness must inform a man in all his activities if he is to live in harmony and peace, from his days in school to his life in society. All social relationships must be realized in a spirit of goodness, as St. Leo the Great so vividly expresses it: "To commit injustice and to avenge it is the world's way, while not doing harm to anyone in return for harm is how the Christian expresses his indulgence. . . . Love humility, therefore, and stay away from arrogance. Put your brother's interests before your own; never seek gain for yourself, but for others. And when benevolence fills everyone, then there will be no room for the poison of hate" (Sermo XXXVII [In Epiphaniae solemn. VII] IV; Migne PL 54, 259).

Humanity must be good. These texts that come down to us through the centuries, and yet speak with modern accents, remind us how important it is that we fulfill our duty to be good. That is to say, just, upright, generous, disinterested, ready to understand and to forgive, and magnanimous.[1]

[1] Radio broadcast, December 21, 1961.

The Sermon

Preaching as part of the priest's mission ought to be marked by decorum; that is, wisdom, simplicity, charity.

1. *Wisdom.* Wisdom is found in the careful selection of themes for the sermon, be it an ordinary one that is homiletic and catechistical, or an extraordinary one prepared for Lent or other major feasts in the calendar.

There is a temptation to wax poetic on more pleasant subjects, or to concentrate on apologetics deriving from older types of sermons, without taking into account at times the tremendous necessity to meet the needs of the present and to make good use of recent pastoral experience.

Let us be careful; people demand the substance of truth from us; let us not give them little pieces or more or less edifying tales that do not really strike the depths of the spirit.

Several of these themes are especially important, such as the idea of guilt and punishment, of "to each his due", public and private worship, the sanctification of the holiday, the sacred duties of marriage, the education of children, the respect for the human person. And they ought to be presented interestingly, not adorned by vague erudition.

The ideal is to frame doctrine in due proportions, not to forget anything and yet keep the sermon on solid intellectual grounds.

When the priest first begins his sermon, the faithful in the congregation—We mean those who realize the importance of religious education as well as the functions of worship and piety—can realize at once how well prepared or not the speaker may be, the timeliness of his subject and his ability to draw up a sound argument, with conclusions that follow sensibly from his premises.

This is a serious responsibility for the priest, which he must realize. As St. Isidore declared; "Just as the value and a seal must be stamped on metal coins, so too in every ecclesiastic doctor must be seen what he teaches and how he lives" (*Diem.* 36).

2. *Simplicity*. Simplicity is a great talent for the preacher who tries to reach directly to the conscience of his listeners. Simplicity does not mean to speak at random, or to wave the arms, as they say in Rome; rather, to preach simply means preparation and study. It means to direct thought to a given end, to use the time at one's disposal carefully, for the primary purpose of instructing the faithful, and not for the pleasure of listening to oneself talk. Simplicity just does not lend itself to the desire for cutting a good figure, or to use a well-turned phrase that will arouse applause. Simplicity makes us terribly aware of the power of grace in the souls listening to us.

3. *Charity*. Does this need repeating for us, who are supposed to be the most convinced apostles of charity? It does, We should say, constantly; above all when tempers are hot. Charity is the sign of the good preacher, in his word, his attitude, in his arguments, in his treatment of them and in his ability to point out guilt and error.

"If you love God," says St. Augustine, "carry off everything for the sake of his love; enrapture everyone you can, by exhorting, by questioning, by disputing, by arguing gently and tenderly" (*Narr. in Psalms* 33, Sermo 2, 6).

There is no greater reward for the preacher of the holy

word than that his listeners will think him the image of Christ; that is, his true disciple, worthy of respect, *mitis et humilis corde* ("meek and humble in heart").

This has been true of all the outstanding priests whom diocesan records and the history of religious orders recall so admiringly. We remember all those We Ourself have met through the years.

The attentive attitude of the congregation, heads lowered in thought, and then their attendance at confession—these are the things that gladden the priest.

Charity goes hand in hand with truth. Do not be afraid to say the same thing this year: we have arrived at the days of health, penance and self-discipline. Say so in respectful but unequivocal terms, just as Christ did in his own time and to his own people.[1]

Let us speak of living sermons

Complaints have been heard all over that sermons and missions have not been attended as they should be. The odd working hours of a large city, the frenetic pace of life, and the leisure time the family would like to use for recreation have made it very difficult to proclaim the word of God to great numbers, or indeed to find even the quiet necessary to contemplate God's teaching.

We must note, however, that at times the form of the sermon is not appropriate to stimulate and satisfy the thirst for the eternal truths.

Everything has its particular role: the language, the rhetoric, the humble and measured pace. The ornamentation of vague erudition has lost the appeal it once had. You must say things clearly, dispassionately, respectfully, and never bitterly or polemically.[2]

I. "*To enlighten souls by teaching*"

The preacher has a very difficult task. He must assume the

roles of teacher, educator, psychologist. He must be able to draw the attention of the faithful, guide their feelings, penetrate their consciences, and expose the truth convincingly.

Explaining doctrine calls for not only intelligence on the priest's part, but his heart and sensitivity as well. The instructor is required to have not so much a literary command of the language as a precise theological command of it, with a sense of propriety as well.

Considering the differences among the congregation, St. Bernardine spoke of three kinds of people: the simple, the average and the more perfect. This categorization is very old and well known, but how frequently forgotten in religious matters. The things that are absolutely needed for salvation, for approaching the sacraments, for sanctifying oneself, should be treated with special simplicity—of word and image—just as we use when we speak with children.

A very devout bishop and excellent speaker recounted to Us how, as a young priest, he was entrusted with the boys who were preparing for the seminary. "I would speak to them with the greatest simplicity," he said, "but I would always be prepared, even in this. As the years passed, and even the quality of my charges changed, I learned that speaking simply was the best method, even to the average and the bright ones, because even though often they were quite learned in profane subjects, they were like children in sacred matters."

It goes without saying, however, that things have improved from many points of view since the time of St. Bernardine.

But the call to "enlighten by teaching" is still a valid one. Each priest must still remember St. Bernardine's warning, no matter how busy he is, night and day, fulfilling the other demands of his ministry: "Where ignorance of religious truth is allowed to grow, morals deteriorate."

Speak simply, clearly. Describe, and enlighten.

After twenty centuries of Christian light, there are still many souls and human institutions shrouded in darkness. We must never delude ourselves, the task entrusted to the Church by her Founder requires always greater efforts in meeting the needs of the times.

The words we use in our sermons are not ours, but come from holy doctrine. In the work of perfecting souls that are entrusted to us, our limbs will tire and our tongues go dry before the task is complete.

Let us remain faithful to the traditions of the most famous orators, who were at once learned, practical and saintly. From the ancient to the modern, from the first Fathers of the Church to Bossuet, from the very popular St. Bernardine to the Curé of Ars.

II. "*Console by the word of God*"

God's word is spoken by the priest to console the saddened.

Sadness and desolation are the inseparable companions of those who do not know how to draw hope from on high; it shows in their faces; it constricts their hearts. St. Bernardine's advice is so unusual for us, we must note it, that the word of God will have the greatest effect of consoling when orderliness and regularity are observed in the churches, on the altars, in the ministering of the sacraments, and in the adoration of the Holy Eucharist.

He meant that the preacher must reflect in his sermons the harmony and consolation which appear as part of the Church's functions. The speaker must draw on the art, the liturgy, on everything in the Church which leaves an impression of beauty.

We are made this way. Organ music, a chorus together, and along with them an appropriate and serene word, these are the things that touch the heart, that encourage us, that renew our will.

The pastor's eye should be able to look discreetly into the homes of his congregation; he must know their most acute problems, for they are the signs of the sacrifice we humans are called upon to make in this life. . . .

Pope Leo the Great's words are always true: To live devoutly all the time is to bear the cross with our whole being.

There is great consolation in these words, but how skillfully and gently the eloquent priest must state them.

III. "*To correct the delinquent in the same way*"

What is there to say on the third point? It is, after all, a grave warning. To correct sin by all the means at our disposal.

Do not emphasize the negative aspects of life. In the Breviary, the office we recite for these days recounts the story of the first crime, the killing of Abel.

From that moment, the misuse of free will has led, through the centuries, to many human tragedies. Your task is to know the quality of life, to put things in their proper perspective, to confide in the mysterious but certain intervention of divine grace, if you want to combat evil and avoid its terrible effects.

But you must handle your task with absolute calm. Harsh words, lurid phrasing, acid polemics do not sound appropriate from the pulpit. And it is not necessary to go into detailed descriptions of evil, which satisfies the morbid curiosity of the weak. An allusion and nothing more. One word, not two.

The exemplary conduct of the priest, the spirit of prayer, charity in every situation, and essential courtesy, these are the antidotes to the evils here below..

The humble but powerful Franciscan to whom We have so often alluded, St. Bernardine, reminds us all, bishops and priests alike, of God's warning to the prophet Micah: "Shepherd thy people with thy staff, the flock of thy inheritance . . ." (Micah 7, 14).

But the pastor must temper the sharpness of his sermon

with piety and understanding. Let him hold the club which represents fatherly authority, but let his heart be compassionate. There are those who are carried away by their zeal and indignation. They are mistaken, just as those who turn the corrective word into tacit permission are equally mistaken.

St. Bernardine ends his sermon on a bitter note, reminding us of the conditions of the time he lived in, but he does leave us with a picturesque image of the good shepherd and the good preacher of Lent and the whole year.

The signs of the good shepherd are, *panis in pera, canis in fune, baculus cum virga, cornu cum fistula*; that is to say, bread in the knapsack, or the sermon memorized; the dog by the leash, or restrained zeal; the club and the staff, or authority and guidance; the horn and the shepherd's pipe, or the fear of divine justice and the hope of divine mercy.

These are the implements of the good shepherd, concludes the Saint, *implements to be taken away from the ignorant and stupid pastor*.

These last are really quite harsh words, but we forgive the Saint for them because of his great devotion to the Most Holy Name of Jesus, to which glory and honor forever.[3]

[1] Allocution, February 10, 1959.
[2] Speech, February 13, 1961.
[3] Exhortation, February 19, 1960.

Pius XII

The memory of Pius XII will be honored through the ages. . . . These signs of respect paid to the new Pope . . . are due in large measure to Pius XII, and his long, twenty-year ministry of grace. He imparted great wisdom, and was always concerned in the pastoral care of Christ's fold.

The humble child of the people who was called upon to replace him by Divine Providence . . . will do his best to lead Christians on the road of goodness and mercy. He will do what he can to mitigate the sadness caused by the death of our Father and Pontiff, whom we see already among God's saints in heaven, working, even from there, to renew the energies of the Christians who have survived him and who will never cease venerating his beloved and holy memory.

At the beginning of the Christmas season, His Holiness Pius XII customarily gave a wisdom-filled speech in place of the usual exchange of gifts. He would comment relevantly on a wide range of subjects, from the subtlest theology to the problems of the day, the problems of individuals and families and of society. Modern means of communication brought his talk to all points of the globe and enabled many to think about the meaning of his words, to discern between truth and error, between what we must really be drawn to and what is mere temptation that leads only to disorder and ruin.

To hear his voice alone was a consolation; from 1939 to 1957 he made nineteen such radio broadcasts, along with many other master statements on theology, law, ascetics, politics and society.

The first broadcast—at Christmas 1939—concerned the fundamental requisites for peaceful coexistence. In 1940, he spoke about the presuppositions for a new order in Europe; in 1941, for a new international order. In 1942, he commented on internal national order, and in 1943, on the meaning of the Star of Bethlehem for the deluded, the desolate and the faithful, adding further the principles for a policy of peace. In 1944, the sixth year of the war, he restated the issue of democracy and clarified it. In succeeding years, the issue of peace was the focal point of his addresses.

In 1949, he explained his announcement of a Year of God, a year of renewal and forgiveness. In 1950, he returned to the theme of domestic order; in 1951, the Church and peace; in 1952, he spoke of the plight of mankind living in misery and on Christ's consolation. In 1953, relevant and precise words on technical progress; in 1954, he spoke about co-existence in fear, in error, and in truth. In 1955, he described modern man's attitude toward Christmas and Christ in his history and social life, and the limits of human nature. In 1957, he pointed to Christ as the fount and security for world harmony. This talk summarized his whole thought.

His tomb in the Vatican, next to St. Peter's, could not have a more splendid epitaph than the themes of these radio broadcasts he gave at Christmas.

We are moved to think that these were nineteen expressions of a single doctrine that nineteen packed volumes can barely contain. Truly a marvelous pontificate, both for doctrinal definition and pastoral care, which will assure Pius XII's reputation for posterity. Apart from any official declaration which would be premature, the triple title, "*Doctor optimus, Ecclesiae sanctae lumen, divinae legis amator*" (Most excellent doctor, light of the holy Church, upholder of divine law), would be most suitable to his memory.

To summarize the contents of his nineteen broadcasts and of the twenty volumes of his collected speeches and letters, two words might be adequate: *unity* and *peace*.[1]

[1] Radio broadcast, December 23, 1958.

Art and Religious Art

Undoubtedly, in a matter so broad and universal as this, we must be as understanding as possible. And since the artistic sense is so subjective and reflects such personal attitudes, we must be forbearing, and in criticism we must avoid the excesses of blame and extravagant praise.[1]

Some have hoped for closer contact between men of the Church and the men of art. We do not say between the Church and sacred art, because they have always understood and trusted one another. For her part, the Church never ceases to promote this relationship through her commissions for sacred art, from the Central Pontifical Commission to the diocesan bodies which act as a dense network of organs that are vital to the defense of beauty and good taste. The Church never fails to encourage this understanding by the teaching of the history of art and the principles of sacred art in her schools and seminaries, by the meticulous care with which liturgy is taught, right down to the details of dress and sacred furnishings. She urges her priests to learn to recognize and safeguard the treasures of antiquity that have been entrusted to them, and to continue to enrich that heritage with new and worthy works.

Christian art is of such a character we should almost call it sacramental; certainly not in the strict meaning of the term, but as the vehicle and instrument which God uses to dispose his creatures to the wonders of grace. In art, spiritual values become visible, closer really to the human mentality, which wants to see and to touch. The harmony of the structure, the plastic forms, the magic of the colors are further means that attempt to bring the visible closer to the invisible, the tangible to the supernatural.

This instructive and instrumental value of art enables us to understand why the Church has always defended images and why she is sympathetic to artists, and why she has encouraged a sound and complete humanism, which has had so many rightful triumphs in art itself. The Church seeks nothing else, we repeat, but to carry out her mission of elevating and sanctifying man. And just as angels are the messengers of God and present our prayers to him, so too does Christian art raise itself above the material plane to join God, to attend to his holy purposes, to facilitate and direct our relations with him.[2]

The intention of placing art at God's service is in itself an apostolate and merits encouragement.[1]

[1] Conversation, January 3, 1959.
[2] An audience, IX Commission of Sacred Art, October 27, 1961.

[IV]
CHRISTIAN UNITY

The Gospel

The believers who belong to the Church know that St. Peter lives again in his successor, and so motivated by a feeling that overcomes all obstacles, they come to visit him to perpetuate the testimony of ages before the Savior of the world, his sacrifice and Resurrection, his victory over death.

We find in the Gospel what was to be the design of the Church's history, a history of faith. One of the most compelling episodes concerns the Apostle Peter himself. He had gone to the lake to meet Our Lord, who had called him. Suddenly a strong wind came up and Peter was terrified that he would drown. He called out to Jesus, and Jesus answered, "Ye of little faith, why do you doubt? I am here."

The whole history of the Church is summarized in this episode. Along her course, there have been many storms, and even today many are suffering from adverse elements, but the Church lives. Even where the faithful enjoy a certain peace, they can feel anxiety and fear. But it is our task to keep the faith strong, so that the Lord need not reprove us as he did Peter, after all the signs he has given us of his presence.

Many things are changed in the world, but the Lord's words never fail.

What makes us sure of this certainty? The holy books, the Gospel, where the Church's purposes are all laid out. The popes repeat them, explain them, communicate them. This is the basis of today's civilization and of tomorrow's. Some may imagine the troubles of the future, the catastrophes and the destruction. But we know about this as well. The end of the world is described in detail in the Gospel. Thus our duty is to continue to trust in the Lord's word, to remain faithful to his teaching, and to transmit these fundamentals to the many future generations with great assurance.

Whenever we need light and consolation, let us return to the four Evangelists; let us think of the martyrs, the apostles, the popes, of the Church's living vitality, and along with the Pope, let us bless the Lord.[1]

[1] Speech, February 19, 1959.

The Christian

I am a Christian: the ancient words want to resound with new strength. They do not require, as they did in the early centuries of Christianity, the testimony of blood. They now require the continuous testimony of felt and meditated loyalty to one's ideals, to the calling of Christianity and the teaching of the Church. They demand from each person his convinced and compelling presence in a world that is fascinated by powerful material interests and all the things they imply. They proclaim the presence of generous love and courage when at times it seems that selfish and calculating motivations are winning out, implicitly or explicitly.

Man's highest purposes

Loyalty to one's ideals means the firm intention to follow the high principles set forth in the Old and New Testaments, on which the peace of individuals and the orderly progress of society are based. This loyalty entails a constant desire for a Christian life, nourished at the genuine sources of thought and action by means of a solid doctrinal training, as is demanded of a person in professional preparation, by participating in the sacramental life of the Church, without which professed Christianity is nothing but vain show. This loyalty means knowing what the pontifical documents say about the realities of labor and the social question, and means being ready to put them into practice with good will.

A *convinced presence* is being asked of you, meaning the awareness in your souls of the dignity of God's adopted children and of human responsibility, which ought to diffuse around them an active constructive influence for the common good. We need men who are detached from the seductions the three kinds of lust can practice on the children of this century. These men must be able at the same time to act concretely on earth for the sake of those high purposes which our predecessor St. Pius X proposed for the Catholic laity in the Encyclical Letter, *Il fermo proposito*: "To bring Christ back into the family, into the school, into society; to re-establish the principle that human authority is representative of God's; to take greatly to heart the interests of the people, particularly of the working class and the farmers . . . seeking to dry their tears, soften their pain, improve their economic condition with effective measures; to see to it that public laws are informed by justice, and that those which are not be corrected or discarded."

I am a Christian: but Christianity is essentially love, as God is charity (cf. I John 4, 16). In the double precept of charity the ancient Law and the message of the Prophets are epitomized (cf. Matthew 22, 40), and all the teaching of our Divine Savior.

There are still imbalances and unfairness which must be a thorn in the heart of the true Christian, who is a follower of the Gospels. There is need for greater charity and equity, need for greater economic justice, for these are postulates of the dignity of the human being who was created in the image and likeness of the Most Holy Trinity and redeemed by the Son of God. The Church never ceased nor ceases to proclaim clearly the natural right of man to dependable work and to a dignified way of life, to proclaim that his aspiration to share in the interests of his enterprise is legitimate, so that his role will always be more consonant with that due to an immortal soul which, through Christian faith, is moving toward the eternal life.

This is the goal the Church proposes to her children; this is the program which is waiting to be put into practice by the collaboration of those who can and who know how to, so that—as is written in the Encyclical Letter, *Mater et Magistra* —so that "discredit (will not be cast) on that doctrine, as if it were noble in itself, but incapable of implementation."[1]

We are a people, a Christian people. Amid this people, the faithful represent the great *plebs christiana* (and let it be noted that the Church uses this word *plebs* not in the current sense of "plebeian," but in a very much higher sense to denote the large noble family redeemed by Christ's blood). Here is Jesus, the Son of the Heavenly Father made Man, who offered all of himself on earth, to his very blood, to sanctify, to guard all the souls united to him by the bond of faith and grace, and brought by him to share in his life of merit here below, and in his glory in heaven.

Through the centuries, our Lord continues to distribute his grace to those who become participants in his heritage through Baptism. He calls on all the others to share in this priceless treasure.

We belong to this immense army and therefore we understand that being Christians means living this continuous activity of sanctification. If someone claims he is a Christian but does not sanctify himself, he still bears the name but it has no value. Whoever calls himself a Christian and tramples on God's commandments is not worthy of God and does not sanctify his own life. Who speaks ill of his neighbor, who does not seek the impetus to unity, peace and mutual understanding, whoever prefers to dally with envy, hatred and discord cannot claim to be a Christian.[2]

[1] Speech, June 17, 1962. [2] Speech, July 25, 1962.

Christianity

Christianity . . . is the joining of earth and heaven insofar as it takes man in his concreteness, spirit and matter, intellect and will, and asks him to elevate his mind from the changing conditions of earthly life toward the heights of eternal life, which shall be an unending consummation of happiness and peace.[1]

We must affirm it with the same sureness as did the Apostles; you must be convinced of it as of the most beautiful treasure, the only one that can render our daily existence rich and tranquil: Christianity is not the oppressive force that the unbelieving describe, but rather it is peace, joy, love, everlasting life, like the secret pulse of nature at the beginning of spring. The source of this joy lies in Christ Resurrected, who frees men from the slavery of sin and who asks man to be a new creature with him in anticipation of blessed eternity.

Life and death engaged in a fierce struggle. The Master of life triumphs over death, and his victory is the Church's victory through the ages. Let us release our spirits from any anxiety and open our hearts to the warmest hopes for the future. We may be pressed upon by the world, we shall be so surely. Before his ascension, Jesus, the victor over death, said: "Have faith, for I have won the world." It is true, but a princely figure remains on the battlefield. We recall him often by name. He is a prince. The Divine Rabbi of Nazareth used to call him the "prince of this world." Christ meekly but effectively carries on the struggle against him, for the sake of justice and the triumph of peace. The infernal adversary, however, hates peace and justice. At times his attacks, his strategy, create such confusion that those who are defending themselves against him almost fall prey to exhaustion.

Every good Christian trusts in Christ, fulfills his duty according to the commands of his conscience, which is both religious and social, before God and before his fellow men. The Christian does not make concessions and is wary of compromises; he moves forward sure and unafraid. He works for peace.

To strengthen his resistance against evil and error, he prays. He invokes the heavenly aid of grace which enlightens and sustains the strong.

We know Christ truly arose from the dead. Christ's victory over death is the assurance that we shall triumph over the obstacles that impair human efforts to defend justice, liberty and peace.[2]

[1] Encyclical, *Mater et Magistra*, May 15, 1961.
[2] Allocution, March 18, 1959.

Devotion to the Most Precious Blood

From the very first months of Our pontificate, We have had occasion several times to ask the faithful to turn their attention during their daily devotions to that sign of God's mercy toward men and toward the Church. We mean the devotion to the Most Precious Blood.

This devotion was instilled in Us during boyhood, and We can still remember Our elders reciting the litany of the Most Precious Blood in July.

The Apostle warns us: "Take care, take care of the fold over which the Holy Spirit has named you bishops, to protect the Church of God, which he got with his own blood." Mindful of this warning, We believe that among the concerns of Our universal ministry—second to that of preserving the faith—religious piety in liturgical and private worship should have a privileged place. We should like to draw the attention of Our dear children to the profound tie between the two devotions that are already so popular, that is, to the Most Holy Name of Jesus and to his Sacred Heart, and the devotion in honor of the Most Precious Blood of the Word Incarnate, "that was spilled for many in remission of their sins."

It is of utmost importance that there be full consistency between the precepts of the Apostles' Creed and the liturgy of the Church, and that there never be any form of worship that does not come from the purest sources of the true faith. It is equally true that this consistency should apply among the forms of devotions themselves, so that there are no contradictions or discontinuities among those that are considered as basic and salutary. At the same time, secondary and personal devotions must not be given more weight than those directly related to universal salvation.

If we take a brief look at the wonderful progress the Catholic Church has made in the area of liturgical devotion, in keeping with the increasing study and understanding of divine truths, we find with great satisfaction that in the last few centuries, this Apostolic See has repeatedly and clearly urged the devotions We have just mentioned. These three devotions began in the Middle Ages, and spread from diocese to diocese, from religious order to religious order, and finally received full approval from the Chair of Peter.

Following the example of Our Predecessors in encouraging the devotion to the Precious Blood of the Immaculate Lamb, Jesus Christ, We have approved the litanies according to the order issued by the Sacred Congregation of Rites and have decreed indulgences for their recitation in order to encourage both public and private devotion.

May this new act of "care for the whole Church," undertaken by the Supreme Pontiff himself, re-awaken the faithful to the perennial, universal and supreme value of these three devotions.

If Christians would only heed the warning of the first Pope: "Live in fear during your pilgrimage, knowing that you have not been ransomed by corruptible things like gold and silver . . . but by the precious blood of Christ, of the spotless lamb" or the exhortation of St. Paul: "You have been bought at a dear price. Glorify therefore God, and bear him in your bodies," how much more worthy and decent would their way of life be, and how much more beneficial would the presence of the Church be. If all men would accept God's invitation to grace, God, who sent his only Son to save them with his Precious Blood and who calls them to be part of his Mystical Body, of which Christ is the Head—how much more peaceful and fraternal would their relations with each other be, how much worthy of God and of human nature, which was created in the image and likeness of the Most High.[1]

[1] Apostolic Letter, *Inde a Primis,* June 30, 1960.

The Church

The Mother and Teacher of all peoples, the universal Church, was established by Jesus Christ so that all who have come to her through the centuries would find the fullness of a greater life and the guarantee of salvation.[1]

One Church

The association of several rites in different languages, each with its own history, in the adoration of the Holy Trinity is the first and leading sign of respect for the unity of the holy institution which is the Church. There is no beauty comparable to the many rites, languages, images and symbols abounding in the liturgy, which expresses in various ways the intimate union of the faithful who compose the Mystical Body of Christ. That union confirms the profoundest and surest reason for the closeness of all the races of man called upon to honor Christ, and through him, the Holy Trinity.

The symbol and certainty of unity is the Pontiff who as Peter's successor is at the head of the sacred order: the hierarchy, doctrine, worship, sacraments. *One God, one faith, one baptism!* One of Christ's principal themes was the praise of the sacrament of unity which draws all peoples, all languages and all the natural differences in their histories into one single aspiration. Christ's last invocation to the Heavenly Father affirms it: *Holy Father, keep them in thy name, which thou hast given me, that they may be one, even as we are one.*

The Latin liturgy is therefore, among the various forms of worship, very worthy of respect because a great many of the faithful use it. But unity appears even more perfect, splendid and wonderful when all the eastern liturgies open, as it were, a path for it, and together with the Latin liturgy form a chorus around the same altar.

Holy Church

If in saying *tu solus Dominus, tu solus sanctus, tu solus altissimus* to Christ, founder of the Church, we fail to respond to his grace, the fount of all holiness, we run the risk of reducing these invocations to spiritually empty forms, comparable in a sense to the human distractions dedicated to material things and forgetful of the eternal ones.

Thus the affirmation, which becomes a precept and a sacred duty, that we must bring to our efforts to develop the energies of the Church an underlying sense of the clergy's and laity's holiness and a desire to do her honor according to the teaching of the Lord and the examples of the saints.

Catholic Church

This is the distinction that is characteristic of the Gospel the Lord entrusted to Peter and his successors. This is the deep root which has penetrated the earth everywhere, beyond Palestine where Christ commanded his apostles to go forth, and beyond Rome and Greece which provided Providence with so many witnesses to the evangelic message, even at the price of numberless martyrdoms.

Catholicity has remained intact, by divine grace, through the centuries, just as Jesus predicted and promised, despite the variations in liturgy and pastoral application which ornament it.

Christ's heritage should not be felt or applied merely in terms of this or that nation's needs, its demands or the changing events of its history, but in uncontaminated fidelity to the promises of Christ, who assured us the continuity of his help.

Catholicity does not suffer because the Church expands and increases her activities; rather, it becomes consolidated and enriched. It is precisely this joining of catholicity to other aims which is fundamental and correspondent to the right doctrine: because "like unity, the prerogative of holiness and apostolic succession must shine forth."

Apostolic Church

The apostolic nature of the Church is alive, the reason

why Christ, king of nations and of the centuries, symbolizes and recapitulates in himself everything, as St. Paul said and Pius X made his own motto: *Establish all in Christ!*

When we say Christ rules over all the segments of society, we recall the biblical image, *Filii tui de latere surgent.* From the wound in Christ's side flows the force of virtue.

St. Paul could describe himself as the "least of the apostles," but nonetheless an apostle, and consequently sure of his vocation and of the gift of grace which would make his ministry a fruitful one.

The Catholic Church is not an archeological museum. It is the old village well which still gives water to the new generations, just as it did to the old.[2]

The Church lives, just as her Divine Founder lives! The Church moves forward by virtue of her life, just as Jesus did, when after paying the debt of his mortal nature, he triumphed over the stone barrier his enemies had placed before his tomb. For the Church, too, there have been other enemies through the ages, who have tried to seal her off, as if in a sepulcher, and who have celebrated occasionally her passing away. But she has the strength of her Founder in her, and is reborn with him, forgiving and granting peace to the meek, the poor, the suffering, to all men of good will.[3]

To his Church, the pillar and foundation of truth, the Redeemer has entrusted two tasks: to increase the number of her children and to educate and guide them, caring equally for individuals and nations for whose dignity she has always had the greatest respect and concern.

Christianity is the joining of earth and heaven insofar as it accepts man in his concreteness—spirit and body, intellect and will—and asks him to elevate his mind from the changeable conditions of earthly life toward the heights of eternal life which shall be the consummation of happiness and peace.

And even though the Church's mission is primarily to sanctify the soul and to prepare it for the joys of the supernatural order, she is nonetheless concerned with the demands of our daily lives, not only in continuing life and facing its problems, but also in our prosperity and culture in its various aspects and historical phases.

In realizing her mission, Holy Church carries out the command her founder gave her when he spoke above all of man's eternal salvation: *I am the way, the truth and the life. I am the light of the world.* But elsewhere, as he gazes on the starving multitude, he says: *I have compassion for these people*, thus showing his concern for man's life on earth. And the Holy Savior does not merely show his concern with words but also by his acts, such as the miracle of the loaves and the fish. And those loaves fed to the multitude foreshadowed the food for the soul he was to give mankind on the eve of his Passion.

There is no marvel greater than the Catholic Church, which has imitated Christ and carried out his commands for two thousand years, from the institution of the ancient deacons to our own time. She has kept the flame of charity burning, not only in her teaching but also by her example, a charity that has accorded with her lessons on mutual love and its enactment. And thus she fulfills the dual mission of guidance and social action.

The Church's contribution

The Church, as we know, is universal by divine dispensation, and is so historically as well by the fact that she is present among all nations.

The arrival of the Church among a people has always had positive effects in their economic and social life, as both history and experience prove. The reason is that human beings who become Christians cannot help but feel the need to improve their institutions and their temporal commitments; that is, in order to insure respect for human dignity, to eliminate or reduce the obstacles to the realization of the good, and to increase the incentives toward its fulfillment.

When the Church does become part of a people's life, she does not feel—nor is she—imposed upon them from without. Her presence is felt, after all, in the rebirth or resurrection of the individual in Christ, and whoever is reborn in Christ never feels that he is forced to be. He senses, rather, that he is freed in his deepest being, and so released to God. Whatever value he possesses, no matter what its nature, is ennobled and reaffirmed.

"The Church of Christ," as Our Predecessor Pius XII observed, "the faithful depositary of divine wisdom, would not even think of altering or meddling in the particular traits which every people jealously guards as their sacred heritage. Her only purpose is supernatural unity in universal love that is felt and practiced, and not the uniformity which is purely superficial and in itself pernicious. The Church hails those customs and concerns which serve a wise and ordered development of a culture that has roots deep in the heart of every race, as long as those customs do not contradict the obligations deriving from man's common origin and common destiny."

We note with great satisfaction that today too the Catholic citizens of developing countries usually are second to none in their efforts to improve and strengthen their economic and social condition.

And the Catholics in countries that are already advanced economically are doubling their efforts to support the work being done to help those developing nations. Especially noteworthy are the various forms of assistance being given increasingly to students from Asian and African countries who are now in universities throughout Europe and America, and noteworthy too are the technicians and professional people going into underdeveloped countries to help with their services.

To Our dear children who embody the Church's vitality throughout the world, who are promoting genuine progress and revitalizing their countries, We want to express Our fatherly encouragement and Our affectionate praise.

The social teaching of the Church

The Church fosters a time conception of social existence.

The fundamental principle in this concept—as has been made clear in what has been already said—is that the individual is and must be the basis, the end and the object of all the institutions through which society acts. That is, the individual understood for what he is and what he must be, according to his intrinsically social nature, and according to the decree of Providence that he shall rise to a supernatural order.

From this fundamental principle which insures the sacred dignity of every person, the Church, along with her clergy and enlightened laymen, has formulated, especially in our own time, a social doctrine that clearly points the way toward building a society on universal standards that correspond to the nature and the limits of the temporal order, and to the characteristics of modern society. Thus these standards are acceptable to everyone.

It is necessary however, today more than ever, that her teaching be recognized, assimilated, translated into social reality, in the form and degree that various situations permit or demand. This is a very difficult but very noble task, to which We call not only Our brothers and sons throughout the world, but all men of good will.[4]

Apostolic activity

The Church wants to be looked to for what she is intrinsically, as the embodiment, especially to her children, of enlightening faith and sanctifying grace inspired by those last words (of Christ). Those words express the primary mission of the Church, her qualifications for service and honor; she must enliven, teach, pray.

As for her mission in the world, that is, the Church, in her confrontation of the needs and demands of all peoples—who are being directed by the forces of history toward the enjoyment and appreciation of worldly things—feels compelled to meet her responsibilities in her teaching: *sic transire per bona temporalia, ut non amittamus aeterna* ("to pass through the good things of the world so as not to lose the eternal ones").

This sense of responsibility felt by the Christian called upon to live, a man among men, a Christian among Christians, must be such that others who are not Christians will be inspired to become so.

This is the key to the Church's outward but always apostolic mission, to teach those who are sent to her to serve. The world has need of Christ, and it is the Church which must bring Christ to the world. The world has problems for which it anxiously seeks solutions, but the anxiety to find timely answers that are also moral can provide an obstacle to the spreading of the whole truth and of sanctifying grace.

Man seeks the love of a united family, his daily bread and that of his wife and children; he hopes to live in peace in his own country, and to maintain peaceful relations with the rest of the world. He senses the call of the spirit, which leads him to know and to raise himself. He jealously guards his freedom but does not refuse to recognize lawful limitations that enable him to meet his social obligations.

In the service of man become God's adopted son

These very serious problems are always the Church's concern. . . .

These are some of them: the fundamental equality of all nations in the exercise of their rights and duties within the human family; the defense of the sacred character of matrimony, which demands knowing and generous love from both partners from which children are procreated in the religious and moral sense, within the frame of the great social and eternal responsibilities.

The philosophies that deny God or foster religious indifferentism, the doctrines that ignore the hand of Providence in history and unduly exalt the person of the individual man, with possible damage to his sense of social responsibility, must feel the weight of the Church's courageous teaching, which has already been expressed in the important document, *Mater et Magistra*, where the thinking of two millennia of Christian history is summarized.

Another thing to be said is that the Church presents herself before the underdeveloped nations for what she is and wants to be, everyone's Church, especially of the poor.

Every violation of the fifth and sixth commandments, any shirking from the obligations imposed by the seventh; the miseries of social life which demand God's vengeance; we must identify and deplore them all. The duty of every man, the impelling duty of every Christian, is to consider his unneeded goods in relation to the necessities of others, and to insure that there is an equal distribution among all.

This is what we can describe as the spreading of social and community spirit that is intrinsic to authentic Christianity. It must be vigorously supported.

Justice and peace

What is there to say about the relations between the Church and the body politic? We live in an age of new political realities. One of the basic rights the Church cannot give up is religious freedom, which is not simply the right to worship.

The Church lays claim to and teaches this right, and is being persecuted for it in many countries.

The Church cannot give up this freedom because it is part

of the mission she has been charged to carry out. The service she performs is not merely complementary or corrective to the services that other institutions provide or have appropriated to themselves, but rather is an essential and irrevocable element in the design of Providence to direct man on the path to truth. Truth and freedom are the foundation stones of the edifice we call civilization.[5]

Situations change, but the difficulties the Church must face in performing her divine mission are never lacking. We must remind those who are amazed or who trust naively in some future of easy victories and perfect tranquillity, of the pages of blood and glory written by the martyrs and the Doctors of the Church in defense of and out of love for the sacred deposit of faith which Christ entrusted to his Church.[6]

The internal structure of the Church derives its strength from the conviction that she has remained faithful to the mission her Divine Founder charged her with, and she does fear seeming or being judged severe or too prudent.

This Church, which does not need anyone, entrusts herself not to all her children.

Holy Church is the great Christian family. Jesus founded it and entrusted it to Peter and his successors, and he breathed divine strength into it. What a vision of grandeur and unity she has been throughout the ages![7]

We are just travelers on this earth, and even if we must naturally think about material necessities, we must bear well in mind that at the end of our trip we shall not come upon an abyss or chaos, but rather upon the dazzling light of Paradise.

The Church is firm in this conviction, and all her children are equally certain, trusting in the words Christ spoke to Peter: "You are Peter . . . and the gates of hell shall not prevail." In such granite certainty, Peter's successor will be the first to give his life whenever it is necessary.

This is the real joy for everyone, old and young alike. The Church is solid, peace-making, a guide. The rock has not budged since the day the Lord fixed it and declared it to be solid until the end of time. St. Peter is always with us. And beside him is St. Paul, who extends the word of the first Pope. This is our certainty: *veritas Domini manet in aeternum* (God's truth shall be for eternity). To that truth is anchored for all time the Church, one, holy, catholic and apostolic.[8]

[1] Encyclical, *Mater et Magistra*, May 15, 1961.
[2] Exhortation to the bishops, April 12, 1959.
[3] Radio broadcast, March 28, 1959.
[4] Encyclical, *Mater et Magistra*, May 15, 1961.
[5] Radio broadcast, September 11, 1962.
[6] Conversation, March 24, 1960.
[7] Conversation, May 4, 1960.
[8] Conversation, August 12, 1961.

The Pope

The Pope's mission is universal by divine investiture. Of course, he represents the Church. Naturally, and after centuries of history, his task is recognized as not being limited to those who profess Christianity, particularly Catholicism. He must, indeed, open his heart to all men in order to tell the truth and to point the way to it, according to the example of the Divine Teacher.

The Gospel tells us that Our Lord Jesus Christ never hesitated to condemn error; when he was faced with pain, he never shirked. He spoke to the Pharisee and the tax collector, sharing the richness of his heart, the source itself of charity. Only rarely did he use hard expressions or act with necessary severity, and even then his ultimate purpose was merciful. Faced with human suffering, he shared with others the fullness of his infinite goodness, and participated in their grief.

Following the Savior's example, the Pope opens his embrace to the whole world. He keeps himself informed about everything that is happening as part of his office. And he prays that he can be always in communication with Christ so that he can reflect, as far as possible, his will and his commands, and receive his inspiration.

The Pope's day is filled with prayer.

The Holy Mass and the Breviary lay down precise rules, which the Pope along with all priests must hold to. Then the Rosary with its fifteen Mysteries which constitute episodes in the life of Our Lord Jesus Christ and his Mother, an excellent opportunity for contemplation and absorption in one's soul. The Rosary is, therefore, not only an exercise in spoken prayer but a profound and fruitful meditation. For instance, in reciting the Rosary, the Holy Father says ten Hail Marys in the first part recalling the joyful mystery of Christ's birth, for the intention of all babies born during the last twenty-four hours. Thus for all the newborn, wherever they are, there is a blessing from the man who represents, by divine mandate, the union of man and God.

The Holy Father thinks on the destinies of all of his children; for instance, during the recital of the second Mystery he prays for the intention of families, and in the fourth, for the intention of the rising generations.

And the fifth joyful Mystery, in which we recall the finding of Jesus in the Temple? He recites it for the intention of journalists and the success of their responsible mission. As we read in St. Luke's beautiful account, Mary and Joseph found their twelve-year-old son standing in the midst of the doctors of the Old Law, listening to them and asking questions. Is this not the task of the journalist, to ask about human events and their causes, and can he not fulfill a role of great importance by seeking and spreading the truth? We have examples of how such an apostolate can even lead to the supreme sacrifice.[1]

The Pope knows his task, and is upheld in fulfilling it by the special graces of continuous assistance from God.

The world provides suggestions, advice, criticism, but the faithful know that the Pope, with the help of their prayers, derives the strength and the motives for his acts solely from the Gospel. His is the teaching of Our Lord Jesus Christ, the single and greatest means to salvation. The Pope, therefore, has no need to comply with the clamorous methods of the world, but rather follows the ways of discretion and firmness, enlightened always by divine guidance and departing from a point of the most profound and open union with God. The Gospel tells us that we need humility, sincerity, gentleness, meekness and great patience more than any material resource.[2]

[1] Conversation, October 24, 1961.
[2] Conversation, May 17, 1961.

Relations with Non-Catholics

In such relations, our children should take care to be always certain of themselves so as never to make compromises about their religion or their morality. But at the same time they should be moved by, and show, a spirit of understanding; they should be dispassionate and ready to work toward objectives which are by their nature good, or convertible to the good.

One should never be confused when dealing with a person who has gone astray, not even when he has done so by mistake or through an inadequate understanding of the truth in morality and religion. He is always and above all a human being and in every case retains his dignity as a person. He should always be treated and considered in a way appropriate to that dignity. Furthermore, in every human being the need, that is part of his nature, to break away from the bonds of error to arrive at the knowledge of truth, is never destroyed. And God's action within him is never lessened. So that whoever lacks a clear conception of faith or believes in mistaken opinions in any particular moment of his life, may be enlightened and believe tomorrow. The encounters and the exchanges in the various activities of the temporal order between believers and non-believers, or those whose belief is not adequate because it includes errors, can be occasions for discovering the truth and honoring it.

And it should be borne in mind that false philosophical doctrines about the nature, the origin and the destiny of the universe and of mankind must not be identified with historical movements that have had economic, cultural and political purposes, even if those movements were originated by those doctrines and were inspired then or are inspired even now by them. Because doctrines always remain the same, once elaborated and defined, while the movements of which we have spoken, by acting within the frame of continually changing historical situations, cannot avoid being influenced by them and thus being subject to rather profound changes. What is more, who can deny that there are positive elements worthy of approval in those movements, in the degree in which they conform to the dictates of right reason and they interpret the just aspirations of the human person?

Therefore, it can turn out that an approach or a meeting of a practical nature that was considered inopportune and unproductive yesterday could be opportune today or could become so tomorrow. To decide whether the moment has arrived and the means and the degree of cooperation for the achievement of economic, social, cultural and political purposes that are honest and useful to the good of the community is a problem that can be solved only with the virtue of prudence, which is the guide of the virtues regulating the moral life, whether it be individual or social. On the part of Catholics, therefore, such a decision is the responsibility, in the first place, of those who live or work in the specific areas of society where the problems arise. The decision must always agree with the principles of natural law, with the social teachings of the Church and with the directives of the ecclesiastical authority. No one should forget, moreover, that to the Church belong not only the right and the duty to safeguard the principles of the ethical and religious order, but also to intervene authoritatively in her children's affairs in the temporal order, when the question concerns a judgment about the application of those principles to concrete cases.[1]

[1] Encyclical, *Pacem in Terris*, April 11, 1963.

Concessions to Non-Catholics

The respect we owe to whoever has not reached complete Christian and Catholic conviction, but who is on the threshold of the Church, does not authorize dangerous concessions, compromises or renunciations that do damage to the sacred heritage of the truth, which is the Gospel.

The most serious danger to which Our children are exposed is precisely this; the danger, that is, of intolerance toward a common discipline which becomes, however, tolerance and indifference before the errors and dangerous positions in the various areas of public life, in politics as in entertainment, in literature as in religious practice.[1]

[1] Speech, December 4, 1960.

The Unity of Christians

Jesus founded the Church and impressed on it the character of unity, so that she might embrace all peoples, from sea to sea. Why cannot the unity of the Catholic Church, which is directly and by divine mandate intent on the interests of spiritual order, be turned as well to the re-uniting of the various races and nations which are equally concerned with living together under the laws of justice and brotherhood?[1]

This marvelous unity which distinguishes the Catholic Church and serves as an example to all, and her prayers that God grant the same unity to the world, may move and inspire your hearts as well, you who are separated from the Apostolic See.

Permit Us to call you, with great willingness, Our brothers and sons. Let Us nourish the hope of your return, which We strive for with paternal affection. We turn to you with the same concern, and with the same words which the Bishop of Alexandria, Theophilus, used during the time of a grievous schism: "Let us, who are all participants in the same heavenly calling, each according to his means, let us imitate Jesus, the guide and author of our salvation! Let us embrace that unity which uplifts the heart and that charity which leads us to God, and let us believe firmly in the divine mysteries. Flee from every division, avoid discord . . . with mutual charity. Listen to Christ's words: 'from this they will know you are my disciples, if you love one another.' "

Remember that Our loving invitation to share in the unity of the Church does not call you to a stranger's house, but to your own Father's home. Permit Us this appeal, which We make with "the tenderness of Jesus Christ." Remember your fathers, "who told you about God's word, and knowing what the end of their life was, imitate their faith." The great ranks of the saints, whom your peoples sent to Heaven, especially those who have explained and transmitted the doctrine of Jesus Christ in their writings, also seem to ask you by the example of their lives to re-unite with this Apostolic See, with which your Christian communities were for so many centuries beneficially united. We address all those who are separated from Us as brothers, with the words of St. Augustine: "Whether you want it or not, they are our brothers. Only when they have ceased saying 'Our Father' will they cease being our brothers." "We love our Lord God, we love his church, the one as a father, the other as a mother; the one as a master, the other as his handmaiden, because we are sons of his servant. This marriage finds coherence in great charity: we cannot offend one and still win the other's benevolence. . . . Of what use is it to you if you do not offend the father, if he will revenge the offenses you committed against the mother? . . . Therefore, let us remain unanimously close to God the Father and to our mother the Church."[2]

[1] Radio broadcast, December 23, 1958.
[2] Encyclical, *Ad Petri Cathedram*, June 29, 1959.

[V]
THE CHANGING WORLD

A. THE FOUNDATION

Charity

Charity: ***veritatem facientes in caritate.*** Here is the summation of our life in society. It begins with the contact between brothers, and then with the contact between groups of brothers. If such life is permeated and inspired by the spirit of Jesus, then it is charitable and moves eagerly ahead. But something quite different happens in the ordinary events of an unhappy life: it turns into worry, anger, struggle. And what is more, this exercise of charity takes the form of meekness, tenderness, forgiveness. And thus at the same time gives us the decisiveness to carry out our duties faithfully.[1]

[1] Speech, April 10, 1959.

Love

God has placed three loves in the heart of man . . . which take nourishment from his love and are ennobled by it: marital love, parental love and filial love.

To try to destroy or to paralyze these affections would be a profanation . . . which would lead inevitably to the ruin of nations and humanity.

Let love be that which sustains and warms you, love for one's family, for the Church, for one's country. Love which compels you to reach out, to forget almost your own selves, in the search for God's glory and the well-being of souls. May divine light be your guide, your ideal, your purpose, a light to be kindled in the minds and hearts of your loved ones, of your friends, even those far away, a light that awaits your hand in order to shine forth and cast its rays about you.[1]

[1] Speech, May 1, 1959.

Truth

Everyone knows of the growing attempts to suppress or dilute the truth. Since childhood, we have known the horror any Christian must feel about lies. Very well, then, one could say that the world today enjoys the enactment of one general lie, a conscious and organized one. It is very difficult to get hold of a complete, absolute statement of truth. And so often there are attempts to cover up lies with the guise of truth.

We must, however, honor truth always as we face the final problems of life, death and the beyond. The Lord is the truth. "I am your Teacher," he said.[1]

Truth is the most precious thing. In a Christian and religious sense, we say that truth is grace. Truth is first, because where Christ is, there is truth. Thus, if we really want our own life and the lives of our fellow men to be worthy of the supreme end, we must always and everywhere live up to the clear and inflexible demands of the truth.[2]

The ignorance of the truth is the root and cause of all the evils which poison, so to speak, the lives of individuals, peoples and nations. And not only ignorance, but denial and disdain of the truth at times as well. From these attitudes come mistakes of every kind that affect men and society, upsetting the necessary balance. And yet God did give us the power of reason to recognize natural truths. By obeying reason, we obey God himself, who is its creator and the lawmaker and guide, at the same time, of our lives. But if through foolishness or sloth, or worse yet, through malice, we fail to use right reason, then we deliberately abandon the highest good and moral law.

But we can arrive at natural truths, certainly, by the use of reason, as we said. This knowledge, however, especially concerning religion and morality, is not readily available to everyone, and if they attempt to arrive at it, they frequently mix it with errors.

The truths that transcend the natural capacity of reason cannot be reached without the help of supernatural light. And for this, the Word of God, God who resides in inaccessible light and who—out of compassion and love for humanity—became flesh and dwelt among us in order to enlighten "every man who is born into the world," and to lead us all not only to the fullness of truth but to virtue and eternal beatitude. Everyone must therefore embrace the doctrine taught by the Gospels. If they reject it, the very bases of truth, morality and civilization are endangered.

As is evident, this is a very serious question, inseparably connected with our eternal salvation. Those who, as the Apostle said, "are always learning without ever arriving at the knowledge of the truth," and who deny that human reason can ever know any truth for certain, and repudiate even the truths revealed by God, which are necessary for salvation, these unhappy creatures are very far from Christ's teaching. They are as far from the Apostle, who urged that we all "arrive together at the unity of faith and to the full cognizance of the Son of God . . . so that we may no longer be children, tossed to and fro and carried about by every wind of doctrine, by the cunning of men, by their craftiness in deceitful wiles. Rather, speaking the truth in love, we are to grow up in every way into him who is the head, into Christ, from whom the whole body joined and knit together by every joint with which it is supplied, when each part is working properly, makes bodily growth and upbuilds itself in love."[3]

[1] Speech, September 9, 1962.
[2] Speech, December 6, 1959.
[3] Encyclical, *Ad Petri Cathedram,* June 29, 1959.

Justice

Justice stems from divine light and consists in giving each his own. One's first duty then is to give to God what is God's. To recognize that he is the Creator, the Redeemer, the fount of life. To practice what he preached and to spread his word among one's own and throughout the world. The provident spreading of his word has been going on for two thousand years now, interrupted at times, or now and then, forced to stop, and frequently dyed by the blood of the Faith's confessors. But it is always alive and unstoppable.

After one's duty to God, there is the duty to give to Caesar what is Caesar's. This means that once respect has been paid to God by the practice of religious faith, then relations of a social character must be taken into account. We are on earth, but we live in trust, and this is our strength. We work for eternity, which is not of this world, but in preparing for our final destination we must be able to live with dignity in the midst of the trials of this life, subordinating everything to that which our Lord offers us for our future life. And one of the main elements in insuring our arrival there is the constant respect for the rights of our fellow man.[1]

The fundamental rules for living with one's neighbor, with one's family, in society, and in the body politic must always be borne in mind, not only with regard to our relations with God, with Revelation and with the great teaching that must always lighten our paths, but also with regard to the concomitant of material well-being.[2]

The union of truth and justice constitutes the basis of human society, and also the happiness of a people and the success of their undertakings. This unity is a claim to honor, which is not merely self-satisfaction, but benefits others as well.

This premise is central to the appreciation of the work carried out by the governmental departments which oversee the enactment of justice.

Their task is a very important one, so much so that, in fact, it could be described as almost sacerdotal. It is necessary, certainly, to be concerned with things of this world, but in serving the good of each man and of society in its entirety, they must include more important necessities, such as the European and world social order, which under the guidance of God and his Law renews our consciences and benefits everyone.[3]

[1] Speech, March 20, 1960. [2] Speech, December 8, 1959.
[3] Speech, October 6, 1962.

The Virtues

Along with the basic principles that govern our behavior before God and our fellow man, we must also observe the theological virtues which define the Christian, the perfect Catholic. The three virtues, which you are all familiar with, are faith, hope and charity. It would be well to note the qualities that make them so splendid and so compelling.

Firma fides (firm faith), *spes invicta* (undefeated hope), *caritas effusa* (charity toward all).

Firma fides

From the time we are baptized to our last breath on earth, as each of us returns to the Heavenly Father, we have with us the Apostles' Creed. The priest finds reassurance as he prays by the side of a dying man, so often a poor sinner like so many others, saying: Lord, this man who is dying is an unhappy creature who was beguiled by the temptations of his youth or hardened by the stubbornness of his old age; he has offended you often, and has allowed himself to be taken in by the things of this world, by its pleasures and profits, and *yet he never denied his faith*. Be good and merciful to him.

The good Christian, however, in the enthusiasm of his youth and in the maturity of his later years, must keep his faith profound and active, the light of his progress, of his decisions, of his highest duties, at home and in society, by example and device.

"But my righteous one shall live by faith" (Hebrews 10, 38). To the intellectual, faith is a lamp that helps him in his search for truth in all branches of human inquiry. The expression "faith seeks intellect" has implications for much of science. It is not an honor for a scientist to be, or claim to be, an unbeliever. It betrays a poverty of spirit, an ignorance of the self and dangerous presumption.

Then there is the defense of the faith which is to be regarded as a true fortress, *firma fides*; the spreading of the faith which is the worthiest apostolate, the perfection of the Christian spirit, and a source of honor in God's Holy Church, which requires workers for its apostolate throughout the world.

And what must we say about those who must suffer terrible persecution in their defense of the truth and of the Catholic faith, persecutions which equal, if not exceed, those of ancient times? On this third day of the Synod, We, along with the entire assembly of Our clergy, send our assurances of solidarity and our encouragement to our troubled brothers, priests and laymen, in the Church of Silence.

These people are worthy of admiration and pity, but their persecutors merit even greater commiseration, for they are brothers in God as well, who—after two thousand years—are just as blind as ever in not recognizing that Christ shall always be the glorious and immortal King. This is and always shall be the faith that conquers the world. "This is the victory that overcomes the world: our faith" (1 John 5, 4).

Spes invicta

Christian faith is well defined: "the assurance of things hoped for, the conviction of things not seen" (cf. Hebrews 11, 1). Of course, the violence with which anti-Christian error is spreading, the great infatuation with material well-being that is alienating man from Heaven, his obsessive desire to enjoy some earthly paradise, the reduction of ideals to mere self-indulgence, these are all aspects of our modern world which depress us. The courage to do good threatens to give way in those who are weak, tired, negative.

But Christ's words fill the Gospels, just as they have filled the world, with impelling courage and with the joy that every soul feels when it has performed its Christian duties, and with the certainty of Christ's promise: "He who believes and is baptized will be saved, but he who does not believe will be condemned" (Mark 16, 16). Among us, the children of light, death holds no fear; theological faith assures us of Christ's promise, and hope is certainty: "I am the resurrection and the life" (John 11, 25). Who believes with faith and love shall live in eternity: "Whoever lives and believes in me shall never die" (*ibid.* 11, 26).

Now that we have arrived at this human and Christian reality, it may seem strange that after two thousand years of religious experience and evangelization there are still those who have the courage to claim that the whole history of the Catholic Church, that all of Christianity, is nothing but a continual fable that must be put aside in order to rebuild the world.

Let us leave these deluded people to their ingenuousness, and let us prepare to keep up our hope, which is undefeated because it is based on Christ's word to us, for whom there shall be the final reward, to the great disappointment of the skeptics and the futility of their efforts. Along the way, we may have to put up with their pressures. "In the world you have tribulation, but be of good cheer, I have overcome the world" (*ibid.* 16, 33). "These things I have spoken to you that my joy may be in you and that your joy may be full" (*ibid.* 15, 11).

Caritas effusa

Our Lord confided to his followers: "This is my commandment, that you love one another as I have loved you. Greater love has no man than this, that he lay down his life for his friends" (cf. John 15, 12–13). This is truly a great lesson in charity. In his concreteness is summarized the living substance of all Christianity, of the whole Church. Ecclesiastical law, on the basis of which are written the constitutions of the synods, emanates from the central concept of charity. Charity makes of the friends of God willing servants and the priesthood into a great service to the Church and the general order of society. The energies of the priest are spent in many ways, from ministering the sacraments, which bear heavenly grace to the world, to performing numerous activities with beneficial effects on society: worship, education, works of various kinds in all areas of human endeavor. At times, perhaps too often, the secular world is too unappreciative of the effort priests make—both secular and religious priests, both equally worthy of respect—for the good of the civic and social order. Many years ago, when We were a young priest, We would hear from several sources that priests should come out of the rectory. Today, however, there has been a change of fashion, and some have demanded that the priest return to his rectory and busy himself strictly with liturgical matters. These people have forgotten that the clergy must obey Christ's precepts and follow his example. Christ, after all, did visit the Temple and did spend his nights praying, but during the day he was concerned with the people, the folk of Judea and Galilee, where he preached and encouraged in the service of charity, and performed miracles. He was the good shepherd, as he himself said, anxious for his flock.[1]

[1] Speech, January 29, 1960.

Today's World

We live in an unfortunately attractive world that deceives us with its charms. According to the world's standards, we should pursue amusement, fortune, success and the other attributes of earthly existence. Intent on this rather limited ephemeral pursuit, we can only keep our eyes on the ground, and never look up. When, however, one lives according to the precepts of faith, one can rise in the morning at the first tolling of the *Angelus* and think of God and invoke his Mother's help. The rest of the day then becomes enlivened by that help and inspiration, and we perform our work obediently, exactly and faithfully. We can truly say that we know life in its essence. We give immense value in this way to every human act, to the least breath, under the influence of God's presence, as well as gain merit for ourselves.[1]

[1] Conversation, December 27, 1958.

Revolution or Evolution?

There are many generous people who—when faced with injustices or with situations in which justice is not fully satisfied—are compelled by the desire to change things with a single stroke, avoiding all the steps in between, as if they preferred something very much like revolution.

But we must not forget that gradualness is the law of life in all its expressions, and for this reason even human institutions cannot be changed for the better except by working from within and gradually. "Not in revolution," proclaimed Pius XII, "but in an evolution that has been agreed upon, lie salvation and justice. Violence has never accomplished anything but destruction, it has never built anything, it inflames passions and does not calm them, it creates hate and ruin and does not make the combatants brothers. Violence has forced men and their parties to the painful necessity of having to reconstruct slowly—after hard trials—on the ruins of discord.[1]

[1] Encyclical, *Pacem in Terris,* April 11, 1963.

Science

We all at times have heard it said—in a loud, or painfully quiet voice—that the heavens are closed now, that there is no connection between the beyond and us on earth, that what has been taught us about our beginning and our end has all been erased by progress and by our continual discoveries. We mean the discoveries resulting from ever more daring trips into space, and the possibility of space stations, discoveries which, in their own way, are trying to change the so-called indifference or hostility of the heavens.

But each one of us must realize that despite the great new advances and the high goals achieved by human genius, we must always bear in mind our limits. By raising our eyes to heaven, we can see that the world is in the Lord's hands, and that the harmony of the universe is due to him. We may be hearing voices that we did not know of before, but they are always voices coming to us from heaven, reflecting the omnipotence of the Heavenly Father, who sent his Son into the world to speak with men and save them.

It is therefore the great Christian teaching contained in the Holy Gospels that will provide the fundamental element for every real conquest; that is, a union of hearts, language and feeling by which we are able to remember the true end of human life, and not fear the fact that our days are numbered. Of course, we can prolong human life with the new means science offers us, but in the end, we must all wait, hope, and finally depart.

When the final moment of our journey on earth arrives, our hearts more easily reach upwards. We feel the urge to return to him who created us, and our joy is immense at joining all those who have been the lights of the world. Our tradition is firm, because it brings the past back to us, our parents, our families, the church where we received the holy sacraments, and even lets us hear the bells of our parish. How willingly we recall the beautiful moments of our childhood and youth, proving, in short, that "God's truth will be in eternity." Christ always triumphs; he offers us an unsurpassable example, he sanctifies us, he calls us, he gladdens us.[1]

It has been claimed that in an age of scientific and technological triumphs, man can build his civilization without God. But the truth is that this progress creates human problems on a world scale, which can be solved only in the light of a sincere and active faith in God, who is the beginning and end of man and the world.

The fact that the limitless horizons opened to us by scientific research help to convince us that mathematical and scientific knowledge merely hint at but hardly express completely the most profound aspects of reality. And our tragic experience of how the vast means at the disposal of technology can be used for destructive as well as constructive purposes is proof of the prevailing importance of spiritual values in guaranteeing that technical and scientific advances retain their essentially instrumental character with relation to human progress.

The sense of increasing dissatisfaction which is spreading among individuals in highly developed countries is dissipating illusions about paradise on earth. At the same time, however, the consciousness of the inviolable and universal rights of the individual is growing in these countries, along with the yearning for more humane and just relations. These are all reasons which help to persuade us of our own limits and awaken us to the values of the spirit. This alone cannot help but be a good sign for sincere understanding and fruitful collaboration.[2]

Once the Lord is banished from humanity, darkness ensues. We must take care that the Lord is not overlooked by our intelligence, our studies, our research and interpretation of nature and by the import of the various sciences. Because if we go far from Christ, we shall be in ignorance.

The object of advanced study, even if it is not theology or asceticism, is always—for the Christian, the Catholic—Christ himself, who reveals and enlightens all.[3]

[1] Radio broadcast, December 22, 1959.
[2] Exhortation, April 5, 1961. [3] Speech, July 25, 1962.

The Law

Without doubt, a legal system consistent with moral order and corresponding to the level of development of the political community is a basic element in achieving the common good.

Social life in our time is so varied, complex and dynamic, however, that any legal system, no matter how well-organized and far-sighted, will never be adequate.

Furthermore, relations between individuals, between individuals and intermediate groups, and intermediate groups and public authority at various levels, are so complicated and sensitive that they cannot be governed strictly by overly defined legal systems. Such a situation, therefore, demands that the civil authorities have a clear conception of the nature and extent of their official duties, if they want to interpret the law faithfully, considered in its constituent parts and its intention, and to cope with the concrete cases which are continuously arising. They must be men of great equilibrium and integrity, competent and courageous enough to see at once what the situation requires and to take necessary action quickly and effectively.[1]

[1] Encyclical, *Pacem in Terris*, April 11, 1963.

Man Today

Every individual is a person with rights and duties

In an ordered and productive society, the primary assumption must be that every man is a *person;* that is, he possesses a nature endowed with intelligence and free choice, and is therefore the subject of rights and duties which spring directly and simultaneously from his nature. These rights and duties are therefore universal, inviolable and unalienable.

If we look upon the dignity of the human person in the light of divinely revealed truth, we cannot help but prize it far more highly, for men are redeemed by the blood of Jesus Christ, they are by grace the children and friends of God and the heirs of eternal glory.

RIGHTS

The right to life and a decent standard of living

Every man has the right to life, to integrity of his body, and to the means necessary and suitable for a dignified way of life. These are primarily food, clothing, shelter, rest, medical care, and necessary social services. A human being also has the right to security in case of sickness, inability to work, widowhood, old age, unemployment, or in any other case in which he is deprived of the means of subsistence through no fault of his own.

Rights concerning moral and cultural values

Every human being has the right to respect for his person, to his good name, to seek after truth, to express his opinion and to publicize it, and to pursue the arts, within the limits laid down by the moral order and the common good. He has the right also to be informed objectively about public happenings.

His human nature gives man the right to participate in all the goods of his culture, and therefore the right to a fundamental education and technical and professional training that is adequate for the levels of development of his own political community. Every effort should be made to insure that those who deserve to go on to higher studies be able to do so, to occupy positions and take on responsibilities in human society in accordance with their natural gifts and the skills they have acquired.

The right to worship God according to the dictates of proper conscience

Every man has the right to honor God according to the dictates of an upright conscience, and thereby the right to worship God privately and publicly. For, as Lactantius so clearly taught: *We were created for the purpose of showing to God who bore us the submission we owe him, of recognizing him alone, and of serving him. We are obliged and bound by this duty to God; from this religion itself receives its name.* On this subject, Our Predecessor of immortal memory, Leo XIII, declared: *This genuine, this honorable freedom of the Sons of God, which most nobly protects the dignity of the human person, is greater than any violence or injustice; it has always been sought by the Church, always been most dear to her. This was the freedom which the Apostles claimed with intrepid constancy, which the Apologists defended with their writings, and which the Martyrs in such numbers consecrated with their blood.*

The right to choose freely one's state in life

Human beings have the right to choose freely the state of life which they prefer, and therefore the right to establish a family, with equal rights and duties for man and woman, and also the right to follow a vocation to the priesthood or the religious life.

The family, founded on marriage freely contracted, monogamous and indissoluble, should be regarded as the primary and natural nucleus of human society. To it should be given every consideration of an economic, social, cultural and moral nature which will strengthen its stability and facilitate the fulfillment of its specific mission.

Parents have prior rights in the support and education of their children.

Economic rights

Human beings have the right to private initiative in economic matters and the right to work.

Indissolubly linked with those rights is the right to working conditions in which physical health is not endangered, morals are safeguarded, and young people's normal development is not impaired. Women have the right to working conditions in accordance with their requirements and their duties as wives and mothers.

Personal dignity claims the right to carry on economic activities according to the degree of responsibility of which the individual is capable. Especially to be emphasized is the right to a proper wage, determined according to the standards of justice, and sufficient, therefore, in proportion to the available resources, to provide for the worker and his family a standard of living in keeping with the dignity of the human person. In this regard, Our Predecessor Pius XII said: *To the personal duty to work imposed by nature, there corresponds and follows the natural right of each individual to make of his work the means to provide for his own life and the lives of his children—so profoundly is the domain of nature ordained for the preservation of man.*

Man's nature gives rise to the right to own private property and the means of production. This right *constitutes the fitting means for the affirmation of the human person and for the exercise of responsibility in all areas. It strengthens the stability and tranquillity of family life, thus contributing to the peace and prosperity of society.*

It is opportune to remember, however, that there is a social duty essentially inherent in the right of private property.

The right of meeting and association

From the fact that human beings are by nature social, arises the right of assembly and association. They have the right also to give the societies of which they are members the form they consider most suitable for the aims they have in view, and to act within such societies on their own initiative and on their own responsibility in order to achieve their desired objectives.

In the Encyclical, *Mater et Magistra*, the point was made on this matter that a wide variety of societies or intermediate bodies be established to pursue objectives that individuals cannot effectively pursue except by joining together. These societies or intermediate bodies are necessary and indispensable elements in assuring the individual a sufficient sphere of freedom and responsibility.

The right to emigrate and immigrate

Every human being has the right to freedom of movement and residence within the political community of which he is a member, and the right to emigrate, when there are legitimate reasons for doing so, to other political communities and to take up residence there. The fact that an individual belongs to a particular state does not in any way lessen his membership in the human family as a whole, nor detract from his citizenship in the world community.

Political rights

Human dignity also claims the right to take an active part in public life and to make a personal contribution toward the common good. *Far from being the object, or passive element, in social life, man as such must be and must always remain its subject, its basis and its end.*

The individual has the basic right to legal protection of his freedom, protection that should be efficacious, impartial and objectively informed by the standards of justice. *That perpetual privilege proper to man, by which every individual has a claim to the protection of his rights, and by which there is assigned to each a definite and particular sphere of rights, immune from all arbitrary attacks, is the logical consequence of the order of justice willed by God.*

DUTIES

The inseparable relationship between rights and duties

The natural rights We have just discussed are inseparably connected in the very person who is their subject with as many related duties. Rights as well as duties have their source, their sustenance, and their strength in the natural law which confers and enjoins them.

The right, for instance, to existence is linked to the individual's duty to preserve it; the right to a dignified standard of living to living with dignity; and the freedom to seek the truth to the duty to do so, in order to know it ever more completely and profoundly.

Reciprocity of rights and duties between persons

In human society, every man's natural right corresponds to a duty in everyone else; that is, the duty to recognize and respect that right. Every basic personal right, in fact, draws its inviolable moral form from the natural law that confers it, and that enjoins a related duty on others. Those who claim their own rights, but fail to carry out their duties, are really building with one hand but destroying with the other.

Mutual collaboration

Since men are social by nature they are meant to live with others and to work for one another's welfare. A well-ordered society requires that men recognize and observe their mutual rights and duties. It also demands that each contribute generously to the establishment of a civic order in which rights and duties are more sincerely and effectively acknowledged and fulfilled.

It is not enough, for example, to recognize and respect every man's right to the means of subsistence. It is equally necessary to do whatever one can to make sure every human being has sufficient food.

Society must not only be well-ordered but also productive for the good of its members. This certainly requires that they observe and recognize their mutual rights and duties, and that they work together in the many enterprises modern civilization permits, encourages, demands.

Sense of responsibility

The personal dignity of every human being demands that he act knowingly and freely. In his social relations, therefore, a man must exercise his rights, carry out his duties, work together with others in the light of his own decisions; that is, he must do these things out of conviction, on his own initiative, with a sense of responsibility, and never by coercion or under pressure from outside sources.

A society founded on power relationships is not human. In such a society, it is inevitable that people are coerced or suppressed instead of being encouraged and stimulated to develop and fulfill themselves.

Living together in truth, justice, charity and freedom

Human society is ordered, productive and in accord with human dignity only if it is based on truth. As the Apostle Paul declared: *Wherefore, put away lying and speak truth each one with his neighbor, because we are members of one another.* This means the reciprocal rights and duties be recognized. Furthermore, the society realizes itself according to the standards of justice, or in real respect for freedom and for the fulfillment of its related duties, if it is motivated and united by charity, which makes the needs and demands of others seem our own, makes us want to share our goods with them, and deepens the communion of the world in spiritual values. This society will be free, in the sense that it will permit its members to develop their own potentiality and to assume responsibility for their lives.

Human society, Venerable Brothers and beloved children, ought to be regarded above all as a spiritual reality in which men communicate knowledge to each other in the light of truth; in which they can enjoy their rights and fulfill their duties, and are motivated to strive for moral good. Society should enable men to share in and enjoy every legitimate expression of beauty, and encourage them constantly to pass on to others all that is best in themselves, while they try to share in the spiritual achievements of others. These are the spiritual values which continually give life and direction to culture, economic and social institutions, political movements, governments, legal systems and all the other outward expressions of society in its continual development.

The moral order has its objective basis in God

The order which prevails in society is by nature moral. Based as it is on truth, it must function according to the norms of justice, it must be motivated and unified in love, it must be ordered on the premise of freedom, with always newer and more human equilibrium.

Now the moral order, which is universal, absolute and immutable in its principles, has its ultimate source in the one true God, who is transcendental and yet personal. God is the first truth and highest good, and He alone is that deepest source from which human society can draw its vitality, if that society is to be well-ordered, beneficial, and in keeping with human dignity. As St. Thomas so clearly says: *Human reason is the norm of the human will, according to which its goodness is measured, because reason derives from the eternal law which is the divine reason itself. It is evident then that the goodness of the human will depends much more on the eternal law than on human reason.*

Sign of the times

The modern age has three distinctive characteristics.

First of all, the rise of the working class on the economic and social scale. They began by claiming their rights in social and economic areas, and then they went on to claim their political rights, and finally the right to participate to an adequate extent in the cultural life of their countries. Today, therefore, workers all over the world refuse to be treated as objects without intelligence or freedom, to be used according to the will of others; they want to be regarded as men with a share in every area of society, in social and economic matters, as well as in public life and education. . . .

When the relations of human society are expressed in terms of rights and duties, men become aware of spiritual values and come to understand what truth, justice, love and freedom are; they feel a part of the world. What is more, they are moving closer to a knowledge of the true God, who is personal and transcendent. Their relationship to God becomes the solid foundation and the highest standard of their lives, both in their own souls and in their life with their fellow men.[1]

[1] Encyclical, *Pacem in Terris*, April 11, 1963.

Life

What is life? It is a time—brief or long, but always limited—to practice the virtues infused in us by Baptism, to acquire perfection, to spread the meaning of charity and of the apostolate to our fellows. It may not last many years, but it can also be very long-lasting. Whatever the case, it is always a journey which must be filled with good works and merit.

This journey does not come to an end, abruptly and forever. At the end of the voyage, when the Angel of the Lord—perhaps the same one who has been our guardian all along—announces that the trip is over, the gate of time closes, but at the same instant the gate of eternity swings open, and then begins the true life, without grief, or tears, or twilights, in the eternal light and joy of God.

Armed with this certainty, the Christian is not sad at the moment of death, but he greets it as the moment of union of his soul with those of the Elect.[1]

Our lives continue, and always, on January 1, each one of us feels the urge to renewal and to greater commitment to his duties. This is certainly a fine decision, but it is even of greater benefit for the soul to kneel before God, the creator of life, to examine our lives as we have led them, in the light of his law and his teachings, and to entrust ourselves to his grace. This is how we can participate in the youth that is the joy of God, who always sustains it, renews it, strengthens it and prepares it for eternal happiness.

Each of us is obliged to examine his past, to reflect on all its failings and to resolve to make up for them. Each one of us thinks of renewing his spiritual life, to pray better, and to perfect himself in the virtues he needs most, such as patience, generosity and willing self-sacrifice. Old and young alike are moved to try again, to be reborn in Christ and with Christ. Thus the wishes of the Father will be well received and will bring happy results. Among them, deep and real understanding, a true and lasting peace among men and nations.[2]

Life is governed by a law common to us all, established by Our Lord, the Son of God, the Divine Word, and—as a man—the son of Mary. He too lived it, and the meaning of his journey through life is found in the Cross. Our lives may be said to be a huge procession, all of us together under the Cross, the same one Christ bore up Calvary.

To bear the Cross is laborious and sacrificial, but still, if we want to move ahead, we must accept it.

The world loves to enjoy itself. No matter what their age, men are urged on by the desire for pleasure. But we must remember that there will be an end: eternity, lasting joy, earned for us by Christ through his Passion and Death.

The greatest event in history was this, the victory of the Savior, because he was crucified and humiliated, and died; he was buried but three days later, there was the glory of the Resurrection, Easter, the moment of a resounding Hallelujah!

Our life is made in the image of Christ's, and even if some pleasure is allowable, we must always remember the sign of the Cross. From their youth, all must learn moderation in eating, restraint, self-denial, which strengthens character and helps spread joy, peace, love.[3]

At times the difficulties and bitterness of life force tears to our eyes and constrict our hearts, but the thought of Christ, prayer and the Christian way of life will mitigate our troubles and enable us to see clearly our true and ultimate end. What greater joy can there be than contemplating Jesus who comes among us, returns to his Father and asks us to follow him and remain with him forever? This is the goal of every man's life. Life is a mere foreshadowing of the harmony of Paradise.

To be worthy of Paradise, we must prove ourselves in the days of trial, suffering and sacrifice; we must always keep the thought of heaven alive in us and remember that for the reward that awaits us, every meritorious act is recorded, not a single tear goes unnoticed, not one bit of suffering is overlooked.[4]

Life is not an adventure, a capricious pastime, the search for ephemeral success and easy profits, rather it is our daily commitment, service to our fellow men, the spirit of sacrifice, the labor of continuous struggle. This is the right way, not the way that would reduce the conscience and distort reality. We must teach that we can find serenity and joy only when we respond generously to our duties and fulfill the talents God has given each of us to the limit. We must all understand that only in a life understood as a consciously-lived vocation can there be great satisfaction, the secret of interior peace and the edification of our fellow man.[5]

[1] Speech, November 15, 1961.
[2] Speech, January 3, 1962.
[3] Speech, May 7, 1962.
[4] Speech, May 30, 1962.
[5] Speech, July 14, 1960.

On Longevity

"*Nos qui vivimus, benedicimus Domino*" (We the living bless God). It is secondary whether we live to 70, 90 or 100. The important thing is that these years be lived in the sight of God and bear his stamp, and be used to spread the splendor of Christian civilization everywhere.[1]

[1] Speech, June 11, 1961.

B. DOUBT AND DISBELIEF

Selfishness

In these days especially, when selfishness threatens to become the universal rule of life, we have the obligation to exercise the spirit of disinterested charity and to perform a Christian service among men. It is still possible today, despite the imposing measures taken by the government and all the public subsidies, for the individual to show that charity does exist, as a sign of his own personal responsibility. "You always have the poor with you" (John 12, 8). Numberless suffering, sick, lonely people require our help constantly, and they should not wait for it in vain. Never forget that it was Christ who said, "as you did it to one of these the least of my brethren, so you did it to me" (Matthew 25, 40).[1]

[1] Speech, August 26, 1962.

Self-indulgence

Unfortunately there prevails here and there the tendency these days to self-indulgence, which would reduce life to the seeking after pleasure and to the full satisfaction of all the passions, with serious damage consequently to the spirit and to the body as well.

On a natural plane, it is wise to exercise sobriety and temperance of the lower appetites; on the supernatural plane, the Gospel, the Church and her whole ascetic tradition demand a sense of mortification and penance, which assures the spirit's dominion over the flesh and offers an effective way to expiate our sins, from which no one is free except Jesus Christ and his Immaculate Mother.[1]

When we see the increase in self-indulgence here and there in the world, it is true we can feel sad and discouraged. But nonetheless, in contrast to these saddening impressions, We are pleased to point out a reassuring fact for those who share the responsibilities for the Church's educational mission with the Pope; that is, the faithful who stream to St. Peter's uninterruptedly are in large part young people, confirming that the general audiences are occasions, above all, for meeting the youth.

Great joy, therefore, because to youth is entrusted the future of the world.[2]

[1] Encyclical, *Mater et Magistra*, May 15, 1961.
[2] Speech, May 19, 1960.

Religious Indifference

There are a number of people who, although not having any grasp of the truth, appear to be very careless and indifferent about it, as if God had not given us reason with which to seek and arrive at it. This rather unworthy behavior leads, almost by a spontaneous process, to an absurdity; that is, that all religions are the same, without any difference between the true and the false. "This notion," to use the words of Pius XII, "leads necessarily to the ruin of all religions, especially the Catholic, which, being the only true one of them all, cannot be considered without dire offense on the same level as the rest."[1]

[1] Encyclical, *Ad Petri Cathedram*, June 29, 1959.

Worldliness

We must be on guard against that worldly spirit embodied in certain currents of thought and fashion in our time, which are trying by every means to lead society away from the influence of Christ's Gospel, from the Church's teaching, from the eternal values of divine truth, love, purity and apostolic mission from which stems Christian culture. These movements claim to be the defenders of an unspecified freedom, but they are ready to deny it to the Church when she seeks to defend revealed truth or the heritage of moral salvation bestowed on her. They proclaim the separation of church and state, but they are continually working to limit her sphere of action, and to cast suspicion and ill-will on her.

In the face of such attitudes, unity is more than ever necessary in order to defend, and help defend, truth, justice and honesty even before religion and the Gospel.[1]

There is a predominance of technical and scientific factors in the orientation of modern culture, as well as a capricious worldly spirit fostered by a press and entertainment industry that are vacuous and superficial when not openly destructive and corrupting. These influences dim the attraction of a greater ideal in many souls, an ideal to which we should give ourselves in our most promising years for a life of generosity and religious mission.[2]

[1] Speech, November 20, 1960.
[2] Speech, April 11, 1961.

Mistaken Ideologies

It has been claimed by some that in this era of scientific and technical triumphs, man can now build his civilization without God. But the truth of the matter is that these very triumphs create human problems on a world scale, which can only be resolved in the light of a sincere and active faith in God, the beginning and end of mankind and of the world. . . .

In our modern age, various ideologies have been born and become popular . . . several of them have already evaporated, like dew in the sun; others are undergoing or have undergone considerable changes, while some are losing their hold quite rapidly.

The reason is that these ideologies consider only part of man's nature, and frequently the least profound part. They do not take imperfections into account, such as sickness and suffering, imperfections which even the most advanced economic and social systems cannot eliminate. Then there is the deep and unextinguishable religious need which is felt everywhere at all times, even when it is opposed by violence or vigorously repressed.

In fact, the most radical error of our times is to consider the religious need of the human spirit as something sentimental or fantastical, or as the outcome of some historical contingency that must be eliminated because it is an anachronism or a hindrance to human progress. In truth, however, human beings reveal themselves for what they really are through their religious need; that is, beings created by God.

Thus, no matter what technical and economic progress is made there will not be peace or justice in the world until men return to the realization that God's creatures and children have dignity. The man separated from God becomes separated from himself and from his fellow men, because the ordered relationships within society presupposed the ordered relationship of the individual conscience with God, the fount of truth, justice and love.

In truth, the decades in which Our Brothers and Children have been persecuted in many countries, even those that have been Christian since the earliest times, have proved how great is the dignity of the persecuted and how habitual the cruelty of the persecutors. Although the persecution has not shown signs of abatement, there is increasing awareness of it.

But the peculiarly typical bent of the modern age is the absurd attempt to found a solid and productive temporal order without God, who is the only foundation on which such an order could be built, and to celebrate man's greatness by stopping the fount from which that greatness springs and from which it is fed; that is, by suppressing and, if possible, extinguishing his aspiration towards God.

Daily events continue to show, with their bitter disappointments and often their violent nature, how true the words of Holy Scripture are: "Unless God build the house, they labor in vain who build it. . . ."

Man is not merely a physical being, but also a spirit endowed with reason and freedom. He requires, therefore, an ethical and religious order which will have an effect greater than any materialist one on the direction and the solutions he must provide for his personal and social problems. . . .[1]

Unfortunately the mistaken ideologies that have exalted reckless freedom on the one hand and urged the suppression of the individual on the other have taken away the worker's importance and reduced him to a simple object of contention or abandoned him to his own devices. They have tried to cause strife and contention by setting one class against the other and they have even tried to turn labor against God, who alone is the defender and protector of the humble, and from whom we receive life, energy and existence. And they have made it appear as if the condition of being a laborer exempts one from the duty of recognizing God, and honoring and serving him.

We are saddened when We think how many of Our sons—upright and honest though they may be—have allowed themselves to be beguiled by such theories, forgetting that in the Gospel, as demonstrated in the social commentaries of the Popes, there exist the guidelines for resolving all of their problems and the will to reform, along with a respect for fundamental values. . . .

Work is a high calling; it represents for man an intelligent and effective way of collaborating with God the Creator, from whom he received the goods of the earth, so that he could cultivate them and prosper. The difficulty and the labor involved in that work form part of God's redemption plan, God who saved the world through the love and the pain of his only begotten Son and who regards human suffering as an instrument of sanctification when it is united with that of his Son.[2]

[1] Encyclical, *Mater et Magistra*, May 15, 1961.
[2] Radio broadcast, May 1, 1960.

Atheism . . . Materialism

In several parts of the world, the most sacred notions of Christian society are smothered or extinguished. Where the spiritual and divine order has been upset, and where men have succeeded in weakening the conception of supernatural life, the beginning of evils can be sadly seen, the evidence of which is by now common knowledge. Even if we want to be restrained in our judgment, in excusing and tolerating the gravity of the *atheistic* and *materialistic* condition to which several countries were or are subjected, and under the weight of which they now tremble, the slavery of individuals and of the masses, the lack of freedom to think and to do, cannot be denied. The Holy Bible recounts that a tower of Babel was built in ancient times on the plain of Senaar and that it ended in confusion. In several parts of the world, more of these towers are still being built today, and they will end surely just like the first one. But the illusion for many is great and ruin is threatening. Only unity and a concerted strengthening of the apostolate of the truth and of true human and Christian brotherhood can stop the grave, inherent dangers.[1]

Let us return to that remark about the great sadness in our heart, in the heart of the whole Catholic Church, that has been caused by what is troubling and threatening destruction to the souls, the communities, which were already on the road to the benefits of liberty and of peace, in the vast and distant but well-known regions of Europe and Asia. Not, thank God, in our beloved Italy so close to us, and in many other nations.

You realize our grief increased from the moment in which We were placed, despite Our unworthiness, in this high office. From here we have been enabled to see, even with some difficulty, a larger horizon that has been stained with blood because of the sacrifice of liberty imposed on so many, whether it be freedom of thought or of civic and social participation or—with greater ruthlessness—the freedom to profess one's own religious faith.

Out of great reserve and out of sincere and considered respect, and in the confident hope that the storm will slowly subside, We abstain from naming the ideologies, the places and the persons. But We are not indifferent to the timely reports that pass continually under Our eyes, revealing the fears, the violence, the annihilation of the human person.

We shall tell you in all confidence that the habitual look of spiritual serenity that appears on Our face, from which our children take pleasure, hides the inner torment and anxiety of Our heart. While it delights in them and comforts them as best it can, Our hearts turn to those others—and there are millions and millions of them—whose fates we do not know. We do not know whether they heard even the echoes of the words with which We greeted all the peoples of the world at the beginning of our pontificate, or the assurance that their tears were spilling into our heart.[2]

The most radical error of modern times is to hold that the religious need of the human spirit is just an expression of sentiment or imagination, or else a product of an historical contingency that is to be eliminated, an anachronism, or an obstacle to human progress. But in reality that human need reveals what men truly are: beings created by God for God, as St. Augustine says: *Thou hast made us for thee, Lord, and our hearts are restless until they rest in thee.*

Therefore, no matter how much technical and economic progress is made, there will not be peace or justice in the world until men return to the sense of dignity of God's creatures and children, the first and last reason for being of the whole reality he created. The man separated from God becomes inhuman to himself and to his fellows, because the ordered relation of living together presupposes the ordered relation of the individual conscience to God, the source of truth, justice and love.

But what is the most typical and sinister characteristic of the modern age is the absurd attempt to set up a firm and productive temporal order that is divorced from God, who is the only foundation upon which it can hold. And the attempt to celebrate man's greatness by closing off the source from which that greatness springs and from which it draws nourishment; that is, by repressing and—if it were possible—

destroying his aspiration toward God. The daily experience of our time continues to bear witness, among the bitterest disillusionments and frequently in terms of blood, to what the Bible says: *Unless the Lord build the house, they labor in vain who build it.*[3]

[1] Radio message, December 23, 1958.
[2] Sermon, January 25, 1959.
[3] Encyclical, *Mater et Magistra*, May 15, 1961.

Religious Persecution

We are struck with sadness when We think that in many countries Our children are being made to suffer for their loyalty to the Savior. We want them to know that We feel their suffering as if it were our own and that We pray for them every day. But We want to point out especially what is happening in China. For some time now, the Catholics in China have had to bear painful and difficult conditions. Even the missionaries have been insulted, imprisoned and expelled, they who were the peaceful heralds of the Gospel; among them were many archbishops and bishops. Eager and courageous Chinese bishops have been thrown in prison, and a number of ordinaries have been confined or otherwise hindered from freely practicing their pastoral office; those who were appointed to substitute for them or replace them have met similar fates. No wonder, then, that if the shepherds have been punished, their flocks should be subjected to enticements, threats, and moral and physical tortures to force them to renounce their faith, to reject their Catholic calling, and to break the bond of love and obedience which unites them to the Chair of Peter?

Unfortunately, We must note with anguish that there have been a number who were more fearful of men's reprisals than of God's judgment, and who have acceded to the demands of their persecutors to the point of accepting sacrilegious episcopal consecration. . . . In the meanwhile, a dark silence has enveloped those dioceses . . . a bitter and saddening occurrence. On the one hand, the violence of the persecutors . . . on the other, the suffering and the torment of the confessors of the faith. . . . If only good people could hear the voices that appeal to Us! The voices of those who are oppressed but not beaten by the extended tortures; they will find the strength to show their love and their loyalty to the Pope. They do not want our prayers for their personal safety, but for their souls. They cry out that whatever happens they shall remain faithful to the Vicar of Christ to their very death.[1]

The things that have been happening for years in the immense lands beyond the Iron Curtain are too well known to comment on.[2]

We want to mention another grievous situation that afflicts Us deeply. In Hungary, the bishops are compelled to carry out their responsibilities under increasingly difficult and cruel conditions, because of the interference, the impositions and the prohibitions which hinder them. Eminent members of the episcopate, including a member of the Sacred College, are kept from their folds; others find it impossible to provide adequately for the needs of the faithful, prevented as they are from utilizing the services of their clergy; many difficulties have been put in the way of training candidates to the priesthood. From these abnormal conditions, it is to be feared that the civil authorities will find still other excuses to interfere in the life of the Church by demanding that pastors comply with acts their consciences could never accept. They would even set over Our Lord's congregation ecclesiastics who are not chosen by this Holy See.[3]

We would not wish to offend anyone; indeed, We would rather grant everyone Our forgiveness by imploring God's. But We are impelled by Our sacred duty to insist that their rightful liberty be granted to Our Brothers and Our Children and to the Church of God. Those who really observe the principles of truth and justice, and are genuinely concerned about men's welfare, the individual's and the nation's, do not deny liberty to them. They have no need to use such means. The truth is that it will never be possible to attain the rightful well-being of the people by violence and oppression.

And it is equally certain that when the sacrosanct rights of God and religion are violated or ignored, sooner or later the very foundations of society will crumble. Our Predecessor of happy memory, Leo XIII, pointed this out: "As a consequence . . . the force of law is weakened and authority lessens whenever the eternal and sovereign reason which is God's authority is repudiated, God who summons the good and forbids evil." Cicero said much the same thing: "You, O pontiffs . . . defend the city more effectively with religion than do the walls."

These considerations take Us back with great sadness to the plight of those who are not allowed to worship, and who must "suffer even persecution for justice's sake" and for the Kingdom of God. We share their grief, their anguish, and their affliction; We pray God that mankind shall see the dawn of better times. May all Our Brothers and Children join Us in prayer, and may a single chorus of pleas rise to heaven, that grace might descend on the suffering faithful of the Mystical Body of Christ.[4]

Prayer for the Church of silence (Three years' indulgence)
O Jesus, the Son of God, who loved your Church and gave

yourself for her to sanctify her and to make her appear before you glorious and spotless (cf. Ephesians 5, 23–27), look mercifully upon the terrible conditions under which your Mystical Spouse must survive in several parts of the Catholic world, but now especially in the great nation of China. You see, O Lord, the dangers that threaten the souls of your faithful, and you know the scandalous insinuations that are made against your pastors, your ministers, and your loyal followers, who desire to spread the truth of the Gospel and your kingdom, which is not of this world. How pernicious and insistent are the attempts to tear the seamless robe of your Bride the Church, one, holy, catholic, apostolic and Roman, by separating the bishops and local communities from the only center of truth, authority and salvation, the See of Peter.

Before the sight of so many evils, we ask you above all to forgive the offenses borne against you. The words you spoke to Saul of Tarsus on the road to Damascus can be so easily repeated today, as they could have been in recent and past history: "Saul, Saul, why do you persecute me?" (Acts 9, 4).

We trust always in the power of the words you spoke to the Father as you hung from the Cross: "Father, forgive them, for they know not what they do" (Luke 23, 34). Just as your sacrifice was the fount of universal salvation, so too through your grace may the martyrdom the Church is suffering in some countries be salutary to all men.

O Prince of Peace, let the bishops and the priests, the religious and the laity, be "eager to maintain the unity of the Spirit in the bond of peace" (Ephesians 4, 3). May your omnipotent virtue win out over every human calculation, so that the shepherds and their flocks will remain obedient to the voice of the only universal Shepherd, who feels the ultimate responsibility of love in his heart: "Holy Father, keep them in thy name, which thou hast given me, that they may be one, even as we are one" (John 17, 11).

Hearken, Our Savior, to the prayers of your Mother and ours, the Queen of Missions and of the universal Church, to the labors, the sacrifices and the blood of so many heralds of the faith who have given you, and give you yet, such heroic witness everywhere. Mindful of your Precious Blood which you shed for the remission of our sins, give to China and to the whole world your peace, because we cannot expect hope, victory and peace except from you, our Lord and immortal King."

[1] Allocution to the Sacred College, December 15, 1958.
[2] Radio broadcast, December 23, 1958.
[3] Lenten allocution, May 17, 1959.
[4] Encyclical, *Ad Petri Cathedram*, June 29, 1959.

The Forces of Evil

At times, it is necessary to mention the devil; in the Gospel the Lord too mentions him and calls him the prince of this world. He called him this again just before his Passion, warning the Apostles that the devil is present and listening.

The prince of this world has not stopped tempting and misleading us, even if we are afraid to say so. We read about and know about these hidden forces of evil, which often hurl themselves against the world and create disasters.

We are, it is true, pursued by these evil forces, by that prince of the world who is the son of prevarication and who was condemned for his pride to fight against God and against the Redemption enabled by God's Son, Jesus Christ. We must be careful, for few of us, unfortunately, take this evil of humanity into account, because they prefer to think only about the facts. Against the wickedness of the evil spirit and temptation, the Christian has an indestructible defense, a sure protection, in grace, in the sacraments, in the Mother of God, in Jesus who redeemed us and ransomed us from sin.

But temptation is always present in the world, and so we must defend ourselves against it with good will and prayer. We must continually invoke our Guardian Angel to be near us in the various vicissitudes of life, and pray to him before we sleep. It is necessary that we guard ourselves against God's enemy, who is also the enemy of our souls.[1]

[1] Conversation, September 24, 1960.

C. URGENT PROBLEMS

The Less Fortunate

Those who are among the less fortunate and decry the poor conditions in which they live should know first of all that We suffer keenly for them in their lot. Not only because We desire with fatherly concern that justice, which is a Christian virtue, govern, direct and qualify relations among the various social groups, but also because it grieves Us that the enemies of the Church exploit the unjust condition of the poor in order to lure them over to their side with deceptive promises and false assertions.

These Our dear children should bear in mind that the Church—far from ignoring their rights—is the loving mother who protects them. She proclaims and instills teachings and social standards which, if they were implemented completely, would eliminate any injustice so that there would be a more equal distribution of wealth. At the same time friendly cooperation among the different social groups would quicken, and every person could consider himself a full citizen of a single community and a brother in the same family.

Besides, if those who live by their daily labor would consider fairly the improvement they have gained in the last few years, they would recognize that these improvements have been brought about by the effective action Christians have been able to exert in the social field by following the wise teachings of Our Predecessors and listening to their continual pleas. And consequently, the men who assume the task of defending the rights of the poor already have, in the teachings of the Church, well defined and positive standards which offer the means for arriving at a just solution of all problems, if they are properly and legitimately put into practice. And for this reason they should never turn to the supporters of teachings the Church condemns. It is very true that these people attract them with false promises. But in reality wherever they wield power they attempt by any means to destroy in the minds of men the supreme good of the conscience—faith and Christian hope and the teachings of the Gospel—and what is more they try to weaken and even destroy what modern men celebrate as a great victory, that is, their rightful liberty and the real dignity of the human person. Thus they undermine the foundations and bases of Christian civilization. And so those who intend remaining faithful to Christ are obliged by conscience to keep away completely from these errors that have already been condemned by Our Predecessors, particularly by Pius XI and Pius XII of blessed memory, and that We equally condemn.

Not a few of Our children who find themselves in more or less serious financial straits frequently complain that the principles of Christian social teaching have not been put into practice yet. And so let every effort be made, not only on the part of private citizens but especially by members of the government, to implement as soon as possible Christian social doctrine which has been repeatedly, clearly and amply re-stated by those same Pontiffs, and which We confirm as well. And even if these social principles are put into practice gradually, it ought to be carried out nonetheless in a real and complete sense.[1]

[1] Encyclical, *Ad Petri Cathedram*, June 29, 1959.

Political Refugees

The feelings of universal fatherhood which the Lord has placed in Our heart is saddened by the sight of so many political refugees. The incidence of such refugees has achieved notable proportions, and always hides numberless and very acute sufferings.

They are evidence of the fact that there are regimes which do not provide sufficient liberty to individuals so that they can live as human beings. In fact, those regimes question or even deny the legitimacy of such freedom, thereby radically inverting the social order, since the reason for the existence of governments is to realize the common good. And a fundamental element of common good is the recognition of freedom and its preservation.

It is not beside the point to recall that political refugees are persons, and that they should have the rights inherent to the person. These rights are not lost when the refugees are deprived of citizenship in the political communities of which they were once members.

Among inalienable human rights is that of joining the political community in which one believes he can best create a future for himself and for his family. Consequently, that political community has the duty of permitting the refugee to join it, as well as helping the new members become part of its life.[1]

[1] Encyclical, *Pacem in Terris*, April 11, 1963.

Hunger

Millions of human beings suffer from hunger in this world. Others—while they cannot be said to be starving—do not have sufficient quantities of food for their needs. These are the facts. They must be made known; they must be shouted from the rooftops, as the Gospel says: ". . . proclaim upon the housetops" (Matthew 10, 27). The conscience of men must be awakened to their responsibility, which weighs upon each and every one, especially on the fortunate. No one can excuse himself by claiming not to know about the needs of his brothers in distant places, or not to be involved in the distribution of aid, when distances no longer count in our modern age. We are all solidly responsible for the underfed peoples of the world. Your organizations are trying to persuade public opinion of this responsibility so that it will demand action and support appropriate measures.

The second aim of the Campaign against Hunger is to put into effect the measures themselves, that is, direct action in raising the levels of production and consumption in underfed areas. At present the world does not produce enough food to meet men's needs, given especially the predictable increase in population in the coming years. Therefore available foodstuffs are not distributed equally. New lands must be tilled and higher yields made possible on lands already under cultivation.[1]

[1] Speech, May 30, 1960.

The Food and Agricultural Organization

The Church takes great interest in the work of the Food and Agricultural Organization (FAO). She is moved by the great and beautiful spectacle of your technicians at work throughout the world, fighting the "battle against hunger" by improving the soil, farming, animal husbandry, fishing techniques, dairying and forestry . . . and all this to help our less fortunate brothers, the uprooted, the hungry, the suffering. . . . Truly a great spectacle that inspires admiration and confidence in the future.

You know that We exhort the pilgrims who come to see Us to work—in the material domain as well as in the spiritual one —for those things dictated by the love for God and for one's fellow man, which religious tradition calls "works of mercy." What is all of FAO's activity if not an immense work of mercy on a world scale! We hardly have to urge you, whose lesson to the world is so eloquent. We should rather like to rejoice with you, congratulate you wholeheartedly, and reassure you that We bless your labors.

We rejoice, first of all, and We thank God, that an undertaking like FAO could come into being and develop so soon after the horrible war which drenched the earth in blood. It is undoubtedly one of the most remarkable and happy developments of the post-war years that the responsible authorities should have been so aware of the great differences among the living standards throughout the world, of the economic deprivation of the less fortunate—or "underdeveloped" as they are called—nations, in comparison to those countries with the principal sources of wealth.

FAO does not fear difficulties, it faces them. It is not discouraged by the number and size of the obstacles which stand in its way: the ruin and destruction left by the war, the extensive misery of certain areas, the epidemics aggravated by malnutrition, without mentioning the problems posed by the constant increase in the world population. FAO has studied the best ways of growing and distributing food and improving crops, and it has placed this knowledge at the disposal of the governments who ask for it. The Church appreciates this positive spirit of accomplishment and this confidence in man's ability to resolve his problems. The Church is equally optimistic.

One of the valuable results of your work—and it is also, We know, one of your organization's aims—is the raising of living standards of rural inhabitants. We Ourself come from a country home and saw with Our own eyes, during Our childhood, and We shall never forget it, the labors and the troubles of those who work the land. To contribute to lightening their burden, to allow those who provide bread to the rest of mankind a greater share of well-being, is a marvelous work of mercy and so worthy of encouragement and praise!

In a world still shaken by the war and its aftermath, mankind anxiously wants to know how to achieve a lasting peace and who will be its architects. The light flickering from the political side is still so unreliable, still so apt to go out after raising such hopes! On the other hand, are not those who promote mutual aid among nations and joint economic planning in the spirit of disinterest and friendly concern, also the people who are showing us the best way toward unity and peace among men?[1]

[1] Audience, November 10, 1959.

The Family

The family is a very precious gift, founded by divine disposition on the different yet complementary aptitudes of husband and wife. In woman the family finds its vigilant custodian. We urge women to love their families, which provide a natural environment for the development of the human personality, and are a refuge against life's storms, a bulwark against uncontrolled indulgence and evil influences. This haven, We must say unhappily, is threatened from so many sides. A campaign, at times unchecked, is carried on through the far-reaching media of the press, the movies and other entertainments, spreading the germs of immorality among our youth in particular. The family must defend itself, women must take courage and assume their rightful place in the work of correcting, watching over, teaching their children to distinguish between good and evil. Whenever necessary, they must seek the protection of civil law.[1]

The family implies a vocation that comes from on high, and it cannot be improvised; it is the only right kind of education. The family is almost everything for man. For the baby, in his awakening to his first unerasable experiences; for the young, who find in the family an example to follow and a defense against evil; for the married couple themselves who together can face the crises and confusion they at times will run into; and for the old, who enjoy in their families the reward for their fidelity and constancy.

Woman fills an irreplaceable role in family life. She will always be listened to, if she has made herself respected. As the dying Moses said to his sons, "I call heaven and earth to witness against you this day, that I have set before you life and death . . . therefore choose life that you and your descendants may live, loving the Lord your God, obeying his voice and cleaving to him" (Deuteronomy 36, 19–20).

When a mother's voice encourages, asks, urges, it is impressed on the hearts of her family and is never forgotten. Only God knows what good she accomplishes and the values of her role to the Church and human society.[2]

Whenever a mother has faith, and prays and educates her children in a Christian manner, there will not be lacking heavenly grace, which comes as a reward after hardship and trials. Society will be more stable and have an indisputable means of defense if families will preserve their responsible and felt faith and through it achieve the secret of serenity that knows no end.[3]

All Christian families are blessed by God, but those in which there are numerous children are especially pleasing to God and are the source of greater understanding and brotherhood.[4]

We ask all families to seek and maintain harmony. If peace, unity and concord do not exist in the family, how can they exist in society? This orderly and harmonious unity must reign in the home; it stems from the indissoluble bond and sanctity of the Christian marriage and it contributes toward the order, progress and well-being of all of society.[5]

[1] Speech, March 1, 1959. [2] Speech, December 7, 1960.
[3] Speech, March 1, 1959. [4] Speech, May 11, 1961.
[5] Encyclical, *Ad Petri Cathedram*, June 29, 1959.

Dangers to the Family

We know of the difficulties and the dangers the Christian family must face. *Of a spiritual nature*, above all, because of the self-denial and renunciation fathers and mothers must be prepared for in educating their children to a Christian life, in being faithful to the immutable law of God, in the midst of the temptations of the worldly mentality which seeks only pleasure, and in shoring up with a solid conscience the weaknesses that appear here and there. We are very aware, furthermore, of the anxiety *of a material nature* that many families feel as a result of economic problems, especially among big families, the unemployed, the underemployed, and the poor.

We have never let an opportunity go by to encourage the responsible authorities to do something to meet these multiple spiritual and temporal needs. We continue to exhort everyone, especially the well-off, to outdo themselves in generosity, to bring to all families the lasting help that is proportionate to their needs.[1]

[1] Speech, January 8, 1961.

Women in Everyday Life

The dynamics of the social and technological evolution of the last fifty years have had the effect, among others, of releasing women from their purely domestic tasks and of placing them in direct contact with public life. We see them at work in factories, in offices and businesses, and in almost all the professions which were at one time fields limited just to men.

We do not mean to consider at this point whether this state of things is ideal for women, much less allow Ourselves any complaints or recriminations. It is the duty of Catholics, rather, to examine this phenomenon, and in the light of Christian teachings to find whatever factors might mitigate the difficulties of woman's position today, and avoid the dangers such a position indubitably entails.

Without going into the details of this large and complex problem, We shall limit Ourself to some points of fundamental importance.

In the first place, a woman's activity cannot depart from the irrefutable characteristics with which the Creator endowed her. It is true that the conditions of life tend to introduce almost absolute equality between men and women. In any case the justly heralded equality of rights—to be recognized in everything that is proper to the person and his personal dignity—in no way implies a parity of functions. The Creator gave woman the inclinations, gifts, natural disposition which are proper to her, or different in degree from man. That is to say she was also assigned different tasks. Not to distinguish clearly this diversity in the respective functions of man and women, indeed their necessary complementary relation, would be to oppose nature, and we would end by reducing woman and taking from her the real basis of her dignity.

We take pleasure in recalling again that the end to which the Creator ordered all of woman's being is maternity. Her motherly vocation is so appropriate and connatural to her that it is active even when she is not reproducing the species. If we ought to provide suitable advice to women in the choice of work, and in the training and perfecting of individual aptitudes, we would say that she must find in the exercise of her profession a means to develop her maternal spirit.

What a great contribution she could make to society, if

she will employ these natural energies, especially in the fields of education, social assistance and religious work, and transform her profession into many forms of spiritual motherhood. Today also, the world has need of maternal sensibility to prevent the violence and grossness into which men sometimes lapse.

And we must always bear in mind the particular needs of the family, which is the center of woman's activities, and in which her presence is indispensable. Unfortunately financial necessities often compel women to work outside the home. There is no one who does not see how this spreading of energies, her prolonged absence from the home, make it impossible for the working woman to perform her duties as mother and wife. Family ties are loosened and the house ceases to be the warm, welcoming place where family members can renew themselves. And to the end of enabling the wife and mother to return to her rightful place in the home, We too have urged that salaries be sufficient for the worker and his family.

Beloved sons and daughters, the structure of modern society is still a long way from allowing women to realize, in their professions and jobs, the fullness of their personalities, and to make the contributions society and the Church expect of them. And it is from this point that we must seek new solutions for reaching an order and an equilibrium that are more consonant with the human and Christian dignity of woman. And from this point comes the necessity of greater participation for Catholic women's groups. Their duties are no longer limited strictly to family matters. The steady rise of women in all phases of public life demands that they participate responsibly in social and political questions. Women no less than men are necessary for social progress, especially in those areas which demand tact, delicacy and maternal intuition.[1]

[1] Speech, September 6, 1961.

The Working Woman

The subject of working women confronts us with new realities, a widening of tasks and therefore of responsibilities which take on different and unexpected aspects.

The problem affects everyone somewhat, but parents especially as they consider their children's future, and the professions and the jobs for which they must be educated.

This or that aspect of the placement opportunities offered to women have been under discussion. But we must look at the reality of the situation, at how many women do work, and how their aspiration to pursue the possibilities for being economically independent and free of need has grown.

But even if the economic independence of women has advantages, there are a number of problems it creates with respect to their fundamental mission, to be the mothers of children. These are the new situations which have become so urgent and which demand forethought, adaptability and the willingness to make certain renunciations. The problems arise in family life, in the care and training of the young; the home is deprived of a very necessary presence, and rest becomes impossible in the face of mounting tasks. Holy days are slighted, along with religious duties, the fulfillment of which is so important to the mother's role as teacher.

Work tires, as is natural, and may also dull the personality, at times even humiliate and mortify one. Coming home after many hours at work, sometimes quite exhausted, will a man find a haven, a place to regain his energies, a distraction from the arid and mechanical things with which he is surrounded?

Here woman's task is a large one. She must not let her rich inner resources, her sensibility, her delicate and candid spirit become hardened by contact with the heavy realities of the working day. She must not forget the values of the spirit which are the only defense of her nobility, or her participation in the sacraments, which enables her to keep pace with her vital mission.

She is called upon to make an effort that is perhaps greater than a man's, when we think of several aspects of her natural frailty and of the variety of things she must do. She alone must be able to face, at any time and under any circumstance, her duties as mother and wife with serene assurance. She must make her house a pleasant and tranquil place after the tiring claims of the working day. She must never shirk her responsibilities for bringing up her children.[1]

[1] Speech, December 7, 1960.

On Birth Control

The imbalance between population and the means of subsistence

In these times there arises frequently the problem of the relationship among demographic increases, economic development and the availability of the means of subsistence, both on a world-wide scale and in the political communities in the process of economic development.

On a world scale many observe that according to reliable statistics the human family will become very numerous in a few decades, while economic growth will continue at a slower rate. They conclude that unless something is done to limit demographic increase, the imbalance between population and subsistence will be felt acutely within the not distant future.

As far as the developing nations are concerned, the same

statistics are quoted to show that the rapid spread of hygiene and sanitary methods has greatly reduced the mortality-rate, especially among infants, while the birth-rate, which is usually high in those countries, continues to remain constant or nearly so for a considerable period of time. Births thus increasingly exceed deaths, while the productive capacity of the economic systems does not increase proportionately. And so developing nations cannot possibly improve their standards of living, and actually these get worse. To avoid deeply critical situations, therefore, some are of the opinion that conception and birth be limited by drastic measures.

The terms of the problem

To tell the truth, when considered on a world scale, the relationship between population increase on the one side, and economic development and availability of the means of subsistence on the other, does not seem at least for now or in the near future to create serious difficulties. In any case the elements upon which to base sound conclusions are too uncertain and varying.

God, furthermore, in his goodness and wisdom, has endowed nature with inexhaustible resources and men with intelligence and ingenuity that are capable of extracting those resources and of using them to satisfy life's needs. And so the basic solution to the problem should not be sought in expedients that offend the moral order established by God, and that undermine the very sources of human life, but rather in renewed efforts, scientific and technological, to extend man's dominion over nature. The progress already made by the sciences and technology open limitless horizons to us.

We know, however, that in certain areas and within countries in the process of development really serious problems of this nature can present themselves and do, which result from an inadequate economic and social structure. Inadequacies cannot keep pace with population increases.

What is more, the problem is partly due to the lack of active solidarity among the people.

But even in this case, We must insist at once that those problems cannot be confronted and those difficulties overcome by recourse to methods that are unworthy of man, methods explicable only in terms of a materialist conception of man and his nature.

The real solution can only be found in economic development and social progress which respect and promote true human values, development, that is, which takes place in a moral atmosphere, in conformity with man's dignity and with the immense value of human life. We need, moreover, world-wide cooperation that will allow and encourage an orderly and fruitful exchange of knowledge, capital and men.

Respect for the laws of life

We must proclaim that human life must be transmitted through the family, which is founded on marriage, one and indissoluble, elevated by Christians to the dignity of a sacrament. The procreation of human life depends on a personal and conscientious act, and as such is subject to God's wise laws. These laws must be recognized and obeyed. And so we cannot employ the means that may be permissible in transmitting the life of plants and animals.

Human life is sacred; right from its beginning, it involves directly the creative action of God. By violating his laws, we offend his Divine Majesty, degrade ourselves and humanity and enfeeble as well the very community of which we are members.[1]

[1] Encyclical, *Mater et Magistra*, May 15, 1961.

Today's Economic Problems

The Church has spoken out, and will always speak out, as her Divine Founder bade her. She will speak frankly, clearly.

We shall say even more, for the Pope wants to allay anyone's fear that the Church will advertise or accentuate the economic problems that need resolving. The suspicion would indeed be shabby. The Church, after all, has no need to apologize for an issue that lies in the historical dominion. As We recently said, "there are important pontifical documents to bear witness to the Church's maternal concern in the area of labor." Her preoccupation is not just recent, nor does it replace her greater concern for the spiritual salvation of all men.

The Church stands by her children during the course of their lifetime with the same solicitude that Christ had for the crowds in Palestine, when he multiplied the loaves and cured the sick. But just as Christ attended to their bodies in order to save their souls and to persuade them of an immortal life, so too the Church does not stand by her children just for their material needs and their present life, which is merely a journey to their eternal one, nor does she seek to delude or deceive them with utopian visions and fantastic promises, as fashionable teachers have always done.

She wants to lead men wisely through ever-present difficulties to the attainment of eternal life.

While national economies are rapidly evolving, in fact more intensely in this later post-war period, We find it an opportune moment to recall the world's attention to a fundamental principle. That is, economic development should be matched by social progress so that all citizens can participate in the growth of production. Every care must be taken, and provision made, that economic and social imbalances do not increase but rather decrease as much as possible.

"The national economy," observed rightfully Our Predecessor Pius XII, "itself the product of men working together in the state community, must aim solely at insuring without interruption the material conditions in which the lives of its citizens may develop fully. Where these conditions are achieved lastingly, the people can truly be said to be economically rich, because the general welfare, and consequently everyone's personal right to material possessions, is realized according to the purposes of the Creator." From this statement it is clear that the economic wealth of a people is not measured solely by the total of its possessions, but more importantly by the distribution of that wealth according to just standards, guaranteeing the personal development of the members of that society, which is the real purpose of a national economy.

We cannot avoid mentioning here that in many economies many middle-sized and large industries achieve—not seldom by any means—rapid and extensive growth through self-financing. We think it proper that in such cases workers be given some credit by their firms, especially when their compensation is not greater than the minimum.

In this regard, it would be well to cite the principle laid down by Our Predecessor Pius XI in the encyclical, *Quadragesimo Anno*: ". . . it is completely false to claim for either capital or labor the achievement brought about by their united efforts; and in fact, it is not just that either side make such claims, denying the part played by the other."

The needs of justice spoken of here can be satisfied in several ways as experience suggests. One of the ways, and among the most desirable, is to allow workers to participate, in the most convenient form and degree, in the property of the enterprises they work for, since today, more than in the day of Our Predecessor, "it is necessary with all our energies to make sure in the future that profits do not accumulate unjustly in the hands of the rich, and that they are distributed broadly among the workers."

But we must bear in mind that in equalizing the compensation for services rendered and net income, the needs of the common good, both within the political community proper and within the whole human race, must be respected.

The requirements of the national common good must be considered: to keep up a high employment level; to avoid the formation of any privileged group, even among workers; to maintain a balance between wages and prices, and to insure that goods and services are within reach of the majority; to eliminate or control the imbalances among the various economic sectors (agriculture, industry and services); to keep the growth of essential public services in step with economic expansion; to modernize production methods in line with technical and scientific advances; to plan improvements in the living standards of the present generation with the objective of preparing a better future for the coming generations.

There are, besides, the requirements of the common good on a world scale: to avoid unfair competition between nations; to encourage economic collaboration among nations by productive treaties; to contribute to the growth of economically underdeveloped countries.[1]

On a world level, it does not appear that the rural agricultural population has decreased in absolute terms. But there has been unquestionably a migration of rural inhabitants toward urban centers, a migration that has taken place in almost every country, and at times in massive numbers, thereby creating complex human problems that are difficult to resolve.

The economic development of political communities

should take place gradually, with proportionate growth among all the productive sectors. That is, new production techniques, new farming methods and organizational improvements should be applied in the agricultural sector, which the economy considered as a whole can allow or demands, and that these advances be proportioned to the requirements of the industrial and service sections.

In order to attain a balanced economy, an economic policy in the area of agriculture is necessary, a policy that covers taxation, credit, insurance plans, price control, promotion of complementary industries, and the efficiency of farming organizations.

The fundamental principle of a tax system is that the rates be adjusted according to the ability to pay.

It is not rare that there exist social and economic inequalities among citizens of the same political community. . . . In such situations, justice and equity demand that the public authorities act to eliminate or reduce them.

Perhaps the greatest problem of the modern age concerns the relations between economically developed nations and the nations still in the process of development. The former enjoy high standards of living, while the latter are faced with difficult if not very bad conditions.

The solidarity that binds all human beings together and makes of them a single family compels the prosperous nations not to be indifferent to the plight of nations whose citizens are faced with difficulties, poverty, misery and hunger, and do not enjoy basic human rights.[2]

[1] Speech, April 23, 1961.

[2] Encyclical, *Mater et Magistra*, May 15, 1961.

Money

Money, as everyone knows, is sometimes dangerous, and in a fearful way. It can be a temptation if it is put unthinkingly at the service of fancy and whim. It is not necessary certainly to dramatize how far one can fall, or to what depths and bitterness one can be reduced, if money is not used wisely and charitably. Money should be used, true, for an orderly and secure life, but should be considered a means for attaining the good, following the example of God himself, the author of all prosperity, the inexhaustible giver of every one of nature's and men's gifts. God therefore expects from man a similar generosity.

The lesson is clear to everyone: live not pursuing fancy, desire and temptation, but rather reflecting and acting on the real welfare of the individual and of the community to which he belongs.[1]

[1] Exhortation, June 18, 1961.

Childhood

How exciting is the mystery of the soul that is becoming conscious of itself and of its own future, that looks confidently to tomorrow, full of hope and promise! What concern we feel for a young life about to begin its journey into the unknown, led, however, by the gentle hand of the Heavenly Father. What anxiety we feel at the thought that the road the child takes will determine the earthly success and happiness of a human being, and often even his eternal happiness!

As Our Predecessor of venerated memory so rightly observed, "the child is the future, a threatening or promising future. As he goes on his way without cares, bearing within him the seeds of all his virtues and vices, many passers-by will ask: What then will this child be? (Luke 1, 66). And you too have asked the same question: What will his future be like, for himself, for society, for the Church?"

And so it is necessary that the problem of the child's calling, that is, his personal fulfillment of his role in God's design so that he can contribute as much as possible to the life of the Church and of society, be kept always in mind in deciding his education, beginning right in the home. And we trust that the schools will increase their effectiveness in guiding boys and girls to a choice of career. Teachers at every educational level can study and assess the qualities of each of their students by virtue of their experience. Much has been done and is being done in this area, and We are grateful for the valuable cooperation that many educators give to the family and the Church.[1]

[1] Speech, July 14, 1961.

Sunday, Day of Rest

To safeguard the dignity of man, who is endowed with a soul in the image and likeness of God, the Church has always insisted on the strict observance of the Third Commandment, "Remember the sabbath day, to keep it holy." It is God's right to demand of men that they dedicate one day a week to worship, a day on which their spirits can be free from material concerns to think about greater things, examining in the depth of their consciences the obligations and relationship they have toward their Creator.

But it is also a right of man's, in fact, a need, to take a rest from his daily labors, to restore his body, to enjoy some honest relaxation, to consolidate family unity that requires being together often.

Religion, morality and health all demand this day of rest, which the Church sanctifies on Sunday in the Holy Sacrifice of the Mass, as a memorial and an implementation of Christ's redemptive act.

In the name of God, and for the material and spiritual sake of men, We call upon everyone—the government, workers and employers—to observe God's commandment and to remember his deep responsibility before God and society.[1]

Since the Pope must think about all Catholics scattered throughout the world, it is only natural that he make a special appeal to those who, especially in cities, observe the commandment cursorily by attending Mass in a merely formal and distracted way.

As they watch the Holy Sacrifice from some remote corner of the church, understanding little or nothing about the beauties of the liturgy, they derive very little from their mere presence. His Holiness has already pointed out this insufficiency before, but it is worth repeating because something can be done about it. True, some people have said that by the simple act of entering the church and listening to the Mass, some Christians appear to be participating in what the priest is saying and reading at the altar, with what the priest does in the act of raising his soul to God. But certainly no one could be satisfied with such superficial participation.

We hope, rather, that thanks to the more active faithful—the members of Catholic Action, for instance—prayers can be better articulated and understood, hymns can be sung well, behavior can be in keeping with the nature of the holy place, and the participation in the events taking place at the altar can be profound. Only in this way can there be a felt relationship, a perfect harmony with the priest.[2]

[1] Encyclical, *Mater et Magistra*, May 15, 1961.
[2] Conversation, August 9, 1959.

Freedom of Education

One of the most burning questions in every country is that of education, the freedom of education and possibility to communicate to others the values we prize in our hearts.

Parents and educators in every country must consider the interests of children. They all understand that the Vicar of Our Lord Jesus Christ does not concern himself with questions of a temporal nature, the technical and immediate concerns of the world. But when the matter concerns the school, the Church is always there, because the Lord stands before us: "I am your Teacher."

Christian society is based on the practice of truth that penetrates the hearts and minds of each of us and brings with it grace. And thus the Pope wants to bless all those who are charged with the proper education of the young. The fathers of families in whatever country must insist that their children be educated according to the solid ancient tradition. Everyone must cooperate with them to insure the freedom of education and the efficacy of the schools.

It is a duty, and everyone shall do it willingly.[1]

. . . We also think that the break between religious belief and secular interests which the faithful feel is the result . . . of ineffective Christian training. It too often happens in many places that there is no proportion between education in the sciences and religious education. Scientific courses continue to increase at every level, while religious education is limited to the elementary grades. It is most necessary that the education of developing children be integral and uninterrupted; that is, that the love of spiritual values and their growing moral consciousness keep pace with their scientific and technical training. And it is equally necessary that they be taught how to fulfill their purposes in the most concrete way.[2]

[1] Speech, July 11, 1961.
[2] Encyclical, *Pacem in Terris*, April 11, 1963.

Sports

We trust that you will never forget, dear sons, that your efforts are not ends in themselves, that the body you use reflects in its harmony and agility a small part of the Creator's beauty and omnipotence. Your body is an instrument, which you must bend to the will of the soul.

Your exercises and competitions, which provide a relaxing break between studies and work, must serve the spiritual and immortal part of your being. If they were to have a bad influence on you, if in your lives as athletes you were not to find a safeguard, but a danger to your souls, or a hindrance to the fulfillment of your religious duties, then you would be radically off course, like the runner who loses the race because he does not keep to the track.

Sports can have a great role in your lives as a means for practicing virtue.

You are always in training to make sure your muscles do not lose their elasticity and response. This kind of continual training aims primarily to keep you in condition to win, to gain prestige, but it should nonetheless have meaning for your spiritual life as well.

In sports too, the true and firm Christian virtues can be developed, which God later renders stable and fruitful. Sports encourage the spirit of discipline—obedience, humility and renunciation. And in working with your team and playing matches, you must learn charity, brotherhood, mutual respect, magnanimity, and at times even forgiveness. Keeping in physical condition, of course, demands that you be chaste, modest, temperate and prudent.

How fortunate you are to be able to live these old virtues with your youthful enthusiasm. Without them, you could, true, still be good athletes, but you would not be real Christian athletes.

Spiritual value can also be gained from the constant striving that is implicit in sporting competitions. During every season, there are always fresh victories and new champions. This experience teaches you never to be satisfied with your achievements, and thus can have great value too as a spiritual lesson.

You learn that we can never be content, in our material and our spiritual interests, with the levels we achieve. We must always seek new goals, with God's help, and look to continuous perfecting of our lives, until we have reached "mature manhood, to the measure of the stature of the fulness of Christ" (Ephesians 4, 13).

Be untiring in doing good, in spreading Christ's word, in convincing those who are indifferent that only in faith and in the Church can be found true equilibrium and true strength, true respect for human dignity and the defense of that dignity from exploitation and threat.

Be mindful of the invigorating energy of your faith and set

a good example in the sports you play. Oppose any influences, contrary to spiritual values, which might attempt to take over sports.[1]

[1] Speech, April 26, 1959.

D. THE SICK AND SUFFERING

The Afflicted and Troubled

We seem to hear rising toward Us the moans of those who are suffering in body or in soul, or who find themselves in such poverty that they cannot have a house worthy of a man, or the work they need to sustain themselves and their children. These sufferings touch Us deeply and move Our spirit.

To the sick, to the handicapped, to the old We want to communicate that consolation which comes from on high. Let them remember that this is not our permanent home, but that we are seeking our future home. Let them remember that the griefs of this mortal life, which serve as expiation, raise and dignify the spirit and make possible the acquiring of eternal glory. Let them not forget that the Holy Redeemer himself submitted to the torture of the Cross and willingly suffered insults, pain and cruel anguish to cleanse the stains of our sins and to purify us. Like him, we are yet called from the Cross to the light, according to his word: "Whosoever would follow me, let him deny himself and take every day his Cross and come after me," and he will have an unfailing treasure in Heaven.

We trust that our exhortation will be accepted willingly and that physical and spiritual sacrifices will not only be so many steps for climbing to Heaven, but that they will contribute as well to the expiating of the sins of others and to the return to the Church of those who are unhappily in error and to the triumph of the Christian faith.[1]

[1] Encyclical, *Ad Petri Cathedram,* June 29, 1959.

The Imprisoned

It is rightly said that the law of life lies in the practice of justice and, naturally, in keeping faith with the requirements of justice. This brings with it an important consideration. Sometimes it happens that the soul is bewildered, or in a given moment loses sight of what is right, of what reality and the laws are, and thus the misfortune. One must be judged and condemned to ugly conditions which produce bitterness, unrest, confusion in one's life.

But never forget that this experience can be elevated and transformed when touched by God's grace.

Jesus had the image of sacrifice, suffering and death always present with him, but he reminded his followers that afterwards there would be rebirth. These are serious words, but how can the Pope speak in any other language but that of the Gospel? And even more, they are words filled with the tenderness with which our Lord spoke them.[1]

[1] Speech, December 26, 1958.

To the Blind

Yours is a burden to offer, a mission to accomplish, for a goal that must be reached.

A burden to offer. It would be useless to mitigate the handicap and the difficulty in which you find yourselves. In a world where sometimes only physical capacities and the splendor of beautiful appearance count, or where at least one must be sound in body and spirit to find a job, a profession, to settle down, you have experienced bitterness, disappointment, discouragement more than the others. Perhaps you even felt alone in a world which seemed to ignore you. You may have shed anxious tears known only to God who sees everything and to your family, who must share with you the grief of your misfortune. We know it is true that society tries to come to your help with various kinds of assistance, especially the worthy Organization for the Social Protection of the Blind, which strives in many ways to raise your living conditions, by finding work, providing cultural pursuits and helping you to progress in the spirit of the times. These efforts get all our applause and encouragement, and We are happy to take this occasion to urge the government and all those who can to do more to meet your just needs.

But even in ideal living conditions, your painful infirmity is always present with you. We ask you, beloved children, to offer it continuously to God, as an incense that rises with its sweet perfume to him. In the words of the Apostle, we must accomplish what is missing in his Passion (cf. Colossians, 1, 24). Thus the Lord has need—in the scheme of the Redemption—of your daily offering that is made with a serene spirit and with conscientiousness, in order to continue his work and save souls.

This is the mission you must fulfill: a silent and beneficent apostolate, an apostolate by example. In life, as you know, the noise that is made, the things we see, do not count, but the love with which God's will is carried out does count. According to the golden words of *The Imitation of Christ*,

"He is truly great who has great charity. He is truly great who is small in his sentiment and places no value on the greatness of honors. He is truly prudent who holds the things of this earth to be refuse in order to gain Christ" (Book I, 3, 6). When one has this conviction, he can enjoy the true light, that which enlightens because it discloses the horizons of eternity. How many have their sight and cannot see! How many get lost in the pettiness and the meanness of life, forgetting God, their souls, virtue; their hearts immersed in the shadows of death! The tears Jesus shed over Jerusalem enable us to understand the only thing necessary: "Would that even today you knew the things that make for peace! But now they are hid from your eyes!" (Luke 19, 42).

Take courage then, dear children. Your faith tells us that the most precious light, the one that never sets, is your guarded heritage, which sustains you in your struggles and your difficulties. Be generous in the mission which awaits you; act in charity and in peace, with the thought that nothing on earth that is done in conformity with God's will is ever wasted.

You have, finally, a goal you must reach: eternal life that has been promised to all men of good will. We have already had the opportunity to tell some blind Belgian pilgrims that Christian hope is founded on Jesus' words: "Who follows me will not walk in darkness, but will have the light of life" (John 8, 12). Every morning during Mass the sweet words of the Psalm re-echo: "Give forth your light and your truth; they took me out and led me to your holy mountain, and into your tabernacle." Such a prayer can well apply to you who do not enjoy physical sight. If you are compelled to live dependent on the help of your fellow man in the plan of Divine Providence, the divine intention then is clear and certain that your life on this earth is transformed in preparation and as a pledge for reaching the great light one day, the light that is not of worldly things, which may sometimes be attractive, but the light emanating from the glorious Christ.[1]

[1] Speech to the World Congress of the Blind, July 29, 1959.

Sickness

Unfortunately, many think that the physical sufferings on earth are all absolute evils. They have forgotten that pain is the heritage of the sons of Adam; they have forgotten that the only evil is the guilt that offends God; that we must look to the Cross of Jesus, just as the Apostles, the martyrs, saints and witnesses did who found consolation and redemption; that in Christ's love, we cannot live without pain.

Thanks be to God, not all souls rebel against the burden of suffering. There are sick people who understand the meaning of pain and realize what possibilities they have for contributing to the salvation of the world; thus they accept their life of pain just as Christ accepted his, just as Holy Mary accepted hers on the day of her Purification and her faithful and chaste spouse, St. Joseph, accepted his. You who are present belong to this select group of fortunate souls. And We say to you, Courage! You are the beloved of the Sacred Heart, because We can say with St. Paul: "For it has been granted to you that for the sake of Christ you should not only believe in him but also suffer for his sake" (Philippians 1, 29).

Is there another word more appropriate for reminding us never to take our eyes from the Crucifix, which the liturgy asks us to contemplate especially during Holy Week?

Look at it, dear children, in your sufferings.

To derive from the meditation on the Cross all the spiritual fruits that have been promised to Christian suffering, you must have within you the gift of grace, which is life itself to the Christian soul. In grace you will find strength, not only for resigning yourselves to suffering but to love it as the saints did. Your pain will not be wasted but will be united with the pain of the Cross, with the grief of the Virgin, the most innocent of all creatures. And thus your lives will truly become the image of the Son of God, the king of grief, and the true means for going to Heaven.

But there is more to it. Christ's Passion will reveal to you the immense possibility suffering has to sanctify souls and to save the world. Look again at the Crucified Redeemer. With his words and deeds he taught mankind, with his miracles he helped them, but by his Passion and Crucifixion above all he redeemed the world. Do you want to be like him? Do you want to be transformed in him? Do you want to help him save souls? Then here in your sickness you have the means offered you by Providence "to complete . . . Christ's sufferings . . . for his Body which is the Church" (Colossians 1, 24). This is the great task of those who suffer, whose generous souls must heroically accept suffering, and make an offering of it. For this apostolate, there is no group that is not available to possible redemption: everyone can receive the benefits of salvation, many of whom would not have been able to save themselves had they not prayed and suffered. Was it not this the Immaculate Virgin insisted on at Lourdes when she asked "prayer and penance" of St. Bernadette? Work and pain are the first penance imposed by God on fallen man. Just as sin calls down God's anger, so too work and suffering draws his mercy on mankind.

Let the suffering realize their mission during their lives: they will never again feel alone. In Paradise they will reap the fruits of their spiritual efforts, there where there are no more tears, or pain, or separation, or the possibility of offending God.

For these reasons, and for the intentions We have indicated, We do count on the efforts of Our co-workers, true, and the prayers of all the faithful, but We count even more on sacred suffering which united to that of Christ will give the greatest meaning to man's labors.[1]

[1] Speech, March 19, 1959.

E. TECHNICAL PROGRESS: BLESSING OR CURSE?

Atomic Energy

Whoever is primarily concerned with the things of Heaven, like the Pope, does not neglect precisely by virtue of his mission an interest in the work of those who study the mysteries of the physical world. That is, those who do so with the intention of harnessing natural forces for the betterment of man's condition and for giving mankind the priceless gift of peace.

According to recent reports, there is talk of the possibility of extending man's life on earth.

These are unquestionably notable advances, but they must be made for the sake of the spirit.[1]

[1] Speech, December 11, 1959.

The Electronic Brain

"The Church," as Our Predecessor Pius XII said in his memorable Christmas message of 1953, "loves and favors human progress." And no one doubts that the technological advances made daily in the field of electronics contribute greatly to that progress. By means of electronics and automation, pieces of information can be collected and handled that permit a greater consideration of human factors in economic planning and the humanization of production. By the same token, the constant and more detailed analysis of the possibilities to be developed and of the needs to be satisfied gives us a broader knowledge of real situations and their foreseeable outcome. Thus more competent decisions can be made, resources can be utilized for the good of peoples who do not have them, and the common good of the entire human race can be better served. In the sense that machines help in coordinating efforts, in linking various activities, and in developing a balanced economy, they respect the ends of human labor and contribute to satisfying the immense needs which in so many parts of the world and in so many sectors of society make an appeal to the wealth of more fortunate countries.

There is also a special application of automation techniques that We take pleasure in speaking about, because it provides a happy example of the valuable aid that electronics have brought to the highest disciplines. We are speaking of the *Index Thomisticus*, conceived and carried out by the Jesuits, particularly through the commendable efforts of Roberto Busa. We know what significant help you bring to this monumental work, which is a milestone in understanding man's cultural heritage and a promise of renewal in the philological and documentary sciences.

And it is here that technical progress is put to the service of humanism, that machines are employed for the benefit of spiritual values, a new and compelling instance of the spirit's domination over matter and the realization of the Creator's command to our first parents: "People the earth and make it grow." Which is to say that technical progress, far from filling us with senseless pride, leads us back to a sense of a creature's humility and to a child's wonder for the gifts bestowed on us, which we use to carry out God's command.

And may we not see it also as an imperative reminder of man's grandeur, man "who was created in nobility and restored in an even more wonderful way" (from the Offertory of the Mass) and redeemed by the Precious Blood of Our Savior Jesus Christ? This is what makes the members of the great Christian family worth something compared to which a machine is nothing, whatever its value may be; that is, the eminent dignity of God's children.[1]

[1] Conversation, March 18, 1961.

F. THE SOCIAL STRUCTURE

Work

It is reassuring to think that in their work every Christian family can faithfully reflect the example of the Holy Family of Nazareth, whose industry even in hardship was united to the most ardent love of God and to the fulfillment of his will.

Work is indeed a high calling. It represents for man an intelligent and effective means for working with God the Creator, from whom he received the goods of the earth to cultivate and to make prosper. The strain and difficulty of work are part of the redemptive plan God has laid down. Having saved the world through the love and suffering of his only begotten Son, God has made of human suffering the precious instrument of sanctification, when that suffering is united to that of Christ.

What great light is thrown on these truths by the events in Nazareth, where work was accepted joyously, as a fulfillment of God's will. What greatness the silent and hidden figure of St. Joseph enjoys through the spirit with which he carried out the mission God entrusted to him. Because man's dignity is not measured by the tinsel of outward events, but by internal order and good will.

Here then, from the brightness of the divine example, we can see what attitude we must have toward work, the burden and honor of each man's life. Unfortunately, the mistaken ideologies that have urged unbridled freedom on the one hand, while repressing the individual on the other, have tried to displace the worker from his greatness by reducing him to an object of contention or abandoning him to his own devices. They have tried to sow discord and disunity by setting one class against the other. They have even tried to separate the working man from his God, who alone is the protector and vindicator of the humble, the God from whom we receive life, energy and existence, as if the condition of labor exempted them from the duty of recognizing, honoring and serving him. We are saddened when we think how many of Our children, upright and honest though they may be, have succumbed to these theories and have forgotten that in the Holy Gospel are found the means to begin resolving all their problems and that there is the desire for fresh reforms that is united with a respect for fundamental values.

Dear sons and daughters, look confidently ahead to the paths open to you. The Church counts on you to spread the teaching and the peace of Christ among your fellow workers. Let your work always be a noble mission for you, of which God alone can be the inspiration and the reward. Let real charity dominate your social relations, as well as mutual respect, a cooperative spirit and brotherly intentions, just as St. Paul wrote to the Colossians: "Whatever you do, in word or deed, do everything in the name of the Lord Jesus, giving thanks to God the Father through him. Whatever your task, work heartily, as serving the Lord, not men, knowing that from the Lord you will receive the inheritance as your reward; you are serving the Lord Christ" (Colossians 3, 17, 23–24).

Working people know the Church follows their lot with maternal affection; that she is especially close to those who perform unseen and thankless labors, which others do not recognize or appreciate sufficiently; that she is concerned for those without a steady job, who must face anxious questions about the future of their growing families; that she is close to those whom sickness or accidents have disabled. As for Us, We shall never cease to ask those with public authority and responsibility to exert themselves to provide you better living and working conditions, and especially to insure that a steady and dignified occupation be available to everyone. And We firmly trust that they will try to understand the difficulties workers must face, that they will willingly meet the legitimate aspirations of free men created in the image and likeness of God and that every effort to alleviate care in a spirit of justice and charity will be made, through cooperation and respect for everyone's rights and duties.

But any effort, even the greatest, would accomplish little without divine help. And so We ask you to pray to God that his protection, through the intercession of St. Joseph, be with you and gladden your labors and fulfill your desires.

St. Joseph, Guardian of Jesus, most chaste husband of the Blessed Virgin, you who have carried out your duty so well, supporting the Holy Family with the labor of your hands, protect those who turn confidently to you. You know their aspirations, their troubles, their hopes. They turn to you because they know they will find in you someone who understands and will protect them. You too have undergone the trial, have felt the fatigue, have labored, but even in the midst of life's cares, your spirit was filled with peace and was gladdened in the presence of God's Son, who had been entrusted to you with Mary, his mother. Let those you protect understand they are not alone in their work, but have Jesus next to them; let them welcome him and care for him as you did. Let everything be sanctified in charity, in patience, in justice wherever Christians work: in the family, in the shop, in the factory, so that heaven's gifts will abound.[1]

Our spirit is considerably saddened by the unhappy sight of so many workers in many countries, even whole continents, who are paid such low wages that they and their families are forced to live in subhuman conditions. It is true that to some degree this is due to the fact that in those countries and continents, the process of industrialization is either just beginning or not advanced enough.

In many of those countries, however, there is a glaring, painful contrast between the extreme deprivation of many and the unbridled luxury of a privileged few; in other countries the present generation is forced to tolerate inhuman privations in order to increase the efficiency of the national economy at a rate that far surpasses the limits imposed by standards of justice and humanity. In other countries a high percentage of the national income is spent to maintain a mistaken sense of national prestige or absorbed by large armaments budgets.

In economically developed countries, it is not unusual to discover that while positions of dubious value are highly paid, the productive and assiduous work of whole sectors of honest and industrious citizens is meagerly paid, and insufficiently and disproportionately in relation to their contribution to the common good, to the profits of their industries, and to the total income of the national economy.

We hold, therefore, that it is Our duty to re-affirm once again that compensation for work cannot be left to the laws of the market-place, nor can it be fixed arbitrarily, but must be determined by standards of justice and equity. This means that workers must be paid enough to maintain really human living standards and to permit them to meet their family responsibilities adequately, but it also means that in determining their wages, their contribution to the production and economic situation of the industry in which they work be taken into account. The demands of the common good of the respective political communities, especially with regard to the effects on the general employment rate throughout the country, must also be taken into account, along with the demands of the universal common good; that is, of the international communities with differing characteristics and size.

It is clear that the criteria laid down here hold always and everywhere, but the extent to which they are applied in concrete cases can only be determined in relation to the wealth available, wealth which in quantity and quality can in fact vary from country to country, and within the same country from time to time.[2]

[1] Allocution, May 1, 1960.
[2] Encyclical, *Mater et Magistra*, May 15, 1961.

Property

The changed situation

In the past few decades, as is well known, the ownership of the means of production and the management of them have become, increasingly, separate functions. We know that this creates difficult regulatory problems for the government, which must see to it that the management of large companies, especially those with an effect on the whole economy, pursue objectives that are not harmful to the general welfare. These problems exist, as experience shows, whether the capital that supplies the large enterprises comes from private sources or from public ones.

It is also true that a large number of citizens, and the number is increasing, can look to the future with a sense of security because of their participation in insurance plans and social security programs. In the past their confidence depended on their savings, modest though they may have been.

And we can observe too that in our day people are more interested in professional training than in acquiring property, and are more confident about the salaries they earn by working than about the incomes they derive from capital investment or from rights based on capital.

This is only consonant with the main characteristic of work as direct personal expression in relation to capital, which by its nature is an instrumental good. We can consider it, therefore, as a step forward in human advancement.

The changes in the economy mentioned here have certainly contributed to spreading the notion that a principle of the economic and social order upheld constantly by Our Predecessors has today lost its importance or validity; that is, the principle of the natural right to own property privately, even the means of production.

Re-affirmation of property rights

That notion has no reasonable grounds. The right to own property, including the means of production, has permanent validity, precisely because it is a natural right founded on the ontological and final priority of the individual over society. It would be pointless to talk about free initiative in economic matters, if such initiative were not permitted to employ freely all the means necessary to its realization. Furthermore, both history and experience have shown that in those countries where the right to own property and the means of production privately is not recognized, the fundamental expressions of freedom are suppressed or abridged. It can be assumed, therefore, that freedom finds incentive and security in that right.

And here we find the explanation why the social-political movements for securing justice along with freedom in society, which were until recently quite negative about the right to own goods of an instrumental nature, have changed their attitudes more and more. Today more aware of social realities, they have revised their stand and taken a more positive view of the right to private ownership.

The observation of Our Predecessor, Pius XII, is relevant, and We concur with him: "In defending the principle of private property, the Church is pursuing an important ethical and social end. She does not intend merely to uphold the present state of things, as if it were the expression of God's will, or to protect on principle the rich and the plutocrats against the poor and the propertyless. . . . The Church aims rather to insure that the institution of private property is what it ought to be according to the scheme of Divine Wisdom and the dispensation of nature." Which is to say, that private property should be a guarantee of the individual's essential freedom, and at the same time an irreplaceable element in the social order.

As We have already noted, the economies of many countries are now rapidly expanding their productive capacities. As national income increases, justice and equity demand, as we have seen, that the compensation paid to labor should also be increased, within the limits allowed by the common good. This would permit workers to have the money they need for savings. It is difficult to understand, consequently, why the natural character of a right that has labor as its source and sustenance should be questioned. This right provides the ideal means for the affirmation of the individual and for the exercise of responsibility in all areas, and constitutes a stabilizing force in family life and in the development of society.

Effective distribution

But it is not sufficient to reiterate the natural character of the right to own property and the means of production privately. It must also be asserted that this right be applied among all the social classes.

As Pius XII affirmed, the dignity of the individual demands "the right to the use of the goods of this earth normally, as the natural basis for living, a right which in turn makes it a fundamental obligation to allow private property possibly to everyone." Among the rights deriving from the moral nobility of work is the "securing and perfecting of a social order that will insure an even modest amount of property to all classes of society."

The distribution of property should be promoted and carried out especially in a time like ours, when, as has been pointed out, the economies of a growing number of nations are developing rapidly. By using a variety of methods that have proved effective, it would not be difficult to establish an economic and social policy that would encourage and implement a greater distribution of durable goods, housing, power, modern machinery to farmers and craftsmen, and the common stock of middle-sized and large corporations, as has been amply tested in several economically developed and socially advanced nations.

Public property

What has been said heretofore does not exclude, obviously, the possibility that the state and other public agencies can legitimately own instrumental goods, *especially when their economic influence is so great that they could not be left in private hands without danger to the common good.*

In modern times, there is a tendency toward greater state ownership of property, or ownership by other public agencies. The explanation for this lies in the increased range of services the common good demands of the government. But even in this matter, the principle of subsidiarity must be observed, as explained earlier. The state and other public agencies should not extend their ownership of property unless required absolutely for the common good, and *not for the purpose of reducing or much less eliminating private ownership.*

It must not be forgotten that the economic enterprises sponsored by the state or other public agencies should be entrusted to persons who bring to their task tested competence, unassailable honesty and a keen sense of responsibility toward their country. Furthermore, their work must be carefully and constantly checked, also to avoid the formation in a state organization of centers of economic power that would prejudice its value to the community, which is its very reason for being.[1]

[1] Encyclical, *Mater et Magistra*, May 15, 1961.

The Social Classes

Unity and peace among the social classes

It is absolutely necessary to restore among the various social classes the same peace that we desire among peoples and nations. If this does not take place, there will be—as we already see—mutual hate and discord, from which can arise riots, destructive upheavals and perhaps even bloodshed, to which would be added the progressive wasting of wealth and a crisis in the public and private economy. Our Predecessor already observed rightly: "God willed that in the human community there would be a disparity of classes, but at the same time friendly relations of equity among them." In fact, "just as in the body, the various parts work together and form that harmonious disposition called symmetry, so too nature demands that in civil existence the classes supplement each other and work together toward a just balance. Each one needs the other: capital cannot be without labor, or labor without capital. Accord produces the beauty and order of things." *Whoever dares deny the disparity of the social classes contradicts the very order of nature. Whoever opposes the friendly and undeniable cooperation among the classes themselves tends without doubt to upset and divide human society, with serious disturbance and damage to public and private welfare.* Our Predecessor wisely noted too that "In a people worthy of the name all the inequalities that do not derive from choice but from the nature of things—inequalities of culture, possessions, social position—without prejudice of course to reciprocal justice and charity, are not at all an obstacle to existence and to the predominance of an authentic spirit of community and brotherhood." *The classes and the various kinds of workers can certainly safeguard their own rights as long as they do it legitimately and not violently, as long as they do not invade the rights of others, which are also inalienable.* All are brothers, and therefore all issues must be resolved peacefully with mutual brotherly charity.

Today, in reality, the distance between classes is somewhat lessened, and they cannot simply take two diametrically opposite sides on the relations between capital and labor. Rather, as it turns out, there is an ever-growing multiplicity of groups, and within the groups themselves there is a broadening, with the result that the most qualified and trained now have the opportunity of getting to the highest positions. As far as labor itself is concerned, it is reassuring to point out the movements that have emerged recently which aim to relocate the questions of labor relations on a higher level that is not exclusively an economic one.

Reflections on important problems in the field of labor

There is a long way to go yet, since there are still too many inequalities among salary levels, too much dissension among the sectors of the economy, at times on account of an imperfect or an unjust conception of property rights that stems from the tenacious endurance of selfishness and individualism. And to this is added the painful incidence of unemployment which is the cause of serious hardship for many, and a problem that the rapid rate of progress in technology—for the moment at least—might even aggravate. This touches upon a source of great sorrow to Our Predecessor Pius XI, who said, "We see so many willing and honest workers forced to idleness and then poverty, along with their families, who would want nothing else but to earn honestly, with the sweat of their brow according to the divine command, their daily bread which they cry for each day from their Heavenly Father. Their cries move Our paternal heart and make Us repeat, with the same tender commiseration, what has already come from the loving heart of the Divine Master when he said about the multitude wasting away with hunger: 'I have compassion for these people.' "

If therefore we desire and we seek as we all must harmony among the classes by uniting public and private efforts and helping courageous undertakings, then we must take action in the best way possible so that even those in the humblest condition can earn the necessities of life and provide for their future and the future of their families honestly and securely with their labor and the sweat of their brow. And all the more so since in our day there are so many means for a comfortable life, from which the less fortunate cannot justifiably be excluded.

We especially urge those who have responsibility in enterprises, and upon whom at times even the lives of workers may depend, not to evaluate a worker solely from the economic standpoint, not to limit his considerations just to recognizing the workers' rights as far as a fair wage is concerned, but to go further and to respect the dignity of his person and to consider him really as a brother. Let them allow the workers to participate more fully in the fruits of the enterprise so that they will not feel they are detached from it, but rather have a stake in its life and in its development.

We say this urged on by the desire to see put into practice greater agreement on the mutual rights and duties of the various interests which compose the world of labor. And we say this with the desire that the unions not be understood to be "arms that are dedicated exclusively to defensive and offensive warfare, that provoke reactions and reprisals, or understood to be a torrent that widens and separates, but rather as bridges that unite."

Above all, however, we must be sure that keeping pace with the favorable developments on the economic plane is comparable progress on the plane of spiritual values, as is required by the dignity of Christians, the dignity of mankind.

The father, as head of the family, is among his own almost the representative of God. He is over the others not only in his authority but also in the example he provides of the complete life. The mother, with the gentleness of her heart and with her domestic virtues, should be kind and loving to her husband and guide their children with him with strength and tenderness, for they are God's most precious gifts. She ought to educate them to an honest and religious life. Children should always be obedient, as their duty demands, to their parents, should love them and be not only their comfort, but if necessary, their help. Within the home there should breathe the same charity that moved the Holy Family of Nazareth. Let all the Christian virtues thrive there, let their hearts be as one and there will live the example of honesty. We pray God that such harmony never be disturbed, for when the Christian institution of the family falters, when the Redeemer's commandments about the family are neglected or rejected, then the very bases of civilized existence can crumble. Such is the serious threat which can bring untold harm to everyone.[1]

[1] Encyclical, *Ad Petri Cathedram*, June 29, 1959.

Management and Labor

Even if we are managers and directors, we are all workers in the cause of social well-being in our homelands, in anticipation of the greater good which awaits us.

We know full well how great is the concern for the problems that beset those who are involved in industry, problems of the conscience and problems of human and Christian brotherhood.

Mistaken and saddening in its consequences—as Pope Pius XII said on March 7, 1949—the unfortunately prevalent prejudice remains that the forces of production are irreconcilably opposed in their interests.

Their differences, as Our Predecessor added, are just on the surface. Economically speaking, theirs is a common end and common interest.

Capitalists, managers and laborers are not and ought not be, We insist, irreconcilable antagonists. They cooperate in a common effort, which demands above all mutual comprehension and a sincere attempt to overcome the temptation and the impulse to seek personal advantages to the detriment of the other participants.

It is a question of justice and Christian spirit, applied and active.[1]

Pius XII has already justly observed: "God decreed that there would be a disparity of classes in society, but that they would together maintain friendly relations of equality." And "just as in the body the various members function together and form that whole we call symmetry, so too nature demands that in society the classes work together and bring about a just equilibrium. Each class needs the other:

capital cannot function without labor, or labor without capital. Concord produces the beauty and order of things." Who dares deny the differences among the classes tends without doubt to upset and divide society, with serious disturbance of and damage to the public and private good.

And as Our Predecessor further noted: "In a people worthy of the name all the inequalities that do not arise from choice, but from the very nature of things—inequality of culture, wealth, position—without prejudice, that is, to justice or reciprocal charity, are not at all obstacles to existence and to the dominance of an authentic spirit of community and fraternity." Each class and all citizens in every walk of life are perfectly free to guard their rights, as long as they do so lawfully and without violence or damage to the rights of others, which are equally inalienable. We are all brothers, and therefore all issues must be resolved in a spirit of fraternal charity.

Several signs of good relations

We must point out as a good omen that for some time now the relations among various social groups have been less tense, as Our immediate Predecessor noted in an address to German Catholics: "The tremendous catastrophe which befell you brought with it some benefit, in that conspicuous numbers were liberated from the prejudices and selfishness of certain groups and the differences among the classes have been largely levelled, and men have become closer. Common misery was and is a bitter but sound teacher of discipline."

In reality, the distance between classes is somewhat lessened today and they can no longer take diametrically opposite sides and reduce issues simply to the differences between capital and labor. We can discern a broadening of groups, and within the groups themselves the growth of new opportunities for the capable and the qualified, even in the most important offices. And as for developments in labor circles, it is encouraging to learn that there have been attempts to work out human relations on a higher plane that is not solely economic.

There is still a long way to go.[2]

[1] Speech, January 30, 1959.
[2] Encyclical, *Ad Petri Cathedram*, June 29, 1959.

Domestic Help

The faithful from all walks of life are welcomed by Us because they are members of the Mystical Body of Christ, which is the Church; all of Our children are very dear to Us, but We can well say that they are dearer as they are more humble, because they recall more closely the humility and meekness of the Savior, who made himself poor for us, so that we could become participants in his infinite riches (cf. 2 Corinthians 8, 9).

Do you remember how Our Lord, at the beginning of his Passion, wanted to give a sign of his great love for his own (cf. John 13, 1)? Before establishing the Eucharist and before starting out on his grievous Passion on Gethsemane, he performed an act of extreme humility. The Son of God and the King of Glory kneeled to wash the feet of his apostles. Then he said to them, "Do you know what I have done to you? You call me Teacher and Lord; and you are right, for so I am. If I then, your Lord and Teacher, have washed your feet, you also ought to wash one another's feet. For I have given you an example, that you should also do as I have done to you" (John 13, 12–15). And a few days before this, on his way to Jerusalem to begin his Passion, he had announced: "The Son of man came not to be served but to serve" (Matthew 20, 28). And what service! "and to give his life as a ransom for many," for the ransom of us all who were the slaves of sin.

We are not speaking, of course, about the literal washing of feet, but of the spiritual energies every Christian should expend for his neighbor's sake, in the spirit of humility and charity. Who does not see that a life spent professionally, we might say, in the service of the family, can—if inspired by Our Lord's teaching—facilitate the imitation of Christ, spiritual perfection and holiness?

And what is more, this work has as its ultimate motive the higher obligation to serve God, for which we were created by the Father, redeemed by Christ and sanctified by the Holy Spirit. "My food is to do the will of him who sent me" (John 4, 34) said Jesus, and he taught us to ask that "your will be done, on earth as it is in heaven."

If in leading a Christian life, God's service becomes at times trying, what inspiration we can derive from the example of the Blessed Virgin, who served before us, and from her prompt and generous consent: "Here is the handmaid of the Lord, do unto me according to thy word." And she gave us the Word Incarnate!

Dearest children, if you will fulfill your duties in this spirit, you will be blessed because you are not serving men but God! You will be blessed because in the example and the grace of Christ, in the example and protection of Mary, you will perfect your labors and yourselves.

And your work will become light and you will be able to do it not because you are told to by men, but because God sees you, and thus you will be able to serve even those who are difficult to please.

The fact that today you are no longer called "servants" but "domestic help" is certainly a step forward, in courtesy and in appreciation for your important service. If the word "servant" refers in Holy Scripture especially to God's service, in the Roman world the word meant slavery, the real disgrace of pagan Rome. A servant in Rome did not have any right to his dignity and his honor, and we know how women slaves were treated! So in having put aside the word servant, we have come slowly and—to some—unknowingly to the realization of the Gospels, the spirit of which has permeated our civilization.[1]

Housekeepers

The term . . . reflects a felt and widespread need to respect the human person. It emphasizes the dignity of your work, and your contribution to the social fabric as a whole.

We cannot but be pleased with this undeniable progress. But it would not be worth much if, both for you and your employers, there were not that profound understanding of Jesus' commandment, the sign of recognition among Christians.

If charity is lacking, the outward structure of respect and mutual aid will totter, and we will fall into arid selfishness.

It is charity which makes the observance of rights and duties easier and more complete, because "love is the fulfilling of the law" (Romans 13, 10).

In whatever position he may be, the Christian cannot do what he pleases because he is God's servant and part of his family. Whatever he does, he does for God and for God's love. Read Paul's beautiful letter to Philemon and consider its meaning when you are with your fellow man. You will see what feelings the Apostle had for the young servant Onesimus whom he restored to his owner from whom he had fled: "that you might have him back forever, no longer as a slave but more than a slave, as a beloved brother . . . both in the flesh and in the Lord" (Philemon 1, 16).

Thus, my beloved daughters, you all belong to God's family and bear the seal of your eminent dignity; you must live it with all your strength, out of love and dedication.

It is your duty to live wisely, because your condition has

the importance of a vocation: we are called and we are truly children of God (1 John 3, 1). The work you do is the work of God's children for others of his children, and so must be stamped by the consciousness of individual responsibility, recalling as well the great final goal toward which you are all moving.

We dare ask you even more: be apostles among yourselves. Guide your fellow workers and keep them from bad influences; show them God's way, even in your healthful recreation.

Be apostles in the families for whom you work, beginning with the children who are so often placed in your care. Be apostles by your example and by word when the case demands it.[2]

[1] Speech, 19 April 1959. [2] Speech, June 17, 1962.

Farmers and Farming

The pages of the Bible, especially of the Gospels, are replete with peaceful country scenes, of planting and harvests, of flowers and fruits. Among the most beautiful images are those offered to Christ by rural life, and several of his parables celebrate so well some particular aspects. What is there to say then about the favor the Church has always shown to the good people of the countryside, who are always so generous to her with their best energies and their dearest possessions? Great saints, heroic priests, fervent religious and innumerable nuns have found the ideal ground in their rural family for the development of a lofty vocation.

Dear sons and daughters, always be worthy of God's favor and the Church's.

We know the laudable efforts expended in trying to raise

in every way the civic and social condition of farmers, and to make their labor more productive, in view of the changing conditions of the times. And in this sense, every effort made to achieve greater justice and charity ought not only be approved, but encouraged and blessed.[1]

Agriculture as a depressed sector

Across the world it does not appear that the rural farming population has decreased, in absolute terms. But the exodus of rural populations toward urban centers is unquestionable, an exodus which is substantiated in almost every country, and which sometimes takes on massive proportions, creating complex and difficult human problems.

We know that as an economy develops, the labor force employed in agriculture decreases, while the percentage employed in industry or in providing services grows. We think, however, that the movement of the farming population toward the other sectors in the economy is due not only to the objective factors of economic development but often to multiple factors, among which should be noted the anxiety to get away from an area that is considered closed or without prospects; the desire for novelty and adventure with which the present generation is so taken; the attraction of quick money; the mirage of living in greater liberty because of the means and the facilities which the towns and urban centers offer. But We believe also that it cannot be denied the exodus finds one of its causes in the fact that the agricultural sector is depressed almost everywhere, both as far as the index of productivity of the labor force is concerned, and as far as the standard of living among farming-rural populations is concerned.

And therefore a basic problem which arises in almost every political grouping is the following: how to proceed to reduce the imbalance in efficiency between the agricultural sector on the one hand and the industrial and service sectors on the other and to reduce the gap between the living standards of the rural population and the urban whose incomes derive from industry and services, so that those who farm will not have a feeling of inferiority but rather will be persuaded that as farmers and inhabitants of the country they also can affirm and develop their persons through their work and look confidently to the future.

And so it seems to Us an opportune moment to point out several ways which can help solve the problem:

First of all, it is absolutely necessary, especially by public authorities, to see to it that the essential services are adequately developed in the rural farming areas, such as roads, public transportation, communications, water supplies, housing, sanitation, elementary education, technical and professional education, proper conditions for religious observance, and recreational facilities. And to see to it that the products which will permit the rural household to be furnished and to function in a modern way will be available.

It is important, moreover, that the economic development of political communities be carried out gradually and in proportion to the other productive sectors. That is, it is necessary to put into effect those innovations in productive techniques, the choice of crops and the structure of farming organizations, which the economic system—considered as a whole—can allow or demands. And that they be put into effect in due proportion to the industrial and service sectors.

Agriculture will thus be enabled to absorb more industrial goods and will require a higher level of services. In turn, it will offer to the other two sectors and to the community in general products which will better answer, in quality and in quantity, the needs of consumption, contributing to the stability of the purchasing power of money, which is a positive element in the orderly development of the entire economic system.

In order to achieve a balanced economic development among all the productive sectors, a thorough agricultural policy is very necessary, a policy that deals with taxes, credit, social security, prices, and that promotes skills and the efficiency of farming enterprises.

The fundamental principle in an equitable and just taxing system is that the tax rates be determined according to the ability to pay.

But in determining the needs of the community as a whole when apportioning taxes, public authorities should take into account the fact that a farmer's income is delayed and is subject to greater risks, and that he has greater difficulties in finding the capital necessary to increase his output.

For these reasons the holders of capital are not apt to invest in agriculture, but rather they will invest in the other sectors. By the same token, farmers cannot pay high interest rates, not even as a rule the ordinary market rates, to borrow the capital they need to meet their daily operating costs.

So that the general welfare requires a broad credit policy and credit institutions that will assure farmers the money they need at reasonable rates of interest and fair terms.

It may even be necessary to have two kinds of insurance for farmers: one for their produce and the other for themselves and their families. . . .

We appreciate that social insurance programs must be applied fairly to all citizens, no matter what jobs they perform or from which sector their incomes may derive.

Insurance programs and social security can contribute effectively to redistribute the gross income of a political community according to standards of justice and equity. These programs can therefore be considered instruments for reducing the inequities in the standards of living of the different classes.

Because of the nature of agricultural products, it is necessary that a pricing system be set up that will utilize the numerous means modern economic theory has proposed. The task of regulating prices ought to be primarily in the hands of those directly concerned, but governmental mediation will also have to be called on.

And it is quite relevant to recall that agricultural prices constitute more often payment for work than return on capital.

Since these agricultural products satisfy primarily basic human needs, their price should be such that everyone can afford them. But it is clear that this fact should not provide a reason for compelling a whole class of citizens to lead lives of permanent economic and social inferiority and depriving them of the purchasing power necessary to a dignified standard of living. Such inequity is besides in absolute conflict with the common good.

Furthermore, the industries and services for preparing and transporting farm products and conservation programs should be promoted in farming areas. Various kinds of economic enterprises and professional activities should be encouraged in these areas so that farming families can have the opportunity to supplement their incomes in the places where they live and work.

It is not possible to prescribe which is the best way to organize farming because of the variety of ways agricultural and rural affairs are handled within each political community and, furthermore, among the various nations of the world. But when there is a humane and Christian conception of man and his family, then the ideal cannot fail to be an enterprise held together and functioning as a community of persons and governed by the standards of justice and in the spirit we have spoken of. Working, that is, together as a family. And we cannot fail to strive to make this ideal, as far as circumstances allow, a reality.

At this point we must note that a family-sized enterprise is viable only on condition that its income be sufficient for a decent standard of living for that family. To this end, the farmer must be educated, constantly brought up to date and given technical assistance in his work. Farmers must also develop a healthy network of cooperatives, must participate in farmers' organizations and in the general life of the community, both socially and politically.

But we are convinced that the protagonists in this economic development and in the cause of social progress and cultural improvement among rural inhabitants must be the workers of the land themselves. They themselves can determine how significant their work is, not only because it takes place in the majestic temple of creation itself, but also because it has to do with the life of plants and animals, inexorable life in all its forms, unvarying in its laws, abounding with reminders of God the Creator and Provider. And because farmers produce the variety of foods which feed the human family and supply an ever-increasing amount of raw materials to industry.[2]

[1] Talk to visiting farmers, November 18, 1959.
[2] Encyclical, *Mater et Magistra*, May 15, 1961.

The Small Farmers

Love the earth! is the first thing We say to you. It is the gentle and strong bond which, beside the family, unites you closely to your birthplace and to your work, and to the memories which are passed down as a sacred heritage from generation to generation. Granted that as a consequence of original sin, cultivating the land demands hard work and sacrifice, just as every other kind of labor performed by human strength. It is also true that the income the land yields is often unequal to the labor put into it, thus compelling the farmer to look for a living in the city that has more immediate, if not always secure, economic advantages.

We have confidence that through continual study of rural problems, and with the generous good will of those responsible for their solution, present difficulties can be removed, and in the meanwhile, We say to you, love the earth, the generous and strict mother who holds the treasures of Providence! Love her, because today especially when a dangerous state of mind is spreading everywhere, undermining man's most sacred values, you can find on the land a safe home for the development and safeguarding of your whole being. Love her because through the land and your noble work your spirits can more easily better themselves and be raised to God.

This love does not mean a quiescent and improvident attachment to ancient methods of farming that no longer meet modern demands, but rather means the application to studying the new techniques of cultivation and production in the unfailing rhythms of continual progress.

Our invitation to love the land is directed to all farmers, especially to the young, into whose hands and to whose intelligence and to whose enterprising spirit are entrusted the continuity and the progress of rural life, and therefore of our entire national existence.

Love your families! The second thought We offer you. Without this love what We said before would not have a complete meaning. The attachment to the land can be understood and appreciated only through the love for one's own family, in which is stored the secret of the integrity and strength of every nation. The exodus from the countryside causes as a direct consequence an injury to, and at times even an undoing of, the institution of the family, when damaging habits and ways of thinking replace it.

How marvelous, on the other hand, is the picture before us of innumerable families that are the careful guardians of the most genuine and openly Christian virtues. Where the father is the firm and sure guide, an exemplar of uprightness, sacrifice, hard work; where the mother fulfills in silence her arduous role as educator and worker; where the hardy youth whose contact with nature makes them simpler and more open and less susceptible to danger, grow up pure and strong, the hope and consolation of their parents. And there the young children "will be like olive shoots around the table" (Psalms, 127, 3) and gladden the house, bringing with them the Lord's blessings. This picture We have painted is not an imaginary one, but a reality that is still alive, thanks be to God. To many of these examples We are a pleased and moved witness.

Love therefore your families! We address particularly the rural women, whose Congress has redefined so many delicate problems. The hoped-for improvement in working conditions and incomes, the efforts for cultural and spiritual enrichment, must center here, in the perfect realization of family life. Let your glory and your holy ambition be to have an honest, sound, hardworking family upon whom God's eye may rest with pleasure, a family which will be exemplary in its spirit of piety and goodness, and in its happy harmony —proved through many trials—the harmony that enables the collaboration necessary to a higher standard of living.

As a final thought We say to you: *Love the Church!* Throughout the ages she has always found in the people of the country the solid and capable material from which she has made the majority of her priests and saints. While in the last few centuries there has been a dimming of faith and of the oneness with the Church in the other social classes and the esteem for the great gift of a religious vocation has been lost, the contribution the country people make to the priesthood was and is irreplaceable. By the same token, as an obvious result, the number of saints whom God has willed to choose from rural families has been large; their most fragrant flowers. We would not have the time to name them all, but it is enough to recall—for reasons closer to our heart—the Curé of Ars, Don Bosco and St. Pius X.

Preserve in its original form the blessed heritage of your religion, your greatest treasure. Love the Church and her bishops and her priests. Be active members and participate with profound and joyous awareness in her life. Be foremost in your parish activities. Feed your desire to know always better the maternal teachings of the Church which can give a reassuring answer to all your questions. Be enthusiastic supporters of her social doctrines, from which you can draw light and secure example.

Dearest sons and daughters!
If the love for the land, for your families, for the Church is really alive in you, the greatest peace will fill your hearts and the blessings of God will descend on you in abundance like the beneficent dew which restores your fields in the morning and renews the flowers. We invoke these heavenly gifts on the events, the hopes, the labors of your daily lives.[1]

Your Confederation was not formed for exclusively economic purposes, just to watch over your commercial interests, but ever since its beginning your group has tried to live by the principles of Christian social teaching, which has been announced before the whole world by solemn pontifical documents that are and remain milestones on the road to the Christian enlightenment of the world of labor. This declared faithfulness to the teaching of the Church is a distinctive characteristic of your association and its noblest and most beautiful quality. We would say that in faithfulness lies the secret which is beyond what is in the technical side of the organization, the secret of its growth and its youthful vitality. It never pauses with results already attained, but is continually seeking new ways and new enterprises that will contribute to the welfare of the large family of farmers.

But even in the midst of the multiple aspects of the various problems your daily situation entails, all of them demanding a solution, you must never ignore the urgency of the spiritual side, the search for supernatural and eternal values. We do not mean by this—as some anti-Christian doctrines would lead the unknowing to believe—that while looking at heavenly things, you should ignore the earthly ones. On the contrary, it is necessary to have one's feet firmly planted on earth to work toward one's improvement. The Church repeats this always in defense of her children's material interests as well.

The just defense of your aspirations is sacrosanct. We trust that those desires have the support of those with public authority and that they feel the duty to exercise it with full respect for the rights of all citizens. The provisions of a technical and economic nature that are being studied, as We are told, to improve Italian agriculture are a reassuring confirmation of the widespread interest in your concrete problems and of the concern of your Confederation for a full evaluation of rural life.

This all goes to show that loyalty to Christian principles does not mean passive attachment to obsolete ways, or failure to seek sound progress, but rather can mean work and commitment to improve your own living conditions and to pursue a happy temporal prosperity.

The Christian faces this exciting prospect: a clear look at present reality on the one hand, and on the other, his sights turned to heaven. The Christian worker who intends remaining loyal to Jesus Christ and to the Church knows very well that here below there can never be lasting happiness, and that peace in the heart and in the family cannot be found if the search for earthly prosperity is detached from the holy fear of God, a respect for his law, an appreciation for heavenly grace. The Christian knows all this, and he derives from the knowledge that quiet and thoughtful trait which is the sign of true wisdom, the uprightness and moral soundness reflected in the ordered harmony of the family, in which the new sons of God can grow pure and strong, and thus prepare themselves for life's trials.

This is, in a special way, the way the people of the fields look! Know how to care for the rich treasure of theological and cardinal virtues: faith, hope and charity; prudence, justice, strength and temperance. They will make your family one of the soundest parts of national life and a consolation to the Holy Church.

Even in the troubles of modern times, and during the profound technical and economic revolution that is taking place and will soon be put more fully in your service, keep your sights on heaven, your hearts full of faith and love for God. Only in this way will the applications of technology be the source of lasting and true spiritual progress, without which there can only be disorder and confusion.

As workers of the land, and thus closer to the great mystery of nature, the open book that tells of the Creator's power, you can well understand these words.

Oh, the land, the land! what lessons about life it can teach! How wonderful to think that God wanted the first man to be in the serene haven of a garden "to till it and keep it" (Genesis, 2, 15); how beautiful to know that the most sacred rites of the Church—the Sacraments—instituted by Christ, take their material from the earth, which becomes a sign of effective grace. And so we have the water of the baptismal font, the smell of bread, the odor of the wine which Christ uses to make himself present every day on his altars and to communicate his very life to men, and the precious juice of the olive, it too a humble instrument of grace. And then there are the benedictions with which the Church marks the growth of the earth's fruits and the acts which prepare them.

Keep these great realities close to you: you can understand them in a special way. They can render the love and appreciation of heavenly things easier and more spontaneous. This is the meaning of the joyous Easter announcement which is heard so frequently these days: "If you have been raised with Christ, seek the things that are above, where Christ is, seated at the right hand of God. Set your minds on things that are above, not on things that are on earth. For you have died and your life is hid with Christ in God" (Colossians 3, 1–3).[2]

[1] Audience, April 22, 1959. [2] Audience, April 27, 1960.

Immigrants

We are very concerned for those who have had to leave their native countries because of the lack of work opportunities, or because of adverse political and religious conditions. What sacrifices they must make, far away from their countries and families, and compelled—many of them—to live in the bustle of great cities and large industrial centers, where the way of life is so different for them, and often so corrupting. Their hard lot sometimes causes serious crises, and a steady loss of the sound religious and moral traditions of their native countries. And besides, they must endure long separations from their families, which can lead to the loosening of ties, and become a threat to family unity itself.

We wholeheartedly encourage, therefore, the beneficial work of the priests who themselves have become emigrants—at great sacrifice—in order to carry out the mission entrusted to them by this Apostolic See. They dedicate themselves to the spiritual and material assistance of Our children and make them feel the Church's maternal concern for them whenever they need her support. And We hail the generous efforts that several nations have made for these people, as well as the measures taken internationally to hasten a solution to this grave problem. These efforts should not only open new possibilities for emigration, but also facilitate the reunion of families, which are the cornerstone of the religious, moral and economic stability of the immigrants, as well as being an advantage to the countries which welcome them.[1]

How much We understand of the suffering, hope and expectations that immigrants feel; after all, they are really displaced at first—from their families, from their home towns, from their countries, indeed from their own language. The immigrant is faced with a new job and the necessity to find a home, with new customs that may rub against everything he was taught before. He needs friends to confide in; he must have access to a church or chapel to fulfill his religious needs. Here the priest is always present, ready to offer him advice and comfort.

Immigration is a densely human phenomenon; the men and women involved are feeling, concrete beings, each with his own problems. They are prepared to make great sacrifices in order to secure some kind of economic advantage, to face strange and alien conditions and to adapt themselves to them, as Providence wills. Immigration brings fresh energies and new talents to the foster countries. And since immigrants do make a large contribution to the economies of these countries, it is only just that they be helped to adapt themselves with as little hardship as possible.

We are now entering into a period when Christian precepts are being applied more and more widely. No one is sufficient unto himself, in his own life or in society. The respect that is owned to intellect and physical capacities is succeeding in overcoming traditional prejudices and in erasing the terrible connotations of "alien," "stateless person," and "tolerated workers."

Every effort should be made to see to it that the immigrant can continue his education: religious, cultural and technical.

What is really needed is a coordinated program that will enable him to make a home in his new surroundings.[2]

[1] Encyclical, *Ad Petri Cathedram*, June 29, 1959.
[2] Speech, August 5, 1962.

Employees and Employer

. . . Following the lines laid down by Our Predecessors, We too hold that it is legitimate for workers to want to participate actively in the life of the companies in which they work. It is not possible to predetermine the form and degree of such participation, since that must depend on the concrete situation of each company or enterprise, a situation which varies from company to company, and within each company is subject to often rapid and substantial changes. We think it opportune at this point to call attention to the fact that the problem of worker activity is always present, whether the enterprise be private or public, and in any case the enterprise must be aimed at becoming a community of persons in their relationships, their functions and their positions.

It is important too that the workers have a voice and contribute in the efficient functioning and development of the companies they work for. As Our Predecessor, Pius XII, observed, "the economic and social function that every man wants to fulfill demands that the work each man does not be totally controlled by the will of others." A human conception of the enterprise must without doubt preserve the authority and the necessary efficiency of a unified management, but it must not reduce day-to-day work to a simple, silent carrying out of orders, without allowing any possibility for co-workers to take advantage of their experience, functioning just passively under the decisions assigning them their tasks.

And lastly it is to be noted that the exercise of responsibility by workers not only answers legitimate needs of human nature, but is consistent with the historical evolution that has taken place in economics, politics and society.

Unfortunately . . . the economic and social imbalances that offend justice and humanity are not few in our times. Profound errors inform the behavior, the ends, the structures and the functioning of economic reality. But it is an undisputable fact that production methods are becoming more rapid and modern than in the past under the pressure of technical and scientific progress, demanding greater aptitudes and technical skills from workers.

At the same time, this progress has allowed them greater means and more leisure time for education and retraining, for culture and religious preparation.

There is now more time for basic education and professional training of the new generations. In this way, a human atmosphere is being created that will permit the working class to assume larger responsibilities even within enterprises. . . .

In modern times there has been a notable increase in the labor union movement, and in a general recognition of the unions in the laws of several countries and internationally, with the purpose of encouraging collaboration, primarily through collective bargaining. We must point out how opportune or necessary it is that the workers have the opportunity to express themselves and be heard beyond their own places of work and at all levels.

The reason for this is that single economic enterprises, no matter how large or efficient they may be, are vitally involved in the economic and social context of their respective political communities, and are conditioned by them.

The decisions which most influence that context are not made within single enterprises, but are made by public authorities or by agencies that operate on a world, national or regional scale. Because of this, it is opportune or necessary that in public authority and in those agencies, workers or their representatives be present, as well as capital interests and their representatives.[1]

[1] Encyclical, *Mater et Magistra*, May 15, 1961.

Social Justice

We consider it opportune to acknowledge how difficult it is to understand precisely the relationship between the objective requirements of justice and concrete situations; that is, to specify the degree and the form in which doctrinal principles ought to be applied to reality.

And specifying those degrees and forms becomes even more difficult in our time because of its marked dynamism. Everyone these days ought to make a contribution toward realizing the universal common good. Thus the problem of raising social reality to the objective standards of justice is not available to a permanent solution. Our children must, therefore, guard against being satisfied with objectives that have already been attained.

In fact, men must consider what has been accomplished as little in comparison to what there is yet to do, because the forces of production, trade unions, professional groups, insurance programs, legal provisions, political regimes and organizations concerned with culture, health, sanitation, sport and recreation—all of these—must be updated in this era of the atom and the conquest of space. The human family is well into this new era and has begun its march on a road with limitless prospects.[1]

[1] Encyclical, *Pacem in Terris*, April 11, 1963.

Man and the Public Authorities

Human society can be neither well-ordered nor productive unless there is an invested authority which will assure order and contribute to the enactment of the common good in sufficient measure.

This authority derives from God, as St. Paul teaches us: "There exists no authority except from God." St. John Chrysostom comments on this passage: "What are you saying? Is every ruler appointed by God?" "I do not say that," he replies, "for I am not dealing now with individual rulers, but with authority itself. What I say is, that it is the divine wisdom and not mere chance that has ordained that there should be government, that some should command and others obey." God, further, created man as social in nature, and since no society *can hold together unless some one be over all, directing all to strive earnestly for the common good, every civilized community must have a ruling authority, and this authority, no less than society itself, has its source in nature, and has, consequently, God for its author.*

Authority is not an uncontrolled force; it is, rather, the power of commanding according to right reason and derives its capacity to enforce order from the moral order, which comes from God, its first source and ultimate end. In this regard, Our Predecessor of happy memory, Pius XII, said: *That same absolute order of beings and their ends which presents man as an autonomous person, that is, as the subject of inviolable duties and rights, and as at once the basis of society and the purpose for which it exists, also includes the state as a necessary society invested with the authority without which it could not come into being or survive. . . . And since this absolute order, as we learn from sound reason and especially from the*

Christian faith, can have no origin save in a personal God who is our Creator, it follows that the dignity of the state's authority is due to its sharing to some extent in the authority of God himself.

Authority which is founded on threats or on fear or on promises of rewards cannot effectively move men to fulfill the common good, and if even by chance it should succeed in doing so, their dignity as persons, that is beings with reason and free will, would not be respected. Authority is above all a moral force, and so it must appeal, in the first place, to the conscience, to the duty everyone has of contributing his share willingly to the good of all. And since all human beings are equal by virtue of their natural dignity, no one of them can coerce the conscience of anyone else. Only God can, because he alone sees and judges the intentions of the spirit.

Human authority, therefore, can oblige men morally only if it is intrinsically related with God's authority and shares in it.

Thus the personal dignity of all citizens is safeguarded, since they obey public authority, not as men subject to men, but as an act of homage to God, the provident Creator, who has decreed that men's relations with one another be governed by an order he himself established. In revering God, men do not debase themselves, but rather perfect and ennoble themselves, for *to serve God is to rule.*

Authority, as has been said, is postulated by the moral order and derives from God. Whenever the laws or provisions of the invested authority are contrary to that order and therefore contrary to the will of God, they no longer have the power of binding the conscience, because *we must obey God rather than men.* And when authority does contradict the moral order, it breaks down and degenerates into abuse. *Human law* has the true nature of law only insofar as it corresponds to right reason, and therefore is derived from the eternal law. Insofar as it falls short of right reason, a law is said to be a wicked law; and so, lacking the true nature of law, it is rather a kind of *violence.*

Because authority derives from God, it does not follow, however, that men do not have the freedom to choose those who will exercise it, as well as the form of their government, the limits of its powers, and its methods. Thus the doctrine We have just discussed is fully consonant with every kind of genuinely democratic government.

The attainment of the common good is the purpose of public authority

Individuals and intermediate groups are all obliged to contribute their share to the common welfare. This means that they pursue their own interests according to the needs of the community, and direct their productivity, in terms of goods and services, to the same purpose, which the authorities prescribe, in accord with the standards of justice, in the proper form and within the limits of their competence. That is, the provisions made by the civil authorities should be in the clear form and their contents should be morally sound, and at least conducive to the good.

Essentials of the common welfare

The ethnic characteristics which distinguish one group of men from the other must certainly be respected as elements of the common welfare, but these values and characteristics do not exhaust the content of the common good. This good—in its essential and deepest aspects—cannot be considered in doctrinal terms and determined even less so in its various forms throughout history without regard for man, since it is so essentially bound up with human nature.

In the second place, all the members of a political community have the right to share in the common good, although in different ways, according to each one's task, merit and condition. Public authority is bound to promote the common good of all, without preference for certain individuals or certain groups, just as Our Predecessor, Leo XIII, said,

The civil power must not serve the advantage of any one individual, or of some few persons, inasmuch as it was established for the common good of all. For reasons of justice and equity, however, the government at times may have to give more attention to the underprivileged members of the body politic, since they are less able to defend their rights and to pursue their legitimate claims.

But here We must draw attention to the fact that the common good pertains to the whole man, to the needs of his body and to the claims of his soul. For this reason, the public authority must realize the common good by ways and means that are proper to both; that is, while respecting the hierarchy of values, the authority must promote the spiritual and material welfare of its citizens simultaneously.

These principles are perfectly consistent with what We stated in the encyclical, *Mater et Magistra*; that is: the common good consists in *the sum total of those conditions of social living whereby men are enabled to achieve their own integral perfection more fully and more easily.*

Men, however, composed as they are of bodies and immortal souls, can never in this mortal life succeed in satisfying all their needs or in achieving perfect happiness. The common good can be realized, therefore, so as not to hinder and indeed to help man attain his eternal salvation.

The duties of the individual and of the public authority

In our time, the common good is best realized in the rights and duties of the individual. The main concern of government should be, therefore, to insure that those rights are recognized, respected, defended, promoted and coordinated with other rights, and to contribute, as a consequence, to making the fulfillment of the individual's duties readily possible. For *to safeguard the inviolable rights of the human person, and to facilitate the fulfillment of his duties, should be the essential office of every public authority.*

This means that any act of a government which does not acknowledge these personal rights, or violates them, contradicts its very purpose for being and is therefore totally void of any legal force.

The reconciliation and protection of the rights of the individual
One of the basic tasks of the government is to coordinate social relations so that the exercise of one man's rights does not impede or threaten others in the exercise of their rights and in the fulfillment of their duties. The government must safeguard personal rights, or restore them if they have been violated.

The duty of promoting personal rights
The common good demands that the government act positively toward creating the human conditions under which all the members of society can best exercise their personal rights as well as carry out their respective duties. Experience, in fact, teaches us that whenever the government fails to act properly, the resulting economic, social and cultural disturbances tend, especially in our time, to become acute, and consequently basic personal rights risk being deprived of meaning, and respective duties are compromised.

Thus it is necessary that the government insure that social progress keep pace with economic development. In keeping with the productive capacity of the economic system, therefore, the public authorities should develop such essential services as the building of roads, transportation, communications, water supplies, housing, public health, recreational facilities and guarantee conditions for religious worship. The government should also see to it that insurance programs are available to the people so that in case of misfortune or increased family responsibilities, no one will lack the necessary means to maintain a decent standard of living. The government must make comparable efforts to insure that those who can work will be offered jobs that are in keeping with their abilities, and that wages be determined according to standards of justice and equity. Workers should be allowed to have their proper responsibility in their respective work. The intermediate groups which make living together effective and richer should be encouraged, and the benefits of culture should be made available to everyone, in the form and to the extent possible.

Balancing the two forms of government intervention

The common good requires that the government keep a careful balance between coordinating and protecting the rights of citizens, on the one hand, and promoting them on the other. Any special efforts to safeguard the rights of certain individuals or certain social groups should be watched carefully to avoid creating privileged positions, just as in promoting these personal rights, the government must avoid the absurdity of actually reducing or preventing altogether the exercise of rights. *Nevertheless, it remains true that government intervention in economic matters should be such as not to reduce constantly the freedom of private initiative among individual citizens, but rather to guarantee the greatest possible amplitude to that freedom by protecting the basic personal rights of each individual.*

The government should abide by the same principle in its multiform activities to promote rights and to facilitate the carrying out of duties in all areas of society.

Structure and function of public authority

It is impossible to determine once and for all what the best form of government should be, or how public authority should most properly fulfill its functions; that is, its legislative, judicial and executive functions.

In determining the structure and operation of government, consideration must be given to the historical background of each political community, which will vary at different times and in different places. We believe, however, that it is in keeping with the innate demands of human nature that the state should take a form embodying the threefold division of powers that correspond to the three functions of public authority. The areas in which the government operates or has some competence are also defined in juridical form, and the relations between individual citizens and government agencies should also be similarly defined, so as to guarantee the individual the power to exercise his rights and to carry out his duties.

In order that this structure of law and government may produce the advantages which may be expected of it, public officials must meet the problems that arise in a way that conforms both to the complexities of the situation and the proper exercise of their function. And this means that legislative power should be exercised within normal bounds and constitutional limits and that it should meet the objective requirements of the common good; executive authority should be used, in applying the law, with full knowledge of their intention and after careful evaluation of concrete situations; and that judicial power be used, in administering justice, with humane impartiality and with absolute independence from pressures exerted by vested interests. An ordered society demands that individual citizens and intermediate organizations should be effectively protected by law in the exercise of their rights and the fulfillment of their duties.

Law and conscience

A legal system consistent with moral order and corresponding to the level of development of the political community is a basic element in achieving the common good.

Social life in our times is so varied, complex and dynamic that any legal system, no matter how well-organized and farsighted, will be inadequate.

Furthermore, relations between individuals, between individuals and intermediate groups, and intermediate groups with public authorities, and public authorities at various levels in the state, are so complicated and sensitive that they cannot be governed strictly by legal systems that are too defined. Such a situation therefore demands that the civil authorities have a clear conception about the nature and extent of their official duties, if they want to interpret the law faithfully, considered in its constituent parts and its intention, and meet the concrete cases which are continuously arising. They must be men of great equilibrium and integrity, competent and courageous enough to see at once what the situation requires and to take necessary action quickly and effectively.

The participation of individuals in public life
Personal dignity demands that individuals take an active part in public life, although the way in which they share in it will depend on the level of development of the political community to which they belong.

Men will discover new and extensive advantages in their participation in public life. The members of the government thus come into frequent contact with the citizens and can learn what is really needed for the common good. The fact, too, that the members of the government hold office for only a limited time keeps them from growing complacent and allows for their replacement as social progress demands it.[1]

[1] Encyclical, *Pacem in Terris*, April 11, 1963.

G. PROFESSIONS AND VOCATIONS

The Craftsman

Just the word "craftsman" brings a rather wide horizon to mind. There were craftsmen, we might easily say, from the very dawn of human history, and they are always present at the beginnings of what is really glorious and great in the history of various nations.

Craftsmanship is something very solid, because it does not mean just a piece of work in itself. It is not like certain kinds of art that do not always fulfill what ought to be their true and proper mission, but rather, craftsmanship expresses a luminous correspondence between the heart, the mind, and the capacity for life. Through this kind of work, in fact, we are provided the means to achieve peace, relief, and personal consolation, in every order of society, under the best relations and auspices.[1]

The craftsman and the farmers' cooperative

The craftsman's trade, the family farm, as well as the cooperative associations should be preserved and promoted in consonance with the common good and the technical possibilities at hand.

Here we might say something in particular about the trades and the cooperatives.

First of all, the two kinds of enterprises—in order to remain alive—must keep themselves constantly up to date, in their procedures, their structures, their products, with new situations created by the progress of science and technology and also by the changeable demands and preferences of the consumers. And the task of keeping up to date belongs in the first place to the craftsmen and the members of the cooperatives themselves.

To that end, it is necessary that both groups be well educated, in both the technical and the human sense, and that they be professionally organized. Equally indispensable is an appropriate policy with regard primarily to their training, their tax structure, credit and social insurance programs.

Whatever the public authorities can do for craftsmen and the cooperatives can also be justified by the fact that these groups are the bearers of genuine human values and contribute to the progress of civilization.

For these reasons We invite with fatherly warmth our dear children, craftsmen and members of cooperatives throughout the world, to be aware of the nobility of their calling and of their important role in keeping alive the sense of responsibility and cooperation in their communities, and the desire to work with dedication and originality.[2]

[1] An audience, December 11, 1959.
[2] Encyclical, *Mater et Magistra*, May 15, 1961.

The Teacher

The vocation of teaching, along with the joys it brings to the person who dedicates himself to it, brings exacting requirements as well, which draw on the teacher's whole personality. They can be defined first of all on a general level, then by the respective duties the teacher has to himself, to his student, to his student's family and to society.

The basis of the educator's training—of every Catholic educator—is made up first of all by the absolute necessity to have a sure and solid Christian background which, pulsing like the unseen heart, will give strength and conviction to the teacher's whole life.

Every Christian, in fact, is obliged to consider his own work in a supernatural light, and to prepare himself for it with full personal virtues.

One cannot give what one does not have; so too men cannot be educated to a Christian life if they do not have the qualities which alone render life marvelously beautiful and worthy of being lived. You need, therefore, a supernatural eye to penetrate to the ultimate greatness and dignity of your work, which can be seen as the valuable auxiliary to the work of Christ, of the Church, and of the family in educating young souls. You need the good and precious Christian virtues which shall place you in the right part of the Church's social organism: the theological virtues, faith, hope and charity; and the cardinal virtues, prudence, justice, fortitude and temperance. But above all, and We repeat this, you must participate consciously and fervently in the truly supernatural life through the sacraments; especially through the Holy Eucharist, which fortifies your soul and prepares it for even greater giving.

From this base, you can develop the other duties determining the outcome of your career, especially the duties *to oneself* in the willing practice of what We have just outlined, in order to meet adequately the requirements of your task. This means the continuous deepening of your knowledge—of the arts, of psychology, of educational methods—in order to know the youthful personality and its problems. This means also to learn the spirit of sacrifice, to regard the teaching profession as a giving of the self to those whom Christ himself singled out: "Whoever receives one such child in my name receives me" (Matthew 18, 5), and as one of the most valuable services in imitation of Christ, "who did not come to be served but to serve and to give his life as a ransom for many" (*ibid.* 20, 28).

There are, besides, one's obligations toward one's student,

which are as deep and important as the personal ones because they concern the subject of education. These obligations stem from the main one of developing a good relationship with the adolescent, of giving him that respect which he deserves as a creature made in the image of God, as a growing creature. The classical authors recognized his importance; take, for instance, Juvenal's well-known maxim: "The greatest reverence is owed the boy" (*Satires*, XIV, 47). This respect is born from a recognition of his personal value and particularly of his supernatural end, which must be kept in mind in school, just as in every other human activity, if we do not want to stray from God's established order.

The whole educational process contributes to establishing this balanced relationship, and this means that notions should not be imposed from on high, but that the search for the truth and beauties of life, of culture, of the sciences and letters, of history and anthropology should be conducted with enthusiasm and patience on both sides. The teacher must encourage the adolescent's own efforts by treating him with affection, understanding, justice and mercy, in order to assure his emotional as well as his intellectual growth. The teaching process acquires special importance and validity from the light of example which the educator must set continually to direct the young student on the right road of life. Should the example ever be lacking, the child's education would become soulless. The example becomes even more necessary in the case of a high school student who is at a sensitive point in his growth when he is easily swayed by the things he sees and hears.

And finally the teacher ought to establish important and fruitful contacts with his students' families, which "can go beyond the simple scholastic relationship in order to exert positive Christian influence." The teacher's responsibilities toward society are equally important because in preparing youth for their future careers, he teaches them to honor the

Church and his country. On his quiet but valuable contribution depend the happiness and security of the future, based on a proper and sound religious, moral and intellectual training of the new generations.[1]

You shape the minds of your students, whose development is being accelerated these days by modern teaching methods, by the widespread effects of the press and other communication media. You must, therefore, continue to exert the greatest effort to keep up with your changing profession, which requires, and will require even more in the future, doctrinal soundness and depth.

But your mission involves something even more important, for you shape and nurture the *souls* of your students. The figure of the teacher is one we remember vividly from our childhood, and a figure so much tied to this highest function —to educate souls, by word, by example, by patient work performed despite difficulties and renunciations. How profoundly St. John Chrysostom describes this incomparable mission: "What is greater than directing the souls and shaping the habits of adolescents? I consider him without doubt more excellent than all the painters, sculptors and artists, who knows well the art of modeling the spirit of the young" (*Homilies* 59 al. 60 cap. 18 Matthew). This art is not learned from books or from practice, but comes from the grace of God, from prayer and from the long apprenticeship to a profound Christian way of life, right from the fruitful early years of school and study.[2]

Great literature of every epoch has praised the teacher highly, and art has exalted his simple and majestic figure. All men—and the Pope says this with tenderness—recall with inexpressible gratitude and reverence their childhood teachers, and the teachers who taught their own children, and the teachers who helped their priest in his holy ministry.

These are the effects of your far-seeing service, which last a whole lifetime.

Take heart at the thought that your work is not unimportant or unappreciated. It must number among the highest services man performs for his fellow men, as the Bible tells us: "Incline your ear and hear the words of the wise, and apply your mind to my knowledge, for it will be pleasant if you keep them within you, if all of them are ready on your lips" (Proverbs 22, 17–18).

It can happen that some of you may fear offending others and so will hesitate to teach something honest and wise but cold and almost secular. There is no need to fear. You do not intend to proselytize in a contradictory manner, or force, as they say, the religious feelings of the young. You are trying, rather, to live according to the clarity and imperatives of the Gospel, to give witness before the whole world of the unity and harmony of the faith, and to reflect thought and life coherently.

There is nothing in Christianity which opposes any noble and legitimate aspiration of man. Christianity respects his personal freedom, his inclinations, his choices, and it knows how to be patient and wait.

Let your conduct, your conversation, your contacts persuade even those who—through traditional preconceptions or irrational fear—try to close their eyes and heart to the Church's influence, thinking that by doing so they defend their independence of thought and action. Learn how to demonstrate, with the gentleness of conviction, that Christianity safeguards the whole man, who was elevated to incomparable dignity by the Incarnation of the Word, and that the Church encourages thought that has been enlightened by supernal certainty and urges it to always new conquests.

Be so certain of this truth that you live it at every point of your lives and in every circumstance. Your Christian beliefs will spread in your school and contribute to that homogeneous and complete development of children toward which you have aimed.

Several pedagogical methods which worked well in their time and for men of other ages, which we still respect, required knowledgeable and opportune adaptations. You should employ the new methods willingly, as long as they fit into the wonderful frame of the Christian conception of man and help you in carrying out your vital task. Make them your methods in the name of God. For it is quite clear that more timely standards and methods must come into being—based always on the unshaken principles—that will better answer the needs of the times in which we function.

These new applications increase rather then lessen the personal responsibility and sacrifice of the teacher. They demand, in fact, greater control of the self, more enlightened and cheerful patience, constant presence of mind and readiness in understanding, responding to, directing one's charges.

Treasure the things the Christian ascetics have taught through the ages, even in the matter of adaptability. Be the followers of the "one Teacher" (cf. Matthew 23, 8) in order to participate in the designs of Providence.

In this sense, be impartial, learn the spirit of delicacy and equity in order to attend to the needs of those who are less endowed with intellect and economic means. Man has a quality he can cultivate without danger as long as he guards himself from demagogy and self-satisfaction; that is, his sympathy for the people Christ himself preferred to know: the sinners, the poor, the sick, and the children.

Do not ever be discouraged. The lively, spiteful perhaps, or surly child of today will feel your presence years from now, and he will be able then to appreciate what you did for him in opening up his path to a life in the community.

Pray for and love the children who are entrusted to you. They are promising buds which will one day flower, in the time and place God has determined for each of them. Learn to respect the mystery of heavenly grace which is silently working in those tender and pliable hearts, from which we may expect promise of the good. Do not be alarmed if your work does not have immediate effects. As true disciples of Christ, you too must look to wider horizons, to which—every year without perhaps even understanding how—you bring new light, new splendor.[3]

One last thought We should like to leave with you to encourage you in all these duties. It is simply this, that in educating and shaping your students, you are preparing a place for yourselves in heaven that is among the most luminous. At times, unfortunately, some problems and projects and arguments are put in the foreground which, however useful and urgent they may be, must not be allowed to make us lose sight of the end to which everything must move in order to have meaning. We must look at everything *sub specie aeternitatis*, as the true teachers of all times have taught, everything, that is, in its eternal and unchangeable value, which can never be eliminated. This is why We encourage you to practice your profession with the most vital faith, the surest hope, the most fervent charity, in expectation of Heaven to which our souls aspire.

Let the Bible shine before you: "And those who are wise shall shine like the brightness of the firmament and those who turn many to righteousness, like the stars forever and ever" (Daniel 12, 3). Let this be your secret desire, which shall find fulfillment in the blessed possession of God. When the difficulties of life, the demands of our obligations, the work, the lack of understanding, and the crises disturb your equanimity, let the thought of the glory the Lord prepares for his good and faithful servants renew your strength and courage.[4]

[1] Speech, March 19, 1960. [2] Speech, September 22, 1960.
[3] Speech, September 5, 1959. [4] Speech, September 22, 1960.

To Surgeons

Divine Providence granted that We Ourself could experience life in a hospital and so We came to know the great physical and moral suffering of the sick. Those were hard years in Our life, but rich ones for getting to know the men whom We met then. And rich years for the fulfilling ministry which God granted Us to exercise in that time.

We want above all to ask you to maintain always a fraternal and respectful attitude in the face of human suffering. Never forget the effect you can have on your patients' pain as you become, in part at least, the master who can reduce or eliminate it. Your concern with the body's suffering puts you literally in touch with man in his totality: a body and a spirit united intimately, reacting on each other, one perishable—and all too visible—the other immortal, that one day shall re-animate that body so that it can participate with the just in the glory of the sight of God. Thus your closeness to the profound mystery of human suffering can only impress your spirits with man's great destiny, and, at the same time, the greatness of your mission.

But those among you who are Christians will not fail to see in your patients an image of the suffering Jesus. May you always remember your divine exemplar, Jesus the Redeemer, and may you always be fired with the desire to walk in the footsteps of the Man who on earth "did good and cured the sick" (Acts 10, 38). Jesus, so powerful in his works and so solicitous to all unhappiness; so great and yet so respectful of other persons and so attentive to the freedom of those he benefited: no one was ever cured who did not, at least implicitly, want to be.

Exercise your wonderful profession, therefore, in this

spirit; it is your greatest hope for understanding the Lord when he says: "Come, O blessed of my Father . . . I was sick and you visited me" (Matthew 25, 36). Those words were intended for those who perform works of mercy, an expression of Christ's gratitude for the care he receives through the persons of men, his brothers.[1]

[1] Conversation, May 16, 1960.

To Blood Donors

We are pleased and moved to know of your commitment in the spirit of sacrifice and generosity to the cause of donating blood, a cause that is nobler for being inconspicuous in the eyes of the world, which sometimes recognizes only vain appearances. We express Our esteem and Our encouragement, and We assure you that your sacrifice, performed in the joy of the heart as well as for the sake of the sick, is pleasing above all to the Heavenly Father "who sees in secret" (Matthew 6, 4). From him you will have a reward in "good measure, pressed down, shaken together, running over" (Luke 6, 38).

We do not hesitate to call your donation of blood an act of apostolate. It is done, after all, for the physical and moral good of one's suffering fellow man, for whom the blood may be a means of salvation and renewed faith in Divine Providence. How many lives you save, how much pain you allay, how much hope you restore, in the silence of the hospital and in the anxious vigil of the family. Yours then is a true apostolate. But to attain perfection, it must be rooted in charity, which is the love for God and one's brothers. Just as blood gives life, color and strength to the body, so too charity, the hidden but vital fluid, makes every good deed worthwhile. Without charity, acts of heroism would be as ringing brass and tinkling cymbals. With charity, even a single drop of blood acquires supernatural value in the sight of God.

At times, a sense of inadequacy may burden you because, as We are told, the demand for blood exceeds the available supply. And so while We congratulate you for your efforts in meeting emergencies, We take the occasion to ask those who are good, willing and well-disposed to join their efforts with yours, so that your ranks in the service of life will continue to grow.[1]

[1] March 17, 1959.

The Military Chaplains

Our period of service as chaplain in the hospitals during the war (World War I) was unforgettable. During that time, We learned from the suffering of the sick and the wounded how great is the universal aspiration to peace, the highest good of man. Never as then—and also later, during the second global conflict when We were the instrument of the untiring charity of Our Predecessor of blessed memory in the countries where We were sent as representative of the Holy See—have We felt what desire man has for peace. Especially among soldiers who are laying the foundations for the future with their personal sacrifice, and often with the ultimate sacrifice of life itself.

The lesson wars have given to the world is the harshest warning, and is the lesson that makes military chaplains men of peace who bring serenity to the hearts of men in war. They are the ministers, by grace of the state, of Jesus who brought peace to the world, and they bring the sign of that peace to men's consciences through the sacraments which they administer. And because of military chaplains who must fulfill a very delicate mission of peace and love under conditions that are frequently arduous and difficult, there is yet another reason to thank Providence and to be inspired to accomplish the tasks God assigns each of us with complete and fatherly trust.

The memories and experiences of military life call to mind the fond image of the military chaplain, who represents a new and very valuable aspect of the modern apostolate.

The chaplains of yesterday and today—in the various special ways in which they carry out the spiritual task assigned them—indeed represent a fresh and immense possibility for good which the Church will certainly foster. They meet the innumerable ranks of young souls, hearty and strong, who are exposed to serious spiritual dangers, and point out the way of the good to them.[1]

[1] Conversation, June 11, 1959.

To the Judiciary

Being a judge means being highly qualified, firm and sensitive; and having deep intellectual and moral resources that were developed in the fertile and energetic years of youth. These resources, moreover, must be constantly renewed by study and research.

A judge must interpret the law strictly, defend legal principles and promote legality itself, which is grounded on the Ten Commandments. The Commandments express and confirm natural law, which God has impressed on every soul. The judge must apply those tenets to the specific cases that emerge from the limitless variety of human life. At the same time, he must draw sanctions, in the image of God, who is "a just judge, strong and knowing" (Psalms 7, 11).

Doctrinally secure and practicing Catholics have a special responsibility in judiciary office, which We do not hesitate to call a true and high vocation. In their fidelity to the Law of God and of his Church, they find their consecration and their reward.[1]

[1] Speech, December 8, 1959.

To Students

You are preparing yourselves to fulfill the promises and hopes of these joyous years, and you will deserve their rewards. That is why We are gladdened and encouraged.

The spiritual and material well-being of society depends on the care with which individuals achieve interior perfection and on the discipline they can exert on their personal energies.

The individual wants to be good in order to satisfy the imperative demands of his soul. He develops his mind in school in order to fulfill the potentiality of his intelligence with sound and deep knowledge. From these efforts, the world will ultimately gain some benefit; this is true vitality.

You must have asked yourselves sometimes why are there so many things to study, why spend so many hours laboring over different ideas and subjects. But if you will consider that you are preparing for tomorrow, then you will see the reason for continuing your efforts today. You will be working in the future for the good of all of society.

The Pope, your parents and your teachers, we all take consolation from the ancient saying, "Blessed are the young, for you are strong" (cf. 1 John 2, 14).

Strength is the characteristic of the young. While for most of us the most important cardinal virtue is prudence, for the young it is—and ought to be—fortitude. Which virtue better corresponds to the life of youth, to its physical development, the coordination of the body, to the search and love of truth, justice and equity? How much strength it takes to learn self-discipline, respect for others, the real meaning of "Do unto others what you would have them do unto you" (cf. Matthew 7, 12; Luke 6, 31).

The young person wants to use his energies in the service of great ideals. He does not want to be told: Don't do this, or that. But he remembers Christ's words: "Do this and you shall live" (Luke 10, 28).

We are certain that you too are compelled by the Christian virtue of fortitude, and We trust you will observe it in the morality of will, the purity of body and in continual self-vigilance. The presence of young people here is a sign of good intentions, an expression of the virtue of constancy.

In your families and in school, in the religious, cultural and sport groups to which you belong, it is almost easy to conduct yourselves well, to employ fruitfully the help you get, to carry out your commitments. With a little application on your part, the predetermined structure of your lives channels, and at the same time stimulates, your bounding energies.

When you are adults, you will have to use all your faculties and your particular talents according to the choices you yourselves have made. You will be in difficulties if you are not constant. Everything in your life could become quite flat and meaningless: your piety reduced to mere external worship that does not touch the depths of your soul; your sense of charity subordinated to the needs of ambition; your sense of purity transformed into mere good manners or into a display of honor that is unfelt. Arrogance, superficiality, the lack of commitment could take over your lives.

And then your youth will have ended, because that is

where old age and decrepitude set in, at the point where ideals no longer enkindle the heart and engage the will.

Constancy, therefore, in carrying out a firm intention. It has been said that life is the fulfillment of a youthful dream. Each of you should have your own dream to fulfill: a dream of generosity, morality, idealization; the intention to do well, to construct, to act personally; faithfulness to a principle of conduct that is always pure, upright, uncompromising. For the good of your future, for the sake of your future family and for the society you will work in.

This is what We wanted to present to you as a plan for the future. We are assured that a great many young people will follow it, just as you here will, with ready and generous hearts.[1]

[1] Speech, May 19, 1960.

H. THE MASS MEDIA

The Press

Our ancestors surely had their own problems. Now we have ours, in the numerous violations of the truth that appear in so many and so recognizable ways in the press. If this wonderful medium is used and applied with integrity, it can be a powerful instrument for spreading the doctrine of Christ and revealing the importance of his life and the generosity of his grace. Unfortunately, these days, we are buried under the publications which have entirely different ends in view. We are almost led not to read papers, but we must, and for this reason, there are good papers in the service of the apostolate. Nonetheless, We must warn the faithful that the other side continues to put out their glittering tinsel, and not the truth of Christ and his Gospel; they are not Christians, but just the opposite.[1]

We do not want to linger on the evil produced by the immorality and maliciousness of so much of the press. And We are truly afflicted and anxious on thinking of the great damage being done to readers, especially the young, by the contents and the pictures carried by a certain segment of the press.

May the Lord not allow too many parents to become accomplices of their children's ruination. We know what danger there is in those daily papers or picture magazines which present a seductive mixture of serious and light material, at times even indecent things, with the pretext of presenting the news or just advertisements.

Precisely for the purpose of replacing this kind of publication in the Christian family, the Catholic press must become better organized and more efficient to counteract the seemingly innocuous and therefore more dangerous publications.

We have finally another kind of paper that seriously offends truth and charity by lying in order to stir up rancor. This segment of the press seems to have a single policy: to mislead the minds of simple folk; to alter the truth ever so slightly and misinterpret what the Church says and criticize what she does in order to lessen people's love for Christ; to combat Christ in order to combat God himself. And this often happens under the guise of advice that will hasten the solution of problems that afflict workers, the weak and the defenseless.[2]

In our time—We must say painfully but frankly—the press has not a few times helped in preparing a climate of contention, animosity, and open ruptures![3]

Whoever is duty-bound to evaluate the things of this world by the standard imposed by God's right and to safeguard the morality of a people, cannot help but recall Christ's terrible words: "Whoever causes one of these little ones who believe in me to sin, it would be better for him to have a great millstone round his neck and to be drowned in the depth of the sea. Woe to the world for temptations to sin, but woe to the man by whom the temptation comes" (Matthew 18, 6–7).

For this reason We make a special plea to parents and educators, to the government, to lawmakers and the judiciary, to management and businessmen; in making the following points, We trust in their good will and in their morality.

1. One must above all keep a clear conscience, inspired by the greatest integrity and not allowed to sleep or relax.

The claims of truth and objective moral norms grounded on eternal law precede and are superior to any other claim or demand. The freedom of the press must be framed and controlled in this respect by divine laws which are reflected in human laws, just as the freedom of individuals is modified by law. And just as it is not legitimate for a free citizen—by the simple fact that he is free—to offend or do violence to the freedom, the goods, or the life of his neighbor, so too it is not right for the press—by claiming it must be free—continuously and systematically to make attempts on the religious and moral well-being of humanity.

A clear conscience goes hand in hand with an exact understanding of our individual roles. So publications are not merely informative, but formative as well; that is, of vital educational value. No one can deny that the press is not only a means for expressing public opinion, but also a means for shaping it and educating it, and thus at times for warping it.

Education is no more or less than respect for man's values as he slowly increases his awareness; his progress, however, can be easily blocked if it is not adequately protected from his sinful tendencies. The nature of his education, according to the ancient but still valid method of Socrates, is simply to induce the spirit to know itself, so that it will come to the light, to life, to perfection. Pouring poison into the mind, encouraging bad tendencies, helping to obfuscate, oppress and lower the mind—this is not education.

2. This clear conscience of which We have spoken assumes its own limitations and knows how to keep the freedom of the press within the bounds of respect, order and legality. This means limiting the rather morbid craving for details, for sensationalism and the illicit; curbing the greed for profits, curbing irresponsibility and levity which corrupt the innocence of children and adolescents, with the excuse they would be corrupted anyway.

It is best to be explicit about such things, without mincing words over human respect when it means that silence would be connivance. It is not the love of truth or culture or knowledge that motivates some writers, but the impulse of certain passions, the greedy desire for notoriety and profit, that win out over the insistent appeals of the conscience.

Is it possible that every detail, the minutest description, things that are fit only for the police and court records, must be thrown up to leering curiosity? Is it right that every crime must be described fully, when in fact a merciful curtain should be drawn across it? These extended descriptions can only be a school for crime and an incentive to vice.

This kind of publicity, especially in certain areas, has assumed alarming proportions, and cannot be justified except as an attempt to arouse the senses and titillate, without any thought to the damage that is being done to the soul.

If the authorities and responsible parties would take a close look at this painful situation, they would be forced to a logical conclusion: that the freedom of the press must have certain necessary limitations put on it. These limitations must be determined carefully, on the basis of law, so that in an area as sensitive and important to the future of every nation, the press is not left, dangling, to its own devices and so-called self-control, or worse, to the whims of bad faith and licentiousness.

3. Lastly, *clear policies* and a *positive program* are needed. We are naturally inclined not to speak of many situations of social life in harsh terms, when We are still hopeful that they can change for the best. But in this case We feel the necessity to speak directly, and to confide our anxiety to Our sons and brothers, not only in the faith, but also in their agreement on the need to comment on writers who do not deserve the name.

Catholics are urged to take a firm position, and not to be silenced by those who are too 'scrupulous', and not to hesitate in criticizing certain publications. Therefore, this means not buying, not praising, not recommending, and indeed not even mentioning them. Catholics should take advantage of every means they can to "clean house" in this area. Although We call on Catholics primarily, Our appeal also goes to all those who conscientiously desire to be of service to society. This is one area in which the sin of omission is felt most deeply.

As far as a positive program to follow is concerned, We must first of all draw attention to the fact that although there has been significant legislation protecting individual rights, not much has been done with regard to the press. And yet, here too we are dealing with personal freedom. As Our Predecessor, Pius XII, said in 1947, "The protection of this liberty is the purpose of every legal system worthy of the name. . . . But if the press is allowed to undermine the religious and moral foundations of the nation, then license would be legalized. To understand and acknowledge this does not require a Christian point of view; we need only use our reason and a sound sense of morality and law, freed from any prejudice."

The responsibility we all feel will urge men of learning—along with everyone else of good will and clear mind—to act soon and act well, to be concerned and involved in the apostolate.

The love of truth, firm convictions and sincere interest in

man's fate will be a spur to anyone who cares about the Church's honor and the salvation of society. May your resolution be made firm by the Apostle's words: "And let us not grow weary in well-doing, for in due season we shall reap, if we do not lose heart. So then, as we have opportunity, let us do good to all men, and especially to those who are of the household of faith" (Galatians 6, 9–10).[4]

[1] Speech, October 15, 1959. [2] Speech, May 4, 1959.
[3] Radio broadcast, Christmas 1961.
[4] Speech, December 8, 1959.

Periodicals

Periodicals have rather different characteristics and purposes, because there are those for specialists in various fields and others for the general public. But they all have the sacred duty not to do harm to their readers, no matter who they are, not to betray or vulgarize them, because they are not simply an anonymous mass without faces, but are God's children, our brothers in Christ. They are the untutored young, the mothers and fathers of families anxious for the right advice, a fundamentally good and sound reading public. One cannot imagine a publisher, an editor or a writer in the field of periodicals who does not feel the responsibility, above all, of carrying out his job as a noble profession, as a high calling, by putting aside less worthwhile interests. Because if there should appear in your magazine so much as one article or photograph that violates the conscience, then We must say that no matter what the other merits, or what success these magazines enjoy, they are bad because they are built on dangerous compromises.

Your sense of responsibility in these matters is based on your natural and Christian virtues, which We should like to summarize in one word—honesty. Unflinching honesty, in life as well as in your profession. This honesty is expressed primarily by a respect for God's laws and for other legislation, including the civil, which conform to divine law and to its presence in the conscience of individuals who are enlightened by reason and by faith. In short, this honesty involves a certain consistency, sincerity, a sense of proper limits, humility, thoughtfulness, prudence. It enables us to seek the good and avoid evil, without being sidetracked by opportunism, as the classic writers themselves said, "If we do not allow ourselves to be moved by good and by consideration for what is honest, but by personal interest and profit, then we can say of ourselves that we are shrewd, but not good" (Cicero, *De Legibus*, I, 14, 41).

The love of *truth* We commend to you as the most specific quality of your profession. Let Us repeat what St. Paul wrote to the Ephesians: ". . . so that we may no longer be children, tossed to and fro and carried about with every wind of doctrine, by the cunning of man, by their craftiness, in deceitful wiles. Rather, speaking the truth in love, we are to grow up in every way into him who is the head, into Christ." Speaking the truth means having it in the mind and on the tongue—that is, speaking and writing—in doctrinal certainty, and in an honorable and edifying life.[1]

[1] Speech, November 29, 1959.

The Catholic Newspaper

1. What characterizes and justifies a Catholic newspaper is first of all its positive outlook. As in all of man's undertakings, that the policy should not be evaluated for what it does not

do, or ought not to do—which would be a limitation—but for what it accomplishes, with praiseworthy effort and clear notions about its purposes. Now, the Catholic press exists primarily to present a point of view and to delineate it. In other words, an active, intelligent, wide-awake survey of the numberless problems posed by today's living, and an interpretation based on the criteria of eternal truth as it is reflected in time. A survey, furthermore, that allows nothing to escape its attention so that the paper can inform the reader and help him, through an enlightened conscience, to deal with the questions and confusion arising in today's world. An active role, therefore, orientating, specifying, clarifying everything in the light of revealed truth.

But the press also bears witness; it will take a stand without compromise or personal motivation, loyally and patiently. The Catholic journalist does not follow the fashions of public opinion, much less bend them to his will, but feels it his duty to serve truth, recalling Christ's words: "Let your light so shine before men, that they may see your good works and give glory to your Father who is in heaven" (Matthew 5, 14–16).

2. The dignity of its task is evident in its presentation as well, in the way the paper attracts and vanquishes with a gentle grace. We refer to the *style* that is appropriate to a Catholic newspaper and that gives it an unmistakable character: a style that is always transparent, even when engaged in polemics, a style that is characterized by truth, by charity, by respect for those in error, by a moderate, gentlemanly vocabulary.

Unfortunately, a presentation and style of writing are fast taking hold, even in children's publications, We must say with sorrow, that ignore the most elementary demands of taste, reserve, modesty by using terminology and photographic layouts that are repugnant to the conscience. In the face of this approach, which frequently determines the success of a paper or magazine, the Catholic journalist might for a moment be carried away by the current and give a less severe picture of reality or pay more attention to the less edifying facts of the day than they merit.

The "sons of this world" (Luke 16, 8) can understand, and so continue to respond with your good sense, your faith and your courage. Educate your readers to appreciate what is true, good and beautiful; learn to draw the materials of your columns from the inexhaustible sources of truth, beauty and goodness, that spring from the presentation of the various epochs of history, from the world of art and music, from the triumphs of science, from astronomy, from the travels of explorers and missionaries. Wide horizons can be opened to the educated family without having to weigh down the pages with pedantry of publications that are intended for leisure reading.

Let it not be said that the work of the Catholic journalist is more difficult because it is "bound up" with moral standards and demands; demonstrate how it can be carried out with unbiased information and open viewpoints, because as the Apostle tells us, "everything is yours, but you are of Christ and Christ is of God" (1 Corinthians 3, 22–23).

3. Lastly, the newspaper which expresses and defends Christian doctrine must live on the enthusiasm of Catholics. That is the elementary truth, but in practice not understood by many. We take the occasion of this audience to express a hope close to Our heart. We trust that many of the clergy and the laity, especially those who have the proper sense of what being a Christian means, will understand that one of the sacred duties of a Christian is religious and social instruction. It is true that this instruction, according to the Council of Trent, the Synods and recently the reminders of the Pontiffs, must be given by the pastoral teaching of the bishops and by the catechism taught by the parish priests. But in practice, the live word reaches few people, in some cases because of

working hours or other duties, or because of the moving around that is so frequent nowadays. Very well then, one of the most effective ways to serve the word of God, to reach into the home, to achieve understanding, is precisely the Catholic press.

If this places considerable responsibility on Catholics to support and distribute the press, your own burden is no less, and in fact becomes more vital. Render good service to God's word, let it ring out in all its beauty and novelty without changing or damping it. Let it sound alive and interesting. What an honor, what credit before God and man![1]

[1] Speech, October 18, 1959.

Radio and Television

Thirty years ago, at 4:30 P.M. on February 12, 1931, the voice of the Holy Father Pius XI went out for the first time from these microphones. Preceded by an address by Guglielmo Marconi, who had assisted personally in building the Vatican Radio, the Pope spoke to the world.

Radio broadcasts by the popes were initiated at that time. For the first time in history, the Pope's voice could be heard in several parts of the world simultaneously, to the untold consolation of Catholics everywhere, including those who had formerly been isolated.

After thirty years of both sad and happy events, it is a source of great joy and emotion to re-echo the same words. That inaugural broadcast indeed offered a powerful instrument to this Apostolic See, and opened new paths for the spreading of truth and charity throughout the world.

That is how it had to be, and is, in fact. Vatican Radio was established with far-sighted wisdom, and is at the service of the Pope, so that he may transmit his thoughts quickly and effectively. It is, besides, an eloquent proof of the Holy See's independence and an instrument for making pontifical teachings known.

Right from the beginning, this product of modern technology has furthered the cause of unity among peoples, in the universal sense of brotherhood. Since that moment, the voice coming from the very center of Catholicism, passing over national borders, has awakened a greater sense of brotherhood in the peoples who are believers in the bond of common faith and of charity that is exemplarily lived, and kindled a flame in the hearts of the oppressed. And indeed, while the Second World War raged, the voice of Vatican Radio kept hope alive, without regard for the interests of either side, and encouraged peace, unity, love. It kept up ties among people by broadcasting messages from prisoners, refugees, the exiled, and from grieving mothers and wives, for whom Vatican Radio became a source of support amid the dark uncertainties and anxieties.

Now there is another valuable aid along with radio—television. Television provides a direct and prompt vehicle for transmitting memorable events and sacred functions celebrated with great decorum. Vatican Radio has been pleased by the possibilities of this new communications medium.

We have recalled these various moments in the history of the Vatican Radio for reasons that transcend technical data and events. We are very pleased to be able to speak, on the occasion of this anniversary, to men of good will, on three themes the occasion suggests.

Radio that is here put at the service of the Church sends out an appeal for the *truth*, which alone can save mankind from the danger of surrendering to the claims of the senses, and restore man to his dignity as the son of God. This Radio is equipped to tell the truth and to exist for it.

This Radio appeals for *charity*, for the overcoming—in mutual respect—of the barriers of nationality, race, social distinctions, and for a turning to the great virtue of unity, mutual collaboration, and constructive understanding.

We acclaim the values of science when it is not used for destructive purposes, the violent upsetting of the natural order and the threatening of man's security, but rather is used for the conquest of the mysterious forces God has concealed in creation that they might be of service to man and contribute to his moral betterment and lasting progress.[1]

Radio, movies and television, which can be enjoyed right in the home. These media of communication can offer powerful appeals for the good, and for the Christian way of life. Unfortunately, especially among young people, they serve to promote immorality, corruption, deceit and vice.

In order to neutralize the bad influences that these media are exerting increasingly, it is necessary to arm ourselves with truth and honesty. We must set up a decent and truthful press to combat a lying and indecent one. We must have programs and films defending truth and morality to oppose those that have become instruments of error and corruption. In this way, these new inventions, which can become the implements of evil, will become, rather, the implements of good and the means for clean entertainment; the cure will flow from the same source from which frequently flows the poison.[2]

[1] Speech, February 17, 1961.

[2] Encyclical, *Ad Petri Cathedram*, June 29, 1959.

The Movies

Catholics and films

In past years, one frequently heard said that it is the job of Catholics to be first. For various activities, this has had a certain merit: in more than one instance and in more than one country they have succeeded, but, unfortunately, not without exceptions. Certainly, in these demonstrations of the film art, in this new way of presenting things (which in substance is nothing but an effort to express the ideals of life and its reality), Catholics have arrived, and obviously not last. In fact, they have done rather well. We should congratulate ourselves for having arrived rather than complain about not having gotten into this field right away.

One can well understand how Providence has been guiding right from the start, helping overcome difficulties that various obstacles presented and that even the experience of others created. Providence helped overcome that definite sense of fear that kept Catholics away from the modern means of entertainment and distraction, the fear of an art form that might cause us to lose sight of essential principles.

We are at a good point therefore. The experience we have acquired allows us to believe we are not going to stop on the way but that we will proceed resolutely—even if with discretion and unhurriedness, as we should—and not ignore anything that will provide the least gleam of light we might use to enlighten souls and urge them to the highest intentions.

Whenever we hear someone speak about "the Church and the movies," we think naturally that the term implies two very different things. On the one hand something very old but always timely, on the other, something very modern. Now we must not forget that at times things go well when they are put together, but at others things that go well together are those which know enough to separate: that is to say, they do not encourage confusion. It is only logical that the coupling would legitimately make one think of the damaging results of making the film a part of the church, or even of the danger that movies could practically nullify, or indeed nullify, the spiritual good achieved by the church, if we make the movies out to be something which has not been purified, or distilled as a manifestation of the truth. This is the reason why it is necessary to associate good judgment with enthusiasm; that is, to act so as not to let anyone get confused or to believe that there could be among us the least compromise in our teaching or in our mission. Without forgetting that often one can become the object of malicious barbs which tend to weaken the will to do what is right, to weaken the spirit of a good apostolate.

As a consequence: before anything else keep always in mind the respect for truth and goodness, and for that purpose to subordinate what we mean by useful and delightful. Follow the right path always. As for the criticisms, always be ready to answer them; we must do what we can and try to be worthy of the trust placed in us.

We must remember, true, that we are on earth, but our eyes are turned upward and our spirits intent on the law of God.

What is to the point is to continue, is to work. Shortcomings and insufficiencies will interrupt, but what is most pressing is to know how to eliminate them and move ahead, since this is our intention, to which the grace God gave us tends. That is what Christ wants, above all and everywhere: truth, goodness, beauty, the center of our souls and our lives.

To know how to guide today's youth, the present generation, in this way means to contribute to quickening and renewing in them the old and perennial splendors of Christ Jesus.[1]

[1] Speech, October 27, 1959.

I. THE COMMUNITY OF NATIONS

The World Community and the United Nations

Interdependence among nations

Recent progress in science and technology profoundly affects human beings, compelling them to work with each other and orienting them toward a unified coexistence of world-wide scope. The circulation of ideas, of men and goods, has, in fact, noticeably increased. And so have the relations between individuals, families and the social bodies of various nations, just as among the governments of those nations. Interdependence among national economies is growing, as they mesh together increasingly to the point where they are becoming a single world economy. The social progress, the order, security and peace within each nation is in vital correspondence with the social progress, the order, the security and the peace of the rest of the world.

No country today can afford to pursue its own interests and to develop apart from the others, since the degree of its prosperity and its development reflects, and is a component of, the degree of prosperity and development of all the other countries.

The inadequacy of the present organization of government with respect to the universal commonweal

The unity of the human family has existed in every age because it is composed of human beings who are all equal by virtue of their natural dignity. As a result, there will always exist the objective need to enact in sufficient measure the *universal* general welfare; that is, the common good of the entire human family.

In the past it was believed with good reason that the governments of the different countries could implement the general welfare, either through the normal diplomatic channels, or by means of top-level meetings, employing legal instruments such as, say, conventions and treaties. These instruments are based on natural law, and determined by the law of peoples and international law.

Following the profound transformations that have taken place in the relations among people, the general welfare, on the one hand, raises extremely urgent, complicated, serious problems, expecially in the area of security and world peace. On the other hand the governments of these various countries, equal, legally, to each other, can no longer deal with and resolve the range of problems adequately, no matter how many meetings are called and no matter how much ingenuity they expend in finding new diplomatic instruments. The inadequacy is not due so much to a lack of good will or initiative as to reasons of deficiency in their structure.

We can assert, therefore, that on historical grounds the actual organization and its exercising of the principle of authority (when operating internationally) no longer corresponds to the objective needs of the universal commonweal.

Relationship between the common good and public authority in historical context

There is an intrinsic relationship between the historical context of the public good on the one hand, and the form and operation of public power on the other. That is to say, just as moral order demands public authority in the community in order to implement the public good, it also demands, as a consequence, that the authority be efficient. This postulates that the organs in which public authority is embodied, and through which it operates, must be organized in such a way that they can readily respond to the needs of changing situations.

The universal common good poses problems of world dimension that cannot adequately be confronted and resolved except by governments having the latitude, the organization and the means of the same dimension; that is, governments which are capable of acting efficiently on a world scale. The moral order itself demands, therefore, that such authority be established.

Governments instituted by common agreement and not imposed by force

A public power having authority on a world scale, and equipped to pursue the objectives of the universal common good, must be established by mutual agreement and not imposed by force. The reason is that such a power must be able to operate efficiently, but at the same time its actions must be informed by sincere and effective impartiality; that is, it must be action directed toward satisfying the objective demands of the universal good. There would certainly be fear lest a supernational or world power imposed by force by the bigger countries be or become an instrument of selfish interests, and even if this were not so, it is highly improbable that the power would be immune to suspicions of partiality in any of its acts, and the suspicions would compromise its effectiveness.

Even when nations are markedly different in the degree of their respective economic development and military power, they are nonetheless very sensitive about their juridical equality and their moral dignity. For this reason, they do not readily obey an authority imposed by force, or one in whose creation they did not participate and to which they themselves did not freely and knowingly choose to submit.

The universal welfare and the rights of the individual
Just as the common good of each country, so too the universal common good cannot be determined without regard for the human person. The government of the world community must, therefore, consider as its fundamental objective the recognition, the respect, the care and the promotion of the rights of the individual. By direct action when the case calls for it, or by creating a community on a world scale in which the governments of each country can more easily carry out its specific functions.

The principle of subsidiarity
Just as within all groups of human beings a principle of subsidiarity must hold, in relations between individuals, families, intermediate bodies and the government, so too it must hold in a government of world scope. This means that the government of the world community must confront and resolve economic, political, social and cultural problems which affect the universal common good, problems, however, which are so large, complex and urgent that the governments of single nations would not be able to deal with them effectively.

The government of the world community would not propose to limit the sphere of action of individual governments, much less replace them. Its purpose would be, rather, to contribute to the creation of a situation in which individual governments, their respective citizens and intermediate bodies, can carry out their tasks, fulfill their duties, and exercise their rights with greater security.

Signs of the times
The United Nations was founded, as we know, on June 26, 1945. Then there followed several intergovernmental agencies with large responsibilities with regard to the world's economic, social, cultural, educational and health problems. The United Nations aims to maintain and consolidate peace among

peoples and to develop friendly relations among them that are based on principles of equality, mutual respect and cooperation in all areas of co-existence.

One of the most important acts of the United Nations is the Universal Declaration of Human Rights, approved in the General Assembly on December 10, 1948. In the preamble to the Declaration one of the ideals put forth is that all nations and all peoples should pursue the recognition and respect for those rights and their related freedoms.

On some particular points of the Declaration there have been objections and reservations. But there is no doubt that the document marks a step forward on the way toward a legal and political organization of the world community. In it, in fact, personal dignity is recognized for all human beings, and consequently their fundamental right is the freedom to inquire after truth and to implement moral good and justice. They have besides the right to a dignified existence, as well as other enumerated rights.

We trust that the United Nations will always better its ability—in its structure and methods—to meet the vastness and import of its tasks. We trust that one day individual human beings can find in the U.N. an effective guardian of the rights which are immediate to their personal dignity, thus being universal rights, unviolable and inalienable. And more so as individuals, who are participating more actively in the public life of their own countries, are showing signs of growing interest in the affairs of the rest of the world and are becoming more aware of being full members of a world community.[1]

[1] Encyclical, *Pacem in Terris*, April 11, 1963.

International Solidarity

Perhaps the most pressing problem of our day concerns the relationship between economically developed countries and those still in the process of development. The former enjoy a high standard of living while the latter suffer serious want.

The ties that bind all human beings, and make of them members of the same family, compel the political communities which enjoy ample means of subsistence not to ignore those countries whose inhabitants are burdened by poverty, hunger and misery, who do not have even basic personal rights. Given the interdependence among nations in the modern age, it is clear that a lasting peace can never be achieved while there exist such marked imbalances among their economic and social conditions.

In Our role as universal father, We feel compelled to repeat here what We have so emphatically said before: "We all share responsibility for the peoples of the world who are undernourished . . . [Therefore] it is necessary to arouse the conscience of everyone, especially the more fortunate."

Obviously, the duty, which the Church has always affirmed, of helping the needy falls especially on Catholics, since they are members of the Mystical Body of Christ. "In this we have come to know the love of God," said John the Apostle, "that he laid down his life for us; and we likewise ought to lay down our life for our brethren. He who has the goods of this world and sees his brother in need and closes his heart to him, how does the love of God abide in him?"

Therefore, We are very pleased to note that highly productive nations are lending aid to developing nations so that they may improve their situation more quickly.

There are countries which produce consumer goods and farm products in excess of their needs, while there are other nations in which large segments of the population suffer want and hunger. Justice and humanity demand that these richer countries come to the aid of those in need. To destroy or to waste goods that are necessary for survival is to violate every standard of justice or humanity.

We are quite aware that to produce surpluses, especially of farm products, can do economic harm to certain classes. But that is not a reason for failing to carry out our duty to help the starving and the poor in cases of emergency. If anything, such a situation demands that the economic harm be contained as much as possible, and its repercussions be borne by all the people on a fair basis.

Emergency help, of course, is not sufficient to eliminate or even reduce the problems that cause hunger and misery in so many nations. The problems can be located primarily in their technological and economic backwardness, which means that they cannot be solved or lessened except by full-fledged cooperation, with the purpose of training the citizens of those countries in professional, technical and scientific skills which will enable them to confront their own problems. This cooperation also entails the lending of capital which is necessary to begin and accelerate modern economic development.

We know that in these last few years a sense of responsibility toward these less fortunate nations has increased, and greater help is being given for their economic development and social advancement.

World agencies, individual nations, foundations and private companies are offering increasing amounts of technical cooperation in all economic areas. Help is being given to as many young people as possible so that they may study in the universities of more developed countries, thus acquiring a knowledge of the arts and sciences compatible with the needs of our time. Moreover, international banks, single nations, and private sources are making money available to these countries so that they increase their productive capacities. We are glad to take this occasion to express Our sincere appreciation for such generous help.

But We are bound to point out that the technical, scientific and economic cooperation which the developed nations have so far provided to the underdeveloped nations must be increased. We hope that in the future the richer countries will make even greater efforts.

And while on this subject, We would like to make some observations.

Wisdom demands that the countries which are just at the beginning of their economic development keep in mind the example of the countries which have already attained full development.

Reason and need require that more goods be produced, and more efficiently. But it is likewise necessary and just that the wealth so produced be distributed equitably among all the people of a political community. Therefore, economic development must be made to keep pace with social advancement. In order to achieve this, development must take place gradually and coordinately in all the sectors of the economy: agriculture, industry, and the services.

Developing countries usually have an unmistakable nature of their own—their natural resources and geography, their traditions frequently rich in human values, and the characteristics of the people themselves.

In providing help, therefore, the richer nations should recognize and respect that special character, and refrain from exerting too much influence on the countries they are helping.

The more powerful nations must resist the temptation to exploit their technical and economic assistance in order to influence the political situation of the countries in need of help, and thereby gain a foothold.

Whenever this happens, it must be labeled for what it is, a new form of colonialism.

So it is a matter of necessity and justice that any technical and financial aid be provided in the strictest political disinterestedness, so that the developing nations may be able to realize their own economic and social growth.[1]

[1] Encyclical, *Mater et Magistra*, May 15, 1961.

Africa

Africa is profoundly religious, a land blessed by God. Was that the reason why she had the privilege of offering a haven to the Holy Family when they fled from Herod? Soon after the Pentecost, Africa welcomed Christianity, and there also many martyrs gave their lives for Christ, among whom shines the name of St. Cyprian. Flourishing communities rose by the shores of the Mediterranean; the desert became the haven for hermits who fought the devil by fasting and prayer, great men such as St. Anthony; at Hippo, St. Augustine led the church entrusted to him with great wisdom. Following that, Providence allowed the light of Christianity to dim for a time, in several places in Africa. But the love of Jesus Christ soon sent many sons of the Church to those regions which had forgotten our Lord's name, or which had never known it. The missionaries did not spare any pains to bring the gift of the Catholic faith to their brothers; leaving their countries and loved ones behind, facing hunger and thirst and disease, they did not give in. They would have been glad to give their blood for the land they had come to love. And thus the blood of these martyrs, as in the early days of Christianity, nourished new shoots of faith: *Sanguis martyrum, semen christianorum!*

The Church welcomes the Christians of Africa, for she is

the world's common home. As St. Paul reminded the Galatians "you are all sons of God in Christ Jesus, through faith. For as many of you as were baptized into Christ have put on Christ. There is neither Jew nor Greek, there is neither slave nor free, there is neither male nor female, for you are all one in Christ Jesus" (Galatians 3, 26–28).

The Catholic Church has the mission of demonstrating this profound unity of mankind. The responsibility falls to the college of bishops, who have succeeded the Apostles, and primarily to Peter and his successors, who have shown through the ages their concern for Africa. There is no need to repeat what was said in the recent Encyclical Letter, *Fidei Donum*, in which Our Predecessor, Pius XII, drew the attention of the faithful to Africa, "at the moment when it is opening up to modern life and going through the most difficult years of its centuries-old history" (*Fidei Donum*, AAS, XLIX, p. 227). We should only like to say again, as We did recently on the occasion of Togo's independence, how great Our satisfaction is on seeing the progressive independence and the attainment of sovereignty of African nations. The Church rejoices in this, and is confident of the desire of these young nations to take their place among the community of nations, as they deserve.

But the problems they face are not resolved by autonomy alone. Each state must be concerned with the sound development of its resources, by taking account of its real possibilities and above all by respecting the true spiritual values that lie in the soul of a people. The Catholic Church received the capacity from her Founder to meet—within moral and religious bounds, and leaving full responsibility for their acts to the civil authorities—man's serious problems successfully. She puts at their disposal, in a disinterested manner and according to their needs, the principles of action they need for the development of the individual, the family, the professions, society and international ties. These principles are based on a respect for personal dignity, as well as on the demands of the common good. The Church hails the efforts being made to win equality for women, so that they may realize themselves on their own. By the same token, the Church acknowledges the priority of the common good in those countries where differences have led even to violence over the issues of legitimate private interests. The people of these countries must be ready to give up their demands in order to benefit the majority of their fellow citizens, just as many nations must give up geographical or economic claims for the good of the world community of nations.

This brings Us to the important point: the Church feels at home in Africa, just as she does everywhere in the world.

The situation of the Church in Africa now is just a beginning. These parishes will still need the help of the older Christian nations. After the problem of preparing seminarians for the priesthood has been met in some way, the work of convincing the laity of their role in the Church and in society begins, so that laymen will be able to acquit themselves with success. They need Sunday schools for religious instruction, schools for members of Catholic Action and union members, centers for health and social workers, and meeting places where Christian culture can be disseminated. We are aware of all the efforts that are being made already, and of the good will that is being expended to answer the appeal made by Pope Pius in *Fidei Donum.* We want to congratulate and encourage all those who are participating in this work, which so often requires non-Africans.

Thus Pentecost is felt in Africa once again.

With this faith in Africa's future, We pray the Holy Virgin and all the saints of Africa will intercede to obtain heavenly favors for the poor, the humble, and for all those who suffer from sickness and hunger, and for those who must still await their basic rights. We shall never forget the prelates and priests, the nuns and brothers, who have devoted themselves to contemplation or action, and the militant Catholics—all of whom do so much to contribute to the spreading of God's word. We pray God as well for the intention of the civil authorities, who are now so burdened in this critical moment, and who need his strength, his wisdom and his justice. We have you all in Our heart, and We send you Our affectionate Apostolic Benediction.[1]

[1] Radio broadcast, June 5, 1960.

Negro Culture

The Church appreciates and encourages the men who study various cultures in order to identify their achievements, to find historical connections, to single out all the cross-influences, and in some measure to benefit their own countries with their discoveries.

Whenever genuine artistic and scholarly values contribute to enriching the human family, the Church is ready to encourage them as a labor of the spirit. She does not identify herself with any single culture, not even with the Western tradition in which her history is so involved. Because her proper mission is of another order—the spiritual salvation of mankind. But the Church, which by the presence of the Holy Ghost is always fresh and young, is prompt to recognize and welcome whatever work is being done to honor human intelligence and feeling on other shores of the world besides those of the Mediterranean, which was the cradle of Christianity.

We follow your efforts to find a common cultural community in Africa with great interest, hoping, of course, that you are proceeding on just principles.

In this matter, rely on the ancient wisdom of the Church.

Her clear-eyed vision can make out at once the components of new and old artistic and literary expressions that must be purified in order to be reconciled with the dignity of man and his natural rights and duties. Her universality, and her concern for the human resources of all peoples, enable the Church to render great service in the cause of world peace. In aiding the qualified people who turn to her to develop the cultural possibilities of their country or their race, the Church asks them to work together in a spirit of collaboration and empathy with the other forces of their own culture. Is not this the only way the triumphs of the spirit will increase, and the spiritual ties of the human community be secured?[1]

[1] Speech, April 1, 1959.

On the Jews

The Pope remembers well how much he was able to accomplish alone in a circumstance that threatened catastrophe. The commander of a ship laden with thousands of children ran the risk of having to consign the youngsters to an enemy power. But the ship was rerouted and headed toward a port where they would be safe, through the personal intervention and on the word of the Apostolic Delegate.

In gratitude to the Representative of the Holy See for his gesture, the chief Rabbi of Jerusalem traveled to Istanbul to pay honor to the Delegate. The Delegate quickly repaid the visit. In their talks—as happens when there is a sincere meeting of human hearts—there emerged a note of great consolation: the constantly possible triumph of charity which shows itself to be the irrepressible law of life and human brotherhood.

The Chief Rabbi wanted to add a token of his gratitude to

his thanks—His Holiness recalls it vividly—the gift of a book, the ancient *Judaic Antiquities* of Flavius Josephus, which the Holy Father has long kept because it expressed so much sincerity.

His Holiness would like to add another consideration. More than once, he has recalled a moving incident from Holy Scripture: the meeting of Joseph and his brothers when Joseph had become an important personage in the government of Egypt. At first Joseph used some innocent guile to conceal his identity from them, but then he could not contain the feeling in his heart any longer and burst forth saying, *I am Joseph, your brother*, and turned to hide his tears.

It is a touching passage from the Old Testament. To tell the truth there is a large difference between those who admit only the Old Testament and those who believe in the New, as law and supreme guide. But this distinction does not eliminate the brotherhood which stems from the same source, because we are all children of the same Heavenly Father. Among us all there must always be charity.

"Lift up the light of thy countenance upon us, O Lord" (Psalms 4, 7). Such shining truth serves to make us understand the mutual help, the plain solidarity of mankind. It will lead us toward the solution of many problems by uniting men in this basic truth: we come from the Father and we must return to him.[1]

[1] Speech, October 17, 1960.

International Relations

Subjects of rights and duties

We reaffirm what our predecessors always maintained: political communities are subjects of rights and duties in their mutual relations, which ought to be governed by truth, justice, real solidarity and freedom. The same moral law which obtains in the relations between individuals also obtains in the relations among political communities.

This is not difficult to understand when one considers that while the persons who represent their respective countries do so in the name and in the interests of that country, they cannot put aside their own dignity. They cannot, therefore, violate the law of their own nature which is moral law.

It would be absurd even to think that men can renounce their humanity because they have been appointed to the government. They have been chosen for such important responsibility precisely because they are considered to be richly endowed in human qualities and among the best in the body politic.

Furthermore, authority in human society is a demand of the moral order; therefore, it cannot be used against moral order, or if it is, it ceases to be the authority. For God warns us: *Hear, therefore, kings, and understand; learn, you magistrates of the earth's expanse! Hearken, you who rule the multitude and lord it over throngs of peoples! Because authority was given you by the Lord and sovereignty by the Most High, who shall probe your works and scrutinize your counsels?* (Wisdom 6, 2–4).

Finally, one must remember that in regulating the relations among states, authority should be exercised for the realization of the common good, which provides its reason for being. A fundamental element of the common good, however, is the recognition of and respect for the moral order.

Truth

Relations among political communities must be governed by truth. Truth requires first of all that racism be eliminated from those relations; and let it be here affirmed that all political communities are equal by virtue of their natural dignity. For this reason, each of them has the right of existence, of self-development, the right to the proper means for realizing their development and to be the primary agent to do so. And each has the right to a good reputation and the honors associated with it.

There are very often marked differences among human beings in their knowledge, their virtues, their originality and their ownership of worldly goods. But such differences cannot ever justify the attempt to impose one's superiority on others. If anything, they constitute the source of greater responsibility that each and every person has in the job of mutual improvement.

So too political communities can differ from one another in their cultural attainments, their degree of civilization, or their economic development, but again this cannot ever justify some of them unjustly dominating others. Rather, it ought to provide them a reason for being more committed to the task of common betterment.

It is not true that some human beings are superior and others inferior by nature; all human beings are equal in their natural dignity. Consequently there are not some political communities superior by nature and others inferior by nature; all political communities are equal by natural dignity, they being the bodies of which human beings are the members. And here let us not forget that various peoples for good reason are very sensitive about dignity and honor.

Furthermore, truth demands that the many means of communication made possible by modern progress—means by which peoples come to understand one another—be employed with calm objectivity. This does not mean that states may not use them to bring our the positive aspects of their way of life. But any propaganda that falls short of the truth slurs unjustly the name of this or that nation must be rejected.

Justice

Relations among political communities should be governed

by justice, which means that besides recognizing their mutual rights, states must fulfill their respective duties.

Political communities have the right to exist, to develop themselves, to use the proper means, and to have the primary responsibility for doing so, and also they have the right to a good name and the honors due to it. And so at the same time the political communities themselves have also the duty to respect each of those rights and to avoid any action which might violate them. Just as in the relations between individuals it is wrong to pursue one's own interests at the expense of others, so too in the relations among states it is not right for some to develop themselves by exploiting or oppressing other states.

Conflicts of interest may and certainly do arise between states, but these conflicts cannot be overcome or controversies settled by recourse to force, fraud or trickery. Solutions must be found through mutual understanding, objective evaluations and fair considerations, as human beings ought to find them.

The treatment of minorities

Since the nineteenth century an historical trend has emerged, that political communities become nations. But for a number of reasons, it is not always possible that geographical borders can encompass ethnical ones, and so arises the problem of minorities in all its complexities.

It must be clearly stated that any action directed at limiting or smothering the growth and life of these minorities is a serious violation of justice. The injustice is graver still if there is any attempt to bring about their extinction.

The demands of justice can be met, on the other hand, by governments which are willing to promote the human development of minorities by legislating in favor of their language, their culture, their customs, their talents and their economic status.

Here it is to be noted that the members of minority groups

—as a reaction to their present condition or because of their history—are sometimes led to emphasize their ethnic elements to the point where they place them above human values, as if what is proper for humanity were secondary to what is proper for a nation. Reason, however, would indicate that they should appreciate the positive aspects of their condition which allows them to benefit from the gradual and continual assimilation of values that come from other traditions and civilizations. But this exchange can take place only if they act as a bridge to facilitate it to allow life's diverse expressions to travel freely, instead of acting as pockets of resistance which can cause considerable damage and hold up progress and growth.

Active solidarity

Relations among the political communities must be governed in truth and according to justice, but those relations must also be enlivened by an active sense of solidarity, through a thousand ways of cooperating, economically, socially, culturally, in health and sports, all the ways made possible and fruitful in the modern epoch. And it is relevant to bear in mind that the purpose of government is not to limit and close off human beings in the confines of their respective countries. The purpose of governments is to realize the common good of their nations, which must be conceived and acted upon as a component part of the common good of the whole human family.

This obligates each state to pursue its own interests without endangering those of other states, but also to join their efforts with those of other states whenever it is possible to attain an objective that would otherwise be unattainable. In such common efforts, however, care must be taken to insure that what is beneficial to one group of political communities is not injurious to others, indeed that the others can benefit as well.

The universal common good further demands that political communities encourage exchanges in every field of interest between the citizens and their intermediate social bodies.

There exists on earth a notable number of ethnic groups that are more or less markedly differentiated from each other. But the elements which characterize an ethnic group should not become grounds for stagnation, in which human beings are prevented from communicating with other human beings belonging to different ethnic groups. Such isolation would be in glaring contrast with an age such as ours, in which the distance between peoples has almost been eliminated. It must not be forgotten, however, that although human beings are different because of ethnic peculiarities, they do possess essential human traits in common and are led by their natures to come together in the world of spiritual values. The progressive assimilation of those values will open possibilities for perfecting themselves that are unlimited. Their right and their duty to live in communion with one another must be acknowledged.

The balance among population, land and capital

On earth, there are countries, as we all know, which have abundant arable land and little manpower, while in other countries there is no proportion between natural resources and available capital. This situation calls on people to collaborate by facilitating the exchange of capital, goods and men.

We consider it relevant to add here that whenever possible, it would seem that capital should seek work and not vice versa. In this way, concrete opportunities to create a better future would be offered to many, without the necessity of their moving from their own areas to others, which is almost inevitably accompanied by painful separations, difficult periods of readjustment and social integration.

The problem of political refugees

The feeling of universal fatherhood which the Lord has enkindled in Our heart is profoundly saddened in considering the case of political refugees, which is taking on large proportions and hides innumerable and very acute sufferings.

Their condition indicates that there are political regimes which do not guarantee their citizens sufficient liberty to enable them to lead lives worthy of humanity. Those regimes, in fact, call into question or directly deny the very right to liberty. Doubtless their attitude represents a radical inversion of the order of social existence, since the purpose of government is to realize the common good, the fundamental constituent of which is the recognition of that freedom and the assurance of its immunity.

It is not superfluous to remember that political refugees are persons, and that all their rights as persons must be recognized, even if they were deprived of citizenship in the political communities of which they were members.

Among inherent personal rights there is also the right to enter a political community in which one believes he can create a future for himself and his family. Consequently that political community—within the limits permitted by the common good rightly understood—is duty-bound to allow and also facilitate the entry of new members, and their integration.

Disarmament

It is also painful to Us to observe how in the more economically developed countries gigantic stores of armaments are kept and are being made continually, and how a high percentage of spiritual energies and economic resources is absorbed by such enterprises. The citizens of those countries are thereby placed under the burden of heavy sacrifices, while other political communities are deprived of necessary cooperation for their economic development and their social progress.

As we all know, armaments are usually justified by the argument that if peace is possible today, it is a peace based only on the balance of power. Thus if one political community arms itself, the others must keep pace and arm as well. And if a political community produces atomic arms, the others must also produce atomic arms of equal destructiveness.

And so human beings must live in fear of a holocaust that might be unleashed at any moment with unimaginably disastrous consequences. The arms, after all, do exist, and even if it is difficult to convince oneself that there would be anyone ready to assume the responsibility for the destruction and the grief that such a war would cause, some unforeseen and uncontrollable event that would trigger the war cannot be dismissed. We have to bear in mind too that even if a war to the finish does not take place, thanks to the deterrent of those arms, fear is also justified that the continuing nuclear experiments for war purposes can have fatal consequences for life on earth.

Justice, wisdom and humanity demand therefore that the armaments race be stopped, that arms already existing be reduced by all sides simultaneously, that atomic bombs be banned and that there be eventually a carefully controlled total disarmament. Pius XII said: *The calamity of a world war, with the economic and social ruin and the moral excesses and dissolution that accompany it, must not be permitted to envelop the human race for the third time.*

But we have to recognize that stopping the building up of arms, reducing their number, much less eliminating them are impossible or practically so, if at the same time steps are not taken toward total disarmament. That is, if man's spirit is not taken apart as well and every effort made to remove from it the obsession for war. In turn, the argument that peace can only be maintained by a balance of arms must be replaced by the principle that peace can only be built on mutual trust. We hold that this objective can be attained. Since it comes from the imperatives of reason, it is very desirable and of the utmost utility.

An objective demanded by reason: it is evident, or at least should be to everyone, that the relations among political communities, as those among individuals, should be governed not by recourse to force of arms, but in the light of reason; that is, in truth, justice and in active solidarity.

It is a very desirable objective. And truly who does not eagerly desire that the danger of war be eliminated and peace secured and safeguarded?

It is an objective of the greatest utility. From peace everyone can gain advantages; individuals, families, peoples, the whole human family. The warning of Pius XII still resounds: *Nothing is lost by peace. Everything can be by war.*

And so as Vicar of Jesus Christ, Savior of the world and Author of peace, and as interpreter of the most profound aspiration of the entire human family, We are seized by anxiety for the good of all and We feel it Our duty to beseech men, especially those who are invested with public responsibility, not to spare any efforts to insure that events follow a reasonable and humane course.

In the highest and most authoritative assemblies, let men give deep thought to the problem of the peaceful adjustment of the relations among nations on a world level, an adjustment founded on mutual trust, on the sincerity of treaties, on the faithfulness to the commitments made. Let them look into the problem to locate the point from which it will be possible to begin progress toward true, lasting and productive understanding.

Freedom

Relations among political communities should be governed by freedom. This means no one of them has the right to take oppressive action against any other or to meddle unduly. All countries, rather, should contribute to the development within each country of a sense of responsibility, the spirit of initiative, and the commitment to be the first to promote their own advancement.[1]

[1] Encyclical, *Pacem in Terris*, April 11, 1963.

Harmony among Peoples

Only if we really seek peace and not war, as is our duty, and make a common and sincere effort toward brotherly concord among peoples, only then, We say, will it be possible to come to agreement and settle differences. And thus by common understanding and common means we can attain the hoped-for union in which the rights of every state to its liberty, far from being trampled upon by others, will be completely secured. Those who oppress others and strip them of their liberty cannot certainly contribute to this unity. And here the affirmation of Our Predecessor of happy memory, Leo XIII, seems very relevant: "To put an end to ambition, to the lust for the goods of others, to rivalry, which are the strongest incentives to war, nothing is more effective than the Christian virtues, justice above all."

What is more, if nations do not reach this fraternal unity founded of necessity on justice and nourished by charity, the world situation will remain very serious. Sensible men deplore such an uncertain situation, when we can never know whether we are heading toward a real and firm peace or running blindly toward another horrifying war. Blindly, we said, for if—God forbid—another war should break out, the monstrous arms of modern times are so powerful that there would be little left—for victor and the defeated—but vast slaughter and universal destruction.

We beseech everyone, especially the governments of nations, to think carefully about this before God the Judge, and to employ courageously any means that might lead to this important unity. This unity of intention, as we have said, will enable the growth of prosperity among all nations, and can be restored only on condition that the freedom proper to individuals, nations, peoples, the Church will be everywhere a reality.[1]

[1] Encyclical, *Ad Petri Cathedram*, June 29, 1959.

Modern Colonialism

Respect for the individual characteristics of nations

Nations that are in the process of economic development usually present their own unmistakable individuality, not only because of their resources and the specific characteristics of their topography, but also because of their traditions which are often rich in human values, and the typical qualities of their peoples.

Nations that are already developed economically, in helping the underdeveloped countries, must recognize and respect that individuality and overcome the temptation to project themselves—through their aid—on the nations that are still being formed.

Disinterested aid

The major temptation economically developed countries are most prey to is to take advantage of their technical and economic cooperation in order to intervene in the political affairs of the underdeveloped countries with the purpose of dominating them.

Whenever this is the case, We must declare explicitly that

it constitutes a new form of colonialism. No matter how carefully it may be disguised, it is no less binding than the colonialism from which many peoples have recently been freed. Such action would be a negative influence on world affairs and would threaten world peace.

Therefore, the technical and economic cooperation of which We have spoken must be given with the sincerest political disinterestedness for the sake of justice. This disinterest is indispensable to the independent social and economic growth of the developing countries.

In this way, a valuable contribution can be made toward forming a world community in which all the members are knowing agents of their own duties and their own rights, acting for the universal good on an equal plane.[1]

[1] Encyclical, *Mater et Magistra*, May 15, 1959.

J. ON PEACE

Peace is a gift from God, and we all are obliged to plead for it, because along with those who want peace, there are—sadly—others who prefer war, discord, separation and disorder. At times they show their intentions by increasing difficulties that might have been overcome, so that, enlarged and impenetrable, the problems become threats and the near occasion for conflict.[1]

The Holy Father opens his arms and speaks out. He desires world peace, he points the way to it and asks for cooperation. Others speak of peace, too, but they are speaking of peace within their own countries, their own race, so that they can keep their advantages and embarrass those who have less. They encourage, in short, situations of inequality in order to shatter peace and universality.[2]

There are three aspects of true peace:

Peace of the heart. Peace is primarily an interior act of the spirit; a fundamental condition for it is the loving dependence on God's will: "O Lord, thou hast made us for thee, and our heart will not be quiet until it rests in thee" (St. Augustine, *Confessions* I, 1). Anything that weakens, breaks, splits this union of wills, this fundamental obedience, is a contradiction of peace. It is guilt and sin, above all. "Who has hardened against him, can he have peace?" (Job 9, 4). Peace is the happy heritage of those who observe God's law. "Great peace have those who love thy law" (Psalms 118, 165).

Good will, after all, is the intention to respect God's eternal law, to conform to his precepts, to choose his ways, to be, in short, on the side of truth. This is the glory God expects of man. *Peace to men of good will.*

Social peace is solidly based on the mutual respect for man's personal dignity. God's Son became Man, and his redeeming act was not intended just for the collectivity, but for the individual as well. "He loved me, and gave himself for me," said St. Paul (Galatians 2, 20). And if God loved man so much, it means that man belongs to him, and his person must absolutely be respected. This is what the Church teaches; she has always looked to the individual human being in solving social questions and taught that other things, and institutions—property, the economy and the state—are above all intended for men, and not men for them. The disturbances against the peace within nations have their origin almost entirely in the purposes, the products, the miserable cogs of a huge machine, the simple production process. Only when man's personal dignity shall be used to evaluate him and his work, will there be a means for settling civil conflicts and the differences—frequently deep ones—between employers and employees. And there will be the assurance that the institution of the family will have the living, the working, and the community conditions best suited to its role as the nucleus of society and the first community man knows in his development, as willed by God himself.

No, peace cannot have solid foundations unless our hearts are filled with a sense of brotherhood, which ought to exist in men since they come from the same place and have the same end. The awareness that we are all members of the same family would extinguish the greed, the desire, the pride, the aggressiveness in our hearts, the roots of conflict and war. Our sense of family would be a bond of greater solidarity among us.

International peace must be based primarily on *truth.* As Christians know, "The truth shall make you free" (John 8, 32). We must get over certain mistaken conceptions: the myth of power, nationalism or other things that poison the relationships among peoples. We must base peaceful coexistence on moral principles, according to the standards of right reason and Christian teaching.

Lighted by truth, justice must prevail. Justice removes the causes of conflict and war, settles differences, specifies duties, and recognizes the rights of all sides.

Justice, in turn, must be complemented and supported by Christian charity. That is, the love for one's fellow, for one's country, must never retreat into suspicious selfishness, but must move out toward others, toward other peoples, in a vital relationship. In this way we could speak of *living together* rather than of mere coexistence, which, bereft of genuine solidarity, only raises barriers behind which grow mutual suspicion and fear.

Peace is an incomparable gift from God, and man's supreme aspiration. Peace is indivisible. None of the aspects which make up peace can be ignored or excluded.

Since not even the men of our time have been able wholly to fulfill the requirements for peace, it can be deduced that God's ways to establish peace are different from man's. The result is the abnormal international situation we have been living in since the war, with two blocs maintaining an uneasy distance. It is not a state of war, but it is not peace either, true peace, to which all nations aspire.

For the reason that peace is indivisible in its several aspects, it will never be established in society or in the world until it becomes an interior act. In other words, we need men of good will, like the men to whom the angels spoke over Bethlehem: *Peace to men of good will* (Luke 2, 14). Only they can realize the conditions for peace that St. Thomas spoke of: *the ordered concord of citizens* (*Contra Gentiles* III, c. 146); order therefore, and concord. But how can we ever arrive at order and concord if the people who hold public authority do not recognize that they themselves are subject to eternal moral laws, before they weigh the risks and advantages of their decisions?

The obstacles created by man's maliciousness must be removed. These obstacles are present in the propaganda for immorality, in social injustices, in forced unemployment, in the misery that contrasts with excessive luxury and privilege, in the fearful imbalance between technical progress and moral growth, in the unchecked arms race. And there is as yet no solution to the question of disarmament in sight.[3]

All men of good will share an immense common task: the need to live together in truth, in justice, in love and in freedom, and this includes not only the relations between individuals, but also between citizens and their political community, among political communities themselves, among families, intermediate bodies and political communities on the one hand, and the world community on the other. How noble a purpose, to realize true peace in the order established by God.

Those who are working to arrive at these conditions for living together are certainly not many. Our deepest appreciation goes to them, Our encouragement that they persevere in their efforts with renewed enthusiasm. And We hope that their number will increase, especially among the faithful. It is imperative, a demand of Love.

We must not forget that gradualness is the law of life in all its expressions, and so even in human institutions progress toward improvement can only be made from within and gradually. As Pius XII said, "Not in revolution, but in evolution that is mutually agreed upon, lie salvation and justice. Violence has never accomplished anything but destruction; it has never built anything; it can only excite passion, never calm it. . . ."

As Vicar—albeit a humble and unworthy one—of the Prince of Peace, We are duty-bound to spend all Our energies for the achievement of this good. But peace will be merely a hollow word if it is not founded on the order outlined so hopefully in the Encyclical, *Pacem in Terris*, an order founded on truth, built on justice, animated and fulfilled by charity, and enacted in liberty.

This is so noble an enterprise that human efforts alone, no matter how highly motivated, could not put it into practice. As long as human society is not a perfect mirror of God's Kingdom, we must have help from above. For this reason, Our prayer is more fervent in these days; We pray to him, who by his Passion and death conquered sin, the source of conflict and mourning, and who reconciled man to his Heavenly Father by his own blood: "For he is our peace, he, who made one out of two. . . . And he came to preach peace unto you who were far, and peace to those near."

The Liturgy of these days announces: *Surgens Iesus Dominus noster, stans in medio discipulorum suorum dixit: "Pax vobis. Alleluia"; gavisi sunt discipuli, viso Domino.*

He left peace, he brings peace: *Pacem relinquo vobis, pacem meam do vobis, non quomodo mundus dat Ego do vobis.* This is the peace We so fervently pray for.

May he keep away whatever will imperil men, and may he

change them into witnesses of the truth, of justice, of brotherly love. May he enlighten the rulers of nations that they be concerned not only for the rightful well-being of their citizens but also for peace. Fire our wills to overcome the barriers that divide; seal the bonds of mutual charity, mutual understanding and mutual forgiveness. And by virtue of his action, may the peoples of the earth unite in brotherhood and may the peace they crave reign forever.[4]

[1] Allocution, September 16, 1961.
[2] Speech, August 19, 1961.
[3] Radio broadcast, December 23, 1959.
[4] Encyclical, *Pacem in Terris*, April 11, 1963.